Uncovering Nevada's Past

WILBUR S. SHEPPERSON SERIES
IN NEVADA HISTORY

Uncovering Nevada's Past

A Primary Source History of the Silver State

Edited by John B. Reid and Ronald M. James

University of Nevada Press

Reno & Las Vegas

WILBUR S. SHEPPERSON SERIES IN NEVADA HISTORY
Series Editor | Michael Green

University of Nevada Press, Reno, Nevada 89557 USA
Copyright © 2004 by University of Nevada Press
All rights reserved

Manufactured in the United States of America

Design by Omega Clay

The Library of Congress Catalog Number (LCCN) 2003022125,
assigned on application to the Library of Congress Cataloging-
in-Publication Data

The paper used in this book meets the requirements of American
National Standard for Information Sciences—Permanence of Paper
for Printed Library Materials, ANSI/NISO Z39.48-1992 (R2002.
Binding materials were selected for strength and durability.

23 22 21 20 19 18 17 16 15 14
9 8 7 6 5 4
ISBN-13: 978-0-87417-567-7

To Tanya and Susan

CONTENTS

ILLUSTRATIONS

ACKNOWLEDGMENTS

The editors would like to acknowledge and thank all of the people who assisted us with this book. We cannot mention everyone, but the following were especially helpful and deserve special thanks here: Bill Rowley and Michael Green for their many helpful suggestions; Jeff Kintop and Mella Harmon for providing many important documents and several of the introductions to them; Tanya Reid for her excellent editorial assistance; Dawn Ingraham for her tireless administrative assistance throughout; Joanne O'Hare, Sara Vélez Mallea, Sarah Nestor, and the University of Nevada Press staff for getting the manuscript ready for publication; Dean Bill Baines and Dean John Adlish for their support of the project; the Nevada Humanities Committee and the National Endowment for the Humanities for a minigrant to assist in the manuscript's preparation; and all of the contributors for their dedication and willingness to participate in the writing of this book.

Nevada's history lies beneath the surface. This is literally true, of course, in one sense. It is difficult to imagine a Nevada history without mining. Themes that continue to define Nevada—the tolerance for what others have long considered to be socially unacceptable behavior, the cozy relationship between business and government, the live-for-today attitude—are legacies of the mining culture that dominated Nevada's early years. But much of Nevada's history lies below the surface in a figurative sense as well, as do all histories. History's surface consists of those things that are easily identifiable as "historical," such as the actions and pronouncements of governors, legislators, and successful businessmen. This history is important, even crucial, to our understanding of the past, and the general histories of Nevada describe and explain the events and people associated with these subjects extraordinarily well.

Below this surface, though, lies another Nevada history that we must uncover. Consider the following examples—first, Arthur Miller's description of the Nevada desert during the 1950s and its levels of meaning: "Out on the desert, far from any vehicle track, there were sometimes signs of life underground; in the midst of sage and sand a pair of shorts hung on a stick to dry in the sun, or a T-shirt. My friends never ventured close, although they claimed to know some of these residents of holes in the ground. They were men wanted by the law, for murder more often than not." Here we receive a glimpse into a late legacy of Nevada's Wild West past, and at the same time Miller's slightly melodramatic description provides insight into the outsider's view of Nevada as a lawless and otherworldly landscape. Second, consider Zenas Leonard's description of Nevada's geography as he encounters the Barren River (later renamed the Humboldt River) for the first time in 1833: "as the country, natives and everything belonging to it, [the Barren River] justly deserves the name." Again, a rather simple observation speaks volumes about the attitudes of early nineteenth-century whites toward Nevada's geography and its inhabitants. Nevada history is revealed in the nuances, detail, and unself-conscious reporting in these perspectives as much as it is in the writings of governors, senators, or big business owners.

While this book's main purposes are conventional—to introduce readers to some of the more provocative and illustrative sources from Nevada's past; to encourage creative, imaginative, and original thinking about the state's history; and to generate discussion about western history—it also probes below the surfaces of Nevada's past to uncover its underlying nature. The nature that emerges has to do with mining's impact on the state's culture as well as with a series of contradictions: lawlessness and law and order; glittery showrooms and grimy mines; old-timers and the newly arrived; the repugnance of unfettered human behavior and the attraction of forbidden freedoms; the decadent and the sublimely beautiful. It is about the seeming emptiness of the state, the lack of restraints this has always seemed to imply, and the outsider's determination to fill this void with projections of his or her own conceptions of lawlessness. Rather than challenging these projections, Nevadans have often adopted them (sometimes with reluctance, sometimes with enthusiasm). The result is a continually evolving mix of the genuine and fake, real and surreal.

This reader uses primary sources as a means to explore Nevada's history. In order to understand the context of these sources, it might be useful to think about your own personal history for a moment. What are the most meaningful aspects of your past to you? Now consider what record of these things will be available to historians in two hundred years. Would it be possible to construct an accurate picture of your life from these remaining traces of you? The historian faces this dilemma every day and tries to derive the most accurate meaning from the few lingering traces of people's lives. Historians call these things from the past—documents, objects, drawings, and other items—primary sources because they are the source material of history, and they are the first and most important source. They are the raw material from which stories of the past are created; many times they are the only voices to speak to us from the unrecoverable past.

By examining the raw materials of history, readers can see for themselves the ways in which the history and perceptions of Nevada have been constructed. Few people realize the degree to which history is an interpretive act. Historians must take these primary sources, which are only a few surviving details of a complex and fully formed era, and extrapolate a comprehensive history. Interpretation of these sources is full of potential for error and must be treated with caution; primary sources served their own purposes in their historical context, with no consideration that future generations might try to reconstruct the past from them. Some were intended as straightforward communication; others were meant as entertainment, persuasion, or even political propaganda. Sometimes they were inaccurate, misleading, or deceptive. Anyone wishing to interpret history accurately must question these sources as vigorously as a detective examines a witness in a criminal investigation. One must first place such a source within its historical context. Who created it? When and where was it created? Why was it created? Who was its intended audience? Why was it preserved? What or who is left out of the source? How does the source fit with what we already know? Has the meaning of the source changed since its creation? This process of questioning the source helps us to identify inaccuracies, biases, or logical errors in the source and ultimately assess the source's merits. The best interpretation is one most supported by evidence and argued with sound logic, but sometimes we are forced to cope with ambiguous or contradictory information. By providing access to a variety of primary sources, this book allows its readers to interpret Nevada history for themselves and develop their own ideas.

While descriptions in general histories are usually accurate, at least until new information makes the interpretations obsolete, these texts can only provide a brief survey of facts. They cannot convey the complexity and detail of individual incidents. For example, in one of the most widely read histories of Nevada, the author describes an incident in 1833 involving the Walker-Bonneville party and the Native Americans of western Nevada as follows: "Increasing difficulties with the Indians led to an encounter there which cost the lives of thirty or more natives and laid the groundwork for later Indian animosity toward Walker in particular and whites in general." While factually accurate, the primary source description of this meeting, which is included in this reader, provides an immensely more vivid and multilayered description of it. The primary source conveys the mutual fear of both parties as well as the hostile and combative attitudes of the whites that made this and future conflicts possible.

Sometimes primary sources provide a visceral experience of the unrecoverable past. For example, consider Samuel Clemens's description of the execution of John Millian from a document included in this collection:

My own suspense was almost unbearable—my blood was leaping through my veins, and my thoughts were crowding and trampling upon each other. Twenty moments to live—fifteen to live—ten to live—five—three—heaven and earth, how the time galloped! And yet that man stood there unmoved though he knew that the sheriff was reaching deliberately for the drop while the black cap descended over his quiet face! Then down through the hole in the scaffold the strap-bound figure shot like a dart! A dreadful shiver started at the shoulders, violently convulsed the whole body all the way down, and died away with a tense drawing of the toes downward, like a doubled fist—and all was over!

I saw it all. I took exact note of every detail, even to Melanie's considerably helping to fix the leather strap that bound his legs together and his quiet removal of his slippers and I never wish to see it again. I can see that stiff, straight corpse hanging there yet, with its black pillow-cased head turned rigidly to one side, and the purple streaks creeping through the hands and driving the fleshy hue of life before them. Ugh!

This description returns the experiences of real human beings to our understanding of frontier justice. The agony of the prisoner and the simultaneous excitement and revulsion in the spectators make all of the participants seem more human, and the description of his death may be the only remnant of this man's life.

"Nevada–desert, waste, / Mighty, and inhospitable, and stern; / Hiding a meaning over which we yearn"—Frances Fuller Victor's lines resonate as much today as they did in 1869. Nevada continues to invite exploration. Its superficial barrenness and freedoms lead to an inward exploration. Visitors and new residents continue to comment on the contradictions—glittery showrooms and empty desert, ghost towns and crowded new suburbs, the decadent and sublimely beautiful, the repugnance of unfettered human behavior and the attraction of forbidden human freedoms. These contradictions continue in mysterious harmony. Mystery suits Nevada. And today, as always, the secret, the next big thing, lies just beneath the surface and waits to be uncovered.

JOHN B. REID

PART 1 | Beginnings

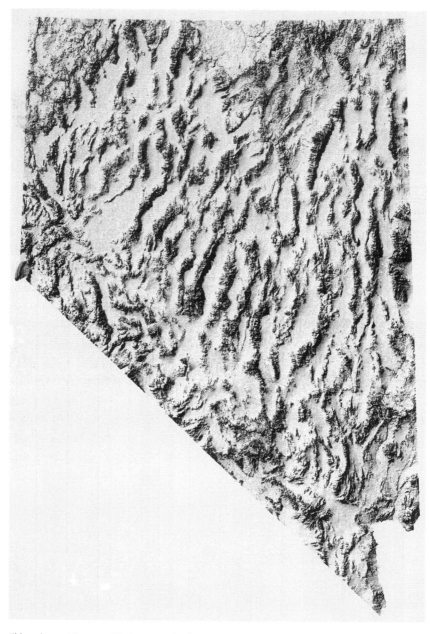

This enhanced topographical map emphasizes Nevada's most historically important geographical feature—its daunting ranges of mountains that crisscross the entire state. Courtesy of Gnomon, Inc.

1

The Physical Environment

A Computer-Enhanced Map of Nevada Geography

Is Nevada's geography a blessing or a curse? For twenty-first-century Nevadans, it is a benefit, without question. The sunny and temperate climate has attracted vacationers, retirees, and others for the last half century. The warm winters in Las Vegas are central to its status as a resort area, and the snowy Sierra Nevada in the winter attracts skiers from around the world. Beautiful Lake Tahoe provides year-round recreation for Nevadans and visitors. However, for nineteenth-century explorers, emigrants, and settlers this positive view of Nevada's geography would have been incomprehensible. The mountains that provide such beauty and recreation today were extraordinary obstacles before railroads and automobiles. The north/south orientation of Nevada's mountain ranges made the journey from the Great Salt Lake to California extraordinarily difficult, and the fact that Nevada's rivers do not drain to the sea prevented water travel as an alternative. The enhanced topographical image included here provides a perspective on Nevada's geography that was unimaginable to early emigrants to the state. If they had seen this image, would they have made the trip?

—John B. Reid

Mark Twain on Nevada's "Harsh Land"

Who would stay in such a region one moment longer than he must? I thought I had seen barrenness before . . . but I was green. . . . Here, on the Humboldt, famine sits enthroned, and waves his scepter over a dominion expressly made for him. . . . There can never be any considerable settlement here.

These are strange words indeed for Horace Greeley (1811–72), the famous nineteenth-century journalist who made "Go West, young man" a national slogan. While he encouraged those seeking opportunity to turn their eyes to an undeveloped frontier, he saw little to recommend the Great Basin to settlers. The same was true for many others who headed to the Pacific Coast in search of cheap land, easy gains, and a temperate climate.

When young Samuel Clemens came west in 1861 with his brother Orion, newly appointed as secretary-treasurer for the Nevada Territory, he found the region shocking in its severity. The following is an excerpt from *Roughing It* (1871), his account of his Nevada sojourn.

—Ronald M. James

My brother had just been appointed Secretary of Nevada Territory—an office of such majesty that it concentrated in itself the duties and dignities of Treasurer, Comptroller, Secretary of State, and Acting Governor in the Governor's absence. A salary of eighteen hundred dollars a year and the title of "Mr. Secretary," gave to the great position an air of wild and imposing grandeur. I was young and ignorant, and I envied my brother. I coveted his distinction and his financial splendor, but particularly and especially the long, strange journey he was going to make, and the curious new world he was going to explore. He was going to travel! I never had been away from home, and that word "travel" had a seductive charm for me. Pretty soon he would be hundreds and hundreds of miles away on the great plains and deserts, and among the mountains of the Far West, and would see buffaloes and Indians, and prairie dogs, and antelopes, and have all kinds of adventures, and maybe get hanged or scalped, and have ever such a fine time, and write home and tell us all about it, and be a hero. And he would see the gold mines and the silver mines, and maybe go about on an afternoon when his work was done, and pick up two or three pailfuls of shining slugs, and nuggets of gold and silver on the hillside. And by and by he would become very rich, and return home by sea, and be able to talk as calmly about San Francisco and the ocean and "the isthmus" as if it was nothing of any consequence to have seen those marvels face to face. What I suffered in contemplating his happiness, pen cannot describe. And so, when he offered me, in cold blood, the sublime position of private secretary under him, it appeared to me that the heavens and the earth passed away, and the firmament was rolled together as a scroll! I had nothing more to desire. My contentment was complete. At the end of an hour or two I was ready for the journey. Not much packing up was necessary, because we were going in the overland stage from the Missouri frontier to Nevada, and passengers were only allowed a small quantity of baggage apiece. There was no Pacific railroad in those fine times of ten or twelve years ago—not a single rail of it.

I only proposed to stay in Nevada three months—I had no thought of staying longer than that. I meant to see all I could that was new and strange, and then hurry home to business. I little thought that I would not see the end of that three-month pleasure excursion for six or seven uncommonly long years!

I dreamed all night about Indians, deserts, and silver bars, and in due time, next day, we took shipping at the St. Louis wharf on board a steamboat bound up the Missouri River. . . .

[*After an eventful trip through the American West, Twain and his fellow travelers approached Nevada Territory's capital city.*]

We were approaching the end of our long journey. It was the morning of the twentieth day. At noon we would reach Carson City, the capital of Nevada Territory. We were not glad, but sorry. It had been a fine pleasure trip; we had fed fat on wonders every day; we were now well accustomed to stage life, and very fond of it; so the idea of coming to a standstill and settling down to a humdrum existence in a village was not agreeable, but on the contrary depressing.

Visibly our new home was a desert, walled in by barren, snow-clad mountains. There was not a tree in sight. There was no vegetation but the endless sagebrush and greasewood. All nature was gray with it. We were plowing through great depths of powdery alkali dust that rose in thick clouds and floated across the plain like smoke from a burning house. We were coated with it like millers; so were the coach, the mules, the mail-bags, the driver— we and the sagebrush and the other scenery were all one monotonous color. Long trains of freight-wagons in the distance enveloped in ascending masses of dust suggested pictures of prairies on fire. These teams and their masters were the only life we saw. Otherwise we moved in the midst of solitude, silence, and desolation. Every twenty steps we passed the skeleton of some dead beast of burden, with its dust-coated skin stretched tightly over its empty ribs. Frequently a solemn raven sat upon the skull or the hips and contemplated the passing coach with meditative serenity.

By and by Carson City was pointed out to us. It nestled in the edge of a great plain and was a sufficient number of miles away to look like an assemblage of mere white spots in the shadow of a grim range of mountains overlooking it, whose summits seemed lifted clear out of companionship and consciousness of earthly things.

We arrived, disembarked, and the stage went on. It was a "wooden" town; its population two thousand souls. The main street consisted of four or five blocks of little white frame stores which were too high to sit down on, but not too high for various other purposes; in fact, hardly high enough. They were packed close together, side by side, as if room were scarce in that mighty plain. The sidewalk was of boards that were more or less loose and inclined to rattle when walked upon. In the middle of the town, opposite the stores, was the "plaza," which is native to all towns beyond the Rocky Mountains—a large, unfenced, level vacancy, with a liberty pole in it, and very useful as a place for public auctions, horse trades, and mass-meetings, and likewise for teamsters to camp in. Two other sides of the plaza were faced by stores, offices, and stables. The rest of Carson City was pretty scattering. . . .

This was all we saw that day, for it was two o'clock, now, and according to custom the daily "Washoe Zephyr" set in; a soaring dust-drift about the size of the United States set up edgewise came with it, and the capital of Nevada Territory disappeared from view. Still, there were sights to be seen which were not wholly uninteresting to newcomers; for the vast dust-cloud was thickly freckled with things strange to the upper air—things living and dead, that flitted hither and thither, going and coming, appearing and disappearing among the rolling billows of dust—hats, chickens, and parasols sailing in the remote heavens; blankets, tin signs, sagebrush, and shingles a shade lower; door-mats and buffalo-robes lower still; shovels and coal-scuttles on the next grade; glass doors, cats, and little children on the next; disrupted lumber yards, light buggies, and wheelbarrows on the next; and down only thirty or forty feet above ground was a scurrying storm of emigrating roofs and vacant lots.

It was something to see that much. I could have seen more, if I could have kept the dust out of my eyes.

But seriously a Washoe wind is by no means a trifling matter. It blows flimsy houses down, lifts shingle roofs occasionally, rolls up tin ones like sheet music, now and then blows a stage coach over and spills the passengers; and tradition says the reason there are so many bald people there, is, that the wind blows the hair off their heads while they are looking skyward after their hats. Carson streets seldom look inactive on summer afternoons, because there are so many citizens skipping around their escaping hats, like chambermaids trying to head off a spider.

2

Contacts and Conflicts

The Adventures of Zenas Leonard, Fur Trader

The first battle between Indians and whites in what is today Nevada took place in 1833, when Nevada was still part of Mexico. By the 1830s, several different fur companies competed fiercely with one another for a diminishing supply of beaver in the Pacific Northwest. Hoping to discover fertile new lands for trapping, Captain Benjamin Bonneville in July 1833 dispatched a party of about forty trappers from an area north of the Great Salt Lake, placing them under the leadership of his lieutenant Joseph Walker. This party entered today's Nevada near Pilot Peak (the first peak described in the excerpt below) and became the first white party to cross northern Nevada from east to west. They traveled along the Humboldt River, which was at that time referred to as the Unknown River, Ogden's River, or Mary's River.

The Walker party was disappointed with Nevada. Unaware that fur trapper Peter Ogden and his men had taken about one thousand beaver from the Humboldt River area several years earlier, the Walker party found the river "barren," and they bestowed the name of Barren River upon it. They also found forage scarce and the landscape desolate. In their ill temper, men in the Walker party were all the more frustrated to discover that Indians were stealing their beaver traps at night. Some hot-headed trappers apparently vowed to kill the first Indian they met and, accordingly, shot and killed an Indian who was fishing, tossing his body into the river. Although Walker scolded the men who committed this act, the party became anxious that the Indians would seek revenge. When they encountered a great gathering of Indians further down the river in the area of today's Humboldt Sink, they feared for their lives and launched the attack described below; they killed thirty-nine Indians by Zenas Leonard's reckoning, while suffering no casualties themselves, and repeated the act the following summer on their return trip from Monterey, California, where they had wintered.

Washington Irving's well-known *The Adventures of Captain Bonneville U.S.A.* (1837) was the first published report of this trip, wherein Irving strongly condemned the

Walker party for the vicious massacre of peaceful and merely curious Indians. Perhaps in defense of his leader, Joseph Walker, Zenas Leonard—a young man from Pennsylvania who served as clerk on the expedition—reported an eyewitness account of the incident that was first published in the newspapers of his hometown in 1839 and is excerpted here. He insists that the party's defensive strike was justified and came only after repeated efforts to avoid violence. Later historians have surmised that the Indians who stole the traps upriver were Shoshones, while the peaceful gathering downriver were innocent Paiutes. Whatever the case, this 1833 massacre set a pattern of mutual mistrust between Indians and white travelers and settlers in Nevada that would break out in repeated acts of violence and war throughout the nineteenth century.

—Cheryll Glotfelty

After traveling a few days longer through these barren plains, we came to the mountain described by the Indian as having its peak covered with snow. It presents a most singular appearance—being entirely unconnected with any other chain. It is surrounded on either side by level plains, and rises abruptly to a great height, rugged and hard to ascend. To take a view of the surrounding country from this mountain, the eye meets with nothing but a smooth, sandy, level plain. On the whole, this mountain may be set down as one of the most remarkable phenomena of nature. Its top is covered with the pinion tree, bearing a kind of must, which the natives are very fond of, and which they collect for winter provision. This hill is nearly round, and looks like a hill or mound, such as may be met with in the prairies on the east side of the mountain.

Not far from our encampment we found the source of the river mentioned by the Indian. After we all got tired gazing at this mountain and the adjacent curiosities, we left it and followed down the river, in order to find water and grass for our horses. On this stream we found old signs of beaver, and we supposed that, as game was scarce in this country, the Indians had caught them for provision. The natives which we occasionally met with, still continued to be of the most poor and dejected kind—being entirely naked and very filthy. We came to the hut of one of these Indians who happened to have a considerable quantity of fur collected. At this hut we obtained a large robe composed of beaver skins fastened together, in exchange for two awls and one fish hook. This robe was worth from thirty to forty dollars. We continued traveling down this river, now and then catching a few beaver. But, as we continued to extend our acquaintance with the natives, they began to practice their national failing of stealing. So eager were they to possess themselves of our traps, that we were forced to quit trapping in this vicinity and make for some other quarter. The great annoyance we sustained in this respect greatly displeased some of our men, and they were for taking vengeance before we left the country—but this was not the disposition of Captain Walker. These discontents being out hunting one day, fell in with a few Indians, two or three of whom they killed, and then returned to camp, not daring to let the Captain know it. The next day while hunting, they repeated the same violation—but this time not quite so successful, for the Captain found it out, and immediately took measures for its effectual suppression.

At this place, all the branches of this stream is collected from the mountain into the main channel, which forms quite a large stream; and to which we gave the name of Barren River [the Humboldt River]—a name which we thought would be quite appropriate, as the country, natives and everything belonging to it, justly deserves the name. You may travel for many days on the banks of this river, without finding a stick large enough to make a walking cane. While we were on its margin, we were compelled to do without fire, unless we chanced to come across some drift that had collected together on the beach. As we proceeded down the river we found that the trails of the Indians began to look as if their numbers were increasing, ever since our men had killed some of their brethren. The further we descended the river, the more promising the country began to appear, although it still retained its dry, sandy nature. We had now arrived within view of a cluster of hills or mounds, which presented the appearance, from a distance, of a number of beautiful cities built up together. Here we had the pleasure of seeing timber, which grew in very sparing quantities some places along the river beach.

On the 4th of September [1833] we arrived at some lakes, formed by this river, which we supposed to be those mentioned by the Indian chief whom we met at the Great Salt Lake. Here the country is low and swampy, producing an abundance of very fine grass—which was very acceptable to our horses, as it was the first good grazing they had been in for a long time—and here, on the borders of one of these lakes, we encamped, for the purpose of spending the night and letting our horses have their satisfaction. A little before sunset, on taking a view of the surrounding waste with a spy-glass, we discovered smoke issuing from the high grass in every direction. This was sufficient to convince us that we were in the midst of a large body of Indians; but as we could see no timber to go to, we concluded that it would be as well to remain in our present situation and defend ourselves as well as we could. We readily guessed that these Indians were in arms to revenge the death of those which our men had killed up the river; and if they could succeed in getting any advantage over us, we had no expectation that they would give us any quarter. Our first care, therefore, was to secure our horses, which we did by fastening them all together, and then hitching them to pickets drove into the ground. This done, we commenced constructing something for our own safety. The lake was immediately in our rear, and piling up all our baggage in front, we had quite a substantial breastwork—which would have been as impregnable to the Indian's arrow as were the cotton bags to the British bullets at New Orleans in 1815. Before we had got everything completed, however, the Indians issued from their hiding places in the grass, to the number, as near as I could guess, of eight or nine hundred, and marched straight toward us, dancing and singing in the greatest glee. When within about 150 yards of us, they all sat down on the ground, and dispatched five of their chiefs to our camp to inquire whether their people might come in and smoke with us. This request Captain Walker very prudently refused, as they evidently had no good intentions, but told them that he was willing to meet them half way between our breastwork, and where their people were then sitting. This appeared to displease them very much, and they went back not the least bit pleased with the reception they had met with.

After the five deputies related the result of their visit to their constituents, a part of them rose up and signed to us (which was the only mode of communicating with them) that they were coming to our camp. At this ten or twelve of our men mounted the breastwork and made signs to them that if they advanced a step further it was at the peril of their lives. They wanted to know in what way we would do it. Our guns were exhibited as the weapons of death. This they seemed to discredit and only laughed at us. They then wanted to see what effect our guns would have on some ducks that were then swimming in the lake, not far from the shore. We then fired at the ducks—thinking by this means to strike terror into the savages and drive them away. The ducks were killed, which astonished the Indians a good deal, though not so much as the noise of the guns—which caused them to fall flat to the ground. After this they put up a beaver skin on a bank for us to shoot at for their gratification—when they left us for the night. This night we stationed a strong guard, but no Indians made their appearance, and were permitted to pass the night in pleasant dreams.

Early in the morning we resumed our journey along the lakes without seeing any signs of the Indians until after sunrise, when we discovered them issuing from the high grass in front, rear, and on either side of us. This created great alarm among our men, at first, as we thought they had surrounded us on purpose, but it appeared that we had only *happened* amongst them, and they were as much frightened as us. From this we turned our course from the border of the lake into the plain. We had not traveled far until the Indians began to move after us—first in small numbers, but presently in large companies. They did not approach near until we had traveled in this way for several hours, when they began to send small parties in advance, who would solicit us most earnestly to stop and smoke with them. After they had repeated this several times, we began to understand their motive—which was to detain us in order to let their whole force come up and surround us, or to get into close quarters with us, when their bows and arrows would be as fatal and more effective than our firearms. We now began to be a little stern with them, and gave them to understand that if they continued to trouble us they would do it at their own risk. In this manner we were teased until a party of eighty or one hundred came forward, who appeared more saucy and bold than any others. This greatly excited Captain Walker, who was naturally of a very cool temperament, and he gave orders for the charge, saying that there was nothing equal to a good start in such a case. This was sufficient. A number of our men had never been engaged in any fighting with the Indians, and were anxious to try their skill. When our commander gave his consent to chastise these Indians, and give them an idea of our strength, 32 of us dismounted and prepared ourselves to give a severe blow. We tied our extra horses to some shrubs and left them with the main body of our company, and then selected each a choice steed, mounted and surrounded this party of Indians. We closed in on them and fired, leaving thirty-nine dead on the field, which was nearly half—the remainder were overwhelmed with dismay—running into the high grass in every direction, howling in the most lamentable manner.

Captain Walker then gave orders to some of the men to take the bows of the fallen Indians and put the wounded out of misery. The severity with which we dealt with these Indians may be revolting to the heart of the philanthropist; but the circumstances of the case altogether atones for the cruelty. It must be borne in mind that we were far removed from the hope of any succor in case we were surrounded, and that the country we were in was swarming with hostile savages, sufficiently numerous to devour us. Our object was to strike a decisive blow. This we did—even to a greater extent than we had intended.

[*The party reached California in November 1833, and after spending almost three months there, set off eastward over the Sierra Nevada. They reached the Humboldt River and began to retrace their steps in mid-1834.*]

June 8th [1834]. This morning we left the California Mountain, and took a northeast direction, keeping our former path, many traces of which were quite visible in places. Here vegetation is growing rapidly, giving our herd abundant pasture, in consequence of which they have greatly improved in appearance, and are enabled to travel quite fast. After continuing our course in this direction for a few days without interruption, we at length arrived in the neighborhood of the lakes at the mouth of Barren River, and which we had named Battle Lakes. All along our route from the mountain this far, we had seen a great number of Indians, but now that we had reached the vicinity of the place where we had the skirmish with the savages when going to the coast, they appeared to us in double the numbers that they did at that time; and as we were then compelled to fight them, by their movements now, we saw that this would be the only course for us to pursue. We had used every endeavor that we could think of, to reconcile and make them friendly, but all to no purpose. We had given them one present after another—made them all the strongest manifestations of a desire for peace on our part, by promising to do battle against their enemies if required, and we found that our own safety and comfort demanded that they should be severely chastised for provoking us to such a measure. Now that we were a good deal aggravated, some of our men said hard things about what they would do if we would again come in contact with these provoking Indians; and our Captain was afraid that, if once engaged, the passion of his men would become so wild that he could not call them off, whilst there was an Indian found to be slaughtered. Being thus compelled to fight, as we thought, in a good cause and in self-defense, we drew up in battle array, and fell on the Indians in the wildest and most ferocious manner we could, which struck dismay throughout the whole crowd, killing fourteen, besides wounding a great many more as we rode right over them. Our men were soon called off, only three of whom were slightly wounded.

The Pyramid Lake War from Two Perspectives: Numaga and Edmund Bryant

The Pyramid Lake War of 1860 was the culmination of several years of deteriorating relations between whites and Great Basin tribes. However, it was the Rush to Washoe in 1859 that directly led to the organized uprising of Northern Paiutes. The rapidly expanding white population in what is now Nevada cut pinyon trees for charcoal to process ore, destroying pine-nut crops used by Native Americans to survive the western Great Basin's harsh winters. White settlers also used Nevada's fertile valleys for farming and ranching, denying Native Americans access to traditional gathering places where nuts, roots, and seeds existed. Whites decimated big-game herds, fish, and waterfowl to feed hungry miners. By the winter of 1859–60, the Northern Paiutes and other tribes of the region were facing starvation.

Increasingly violent encounters between whites and Native Americans occurred throughout the winter months, but the war did not actually begin until keepers of a Pony Express station along the Carson River kidnapped and raped two Northern Paiute women in May of 1860. A band of Northern Paiutes liberated the women and killed the five responsible men. Without any attempt to learn the Northern Paiute side of the story, Major William Ormsby led a company of 105 volunteers from Virginia City to bury the dead at Williams Station and to chastise the Native Americans where they were gathered at Pyramid Lake. Instead, a well-organized force of Northern Paiutes decoyed Ormsby and his men into a trap now known as the Battle of Pyramid Lake and soundly defeated the Virginia City volunteers, killing Ormsby and the majority of the troops. In the letter that follows, eyewitness Edmund Bryant describes the battle and its aftermath.

The first document is an excerpt from Myron Angel's *History of Nevada*, published in 1881. It purports to capture the words of Numaga, "Young Winnemucca," who attempted to lead the Northern Paiutes in the direction of peaceful coexistence. The second document is a little-known letter authored by Dr. Edmund Bryant to his father. Bryant came to Nevada as a volunteer medic in the midst of the Pyramid Lake War. His observations are now available because a copy of his letter was donated to Storey County by a tourist who had rescued the document from garbage on a New York City sidewalk. Bryant is an important historic footnote as the first husband of Marie Louise Hungerford Bryant. After being widowed, she married mining baron John Mackay.

—Alice M. Baldrica

Numaga (from Myron Angel's *History of Nevada* [1881])

You would make war upon the whites; I ask you to pause and reflect. The white men are like the stars over your heads. You have wrongs, great wrongs, that rise up like those mountains before you; but can you, from the mountain tops, reach and blot out those stars? Your enemies are like the sands in the bed of your rivers; when taken away they only give place for more to come and settle there. Could you defeat the whites in Nevada, from over the mountains in California would come to help them an army of white men that would cover your country like a blanket. What hope is there for the Pah-Ute? From where is to come your guns, your powder, your lead, your dried meats to live upon, and hay to feed your ponies with while you carry on this war. Your enemies have all of these things, more than they can use. They will come like the sand in a whirlwind and drive you from your homes. You will be forced among the barren rocks of the north, where your ponies will die; where you will see the women and the old men starve, and listen to the cries of your children for food. I love my people; let them live; and when their spirits shall be called to the Great Camp in the southern sky, let their bones rest where their fathers were buried.

[*As Numaga spoke these last words, an Indian approached on horseback and informed the group that Indians had killed four whites and burned Williams Station the previous night. Numaga continued:*]

There is no longer any use for the counsel; we must prepare for war, for the soldiers will now come here to fight us.

Document 2

Downieville May 31, 1860:

My dear *Father,*

Your letters of April 20th and May 5th have been received. The latter were received today. Most sincerely do Marie and myself thank you for your kind congratulations. In receiving the approbation of my parents we are rendered if possible more happy. We are both well and in enjoyment of reasonable prosperity. I was prevented from writing to you by the last mail by circumstances unavoidable. I left home for a visit to Utah to look after some of my debtors and some mining claims and barely got back with my scalp. I anticipated no danger when I left, but the war commenced about the same time. I did not learn the news until I had arrived in the Indian country. I met trains of people and stock on their way to California, flying from the Indians. I made my way back but did not get time to write before I was obliged to return. How narrowly I escaped I have no time to present to detail. The Major (my father-in-law) was at Virginia City at the time. When I arrived in town, news of the battle and defeat of the whites had reached here. And the excitement was terrible. I found dispatches for me from the Major (as I was the only officer of his staff here) to have all the arms of ammunition of the battalion conveyed immediately to the scene of action. I left on the following morning with an escort of 150 men mostly volunteers under command of the sheriff of the county who was chosen to provide for the men until they arrived in Virginia City. Many who went lost friends or relatives in the battle. The arms were U.S. rifles or muskets. We arrived there after five days march. Our beds were the ground without shelter—one night of snow-storm and our food bacon and flour and water baked together. Ice every night, but all were healthy and hungry. The distance is 100 miles. We escaped from any attack. The details of the trip you will find in the *Sierra Citizen*. I found my Indian boy (who had got frightened and run away the day before I got home) with his tribe on the Truckee River fishing. He told me that he wanted to come back but was afraid some one would kill him because he was an Indian. His tribe (the Wassoos) are friendly. The hostile Indians, the Pah Utes, Shoshones and Pitt River Indians, number in and about 15,000 warriors well armed mostly with rifles from the Mormons and Hudson Bay Co. and abundant ammunition, a great deal of which has been thoughtlessly [illegible] them by our miners. About half of them are well mounted on [illegible] horses. They were apparently friendly until about a month since when in a single night every Indian disappeared from the settlements and mining camps. They assembled at Pyramid Lake a few miles below Virginia City, held a council of war and determined to wipe out the whites. Then came daily news of massacres by the red villains. Ever since the discovery of these silver mines at Virginia City, they have complained and threatened. That neighborhood is their last and only resting place. California being on their west and east of them the great desert. On the 9th of this month, a party of 105 men well mounted and well armed left Virginia City in search of parties of miners who were out prospecting and who were supposed to have been killed by the Indians. On the 12th they fell in with a large band of warriors near the pass where the Truckee River enters into Pyramid Lake. A hard and bloody battle was fought and the whites defeated. An expedition has now started after them under the command of Col. Jack Hays and Major Hungerford aided by a company of U.S. artillery and one of dragoons. I employed or rather found a man to represent me in the battalion as a surgeon and after attending to the wounded returned to my business. Col. Hays was very anxious to have me remain but the Major and myself thought I had better be at home. Last night I received a dispatch that an attack was made upon the camp of the troops on the night of the 27th by 200 mounted Indians. 7 Indians killed and 3 of our men wounded. I expect while I am writing that a bloody battle is going on. The Major is now in his glory. Today is the one appointed for the attack upon Pyramid Lake. Hays you will remember was chief of the Texas Rangers. The Major and him fought side by side in Mexico. The scene of the battleground where the battle of the war was fought is horrible beyond description. The savages were not content with scalping their victims but after stripping them mutilated their bodies in a horrible manner. About 35 of the whites were killed and only about 15 Indians. I can give you further particulars in my next letter . . .

> I am as ever your affectionate son, Edmund Bryant

The Native American Condition: Various Writings by Sarah Winnemucca

Sarah Winnemucca (1844–91) was one of the most influential and charismatic Native American women in American history. Born near the Humboldt River Sink in western Nevada to a legendary family of Paiute leaders at a time when the Paiutes' homeland and way of life were increasingly threatened by the influx of white settlers, Sarah dedicated much of her life to working for her people. During the Bannock war of 1878, she played an influential and controversial role as interpreter, messenger, scout, and close associate of commanding general Oliver Howard. After the war, she traveled to Washington in 1880 with her father and brother and appealed to the secretary of the interior and the president to win the release of Paiutes exiled to Yakama Reservation. Meanwhile, she underwent vicissitudes in her private life, with several failed relationships. She toured the East Coast in the 1880s, giving over three hundred speeches about the plight of her people and heavily criticizing the reservation system. She made the sufferings of a little-known tribe a matter of public concern and finally testified before Congress. In 1883 she produced the first book written by a Native American woman, *Life Among the Piutes: Their Wrongs and Claims*, which combined her autobiography with the ethnohistory of her tribe and preserved the history of her people. Returning to Nevada, she used private contributions to found a Native American school whose educational practices were far ahead of its time. By the time of her death at Henry's Lake, Idaho, Sarah had not achieved all her aims, but she had accomplished a great deal.

Excerpted below are three original documents authored by Sarah Winnemucca. In the first, from *Life Among the Piutes*, Sarah recalls a terrifying flight from white men when she was very small. The second is a letter from Winnemucca to Major Henry Douglas, superintendent of Indian Affairs for Nevada, to provide information on the Paiutes. Her classic statement of their plight impressed Douglas so much that he forwarded it to the commissioner of Indian Affairs in Washington. It was also reprinted in newspapers, and Helen Hunt Jackson included it in her book, *A Century of Dishonor* (1881). The third excerpt comes from an 1879 lecture to a San Francisco audience.

—Sally Zanjani

Life Among the Piutes (1883) by Sarah Winnemucca Hopkins

Oh, what a fright we all got one morning to hear some white people were coming. Every one ran as best they could. My poor mother was left with my little sister and me. Oh, I can never forget it. My poor mother was carrying my little sister on her back, and trying to make me run; but I was so frightened I could not move my feet, and while my poor mother was trying to get me along my aunt overtook us, and she said to my mother: "Let us bury our girls, or we shall all be killed and eaten up." So they went to work and buried us, and told us if we heard any noise not to cry out, for if we did they would surely kill us and eat us. So our mothers buried me and my cousin, planted sage bushes over our faces to keep the sun from burning them, and there we were left all day.

Oh, can anyone imagine my feelings *buried alive*, thinking every minute that I was about to be unburied and eaten up by the people that my grandfather loved so much? With my heart throbbing, and not daring to breathe, we lay there all day. It seemed that the night would never come. Thanks be to God! the night came at last. Oh, how I cried and said: "Oh, father, have you forgotten me? Are you never coming for me?" I cried so I thought my very heartstrings would break.

At last we heard some whispering. We did not dare to whisper to each other, so we lay still. I could hear their footsteps coming nearer and nearer. I thought my heart was coming right out of my mouth. Then I heard my mother say,

"'Tis right here!" Oh, can anyone in this world ever imagine what were my feelings when I was dug up by my poor mother and father? My cousin and I were once more happy in our mothers,' and fathers' care. . . .

Letter to Major Henry Douglas, Superintendent of Indian Affairs for Nevada (from an 1881 reprint), by Sarah Winnemucca

It is needless for me to enter into details as to how we were treated on the reservation while there. It is enough to say that we were confined to the reserve, and had to live on what fish we might catch in the river. If this is the kind of civilization awaiting us on the reserve, God grant that we may never be compelled to go on one, as it is more preferable to live in the mountains and drag out an existence in our native manner.

So far as living is concerned, the Indians at all the military posts get enough to eat and considerable cast-off clothing; but how long is this to continue? What is the object of the Government in regard to the Indians? Is it enough that we are at peace? Remove all the Indians from the military posts and place them on reservations . . . [as they were conducted], and it will require a greater military force stationed around to keep them in the limits than it now does to keep them in subjection.

Speech presented in San Francisco, 1879, by Sarah Winnemucca

You take all the nations of the earth to your bosom but the poor Indian . . . who has lived for generations on the land which the good God has given to them, and you say he must be exterminated. [Thrice repeated, with deep passion, and received with tremendous applause.] The proverb says the big fish eat the little fishes, and we Indians are the little fish and you eat us all up and drive us from home. [Cheers.] Where can we poor Indians go if the government will not help us? If your people will help us, and you have good hearts, and can if you will, I will promise to educate my people and make them law-abiding citizens of the United States. [Loud applause.] It can be done—it can be done. [Cheers.] My father, Winnemucca, pleads with you that the guilty shall be punished, but that the innocent shall be permitted to live on their own lands in Nevada. . . . We want you to try us for four years, and if at the end of that time we don't learn, or don't work, or don't become good citizens, then you can do what you please. [Cheers.]

PART 2 | Bonanzas and Borrascas

3

First Settlements, Territory, and Early Statehood

Captain Nathaniel V. Jones's Report from the Las Vegas Mormon Fort-Mission

Leading his fellow Mormons to the Great Salt Lake in 1846–47, church leader Brigham Young sought independence for his people. One way to achieve this was by leaving the borders of the United States—which proved a failure when the United States won the Mexican-American War and the area west of the Rockies in the process. When faced with this situation, Young planned the "Mormon Corridor," a series of missions from Salt Lake City to San Bernardino that would enable members of his church to come in and out of what would become known as Utah personally or with supplies. Well aware of John C. Frémont's report of his travels on part of the Old Spanish Trail in 1843–44, Young included Las Vegas as a location for a fort-mission to serve as a pit stop on the trail for travelers—imagine Las Vegas catering to travelers—and to teach religion and farming to the Native Americans in the area.

At a meeting in April 1855, church elders made plans to send thirty missionaries to Las Vegas. Their leader, chosen by Young, was William Bringhurst, a longtime and respected church member. The group, arriving in Las Vegas on June 14, 1855, planned to settle at the Las Vegas Springs but found local Paiutes there. Unsure that the Paiutes would be friendly, Bringhurst led his mission four miles northeast to a natural bench, where they built the fort-mission.

The mission proved short-lived for a variety of reasons. One was understandable to anyone familiar with Las Vegas during the summer: It was brutally hot. The local Paiutes stole some of their crops. At least as significant, though, the missionaries began bickering. While exploring the vicinity, they found lead at Mount Potosi. One of the means of independence for Mormons was the availability of lead for bullets, and Young saw an opportunity to foster that independence. He sent a Mormon bishop and veteran miner, Nathaniel Jones, to get the lead out—literally. Jones then argued with Bringhurst, who believed that the missionaries should concentrate on their mission, not on mining. Finally, they took the matter to Young, who dismissed Bringhurst and sent the more agreeable Samuel Thompson to head the mission. Unfortunately for them, the lead proved worthless, and the mission remained divided.

Today, the Las Vegas Mormon Fort State Park includes the oldest building in the state, museum exhibits, a corral, and a replica of the creek that ran through the heart of Las Vegas until the twentieth century. The park serves as a reminder that the beginnings of Las Vegas were similar to those of many western towns—a settlement involving religion and an economy that was linked to travel.

—Michael Green

About the middle of February, 1856, Prest. Young informed me that I was called upon to go to the vicinity of the Las Vegas for the purpose of exploring that region in search of lead, as there had been some specimens sent to him from that quarter. He desired me to start as soon as I could get ready. Accordingly, I set off from this place (G.S.L. City) on the 15th of April, 1856, with the following letter of instruction from the president:

President's Office,
Utah Territory, G.S.L. City.
April 14, 1856.

To the Bishops and Presidents of the Church of Jesus Christ of Latter-day Saints who are beyond Cedar City.

Beloved Brethren:—You are hereby authorized and required to use all reasonable exertions to furnish the bearer, Bishop Nathaniel V. Jones, with such men, animals, tools, etc., as he may call upon you for, to enable him to safely, diligently, and successfully accomplish the purpose of the mission upon which he is now sent, viz: to search for and examine into the location, quality and quantity of different ores and metals, as specimens of rich lead ore have already been brought to me from that region, and it is highly desirable that we be able to make our lead, copper, etc., at the earliest practicable date.

Your brother in the gospel,
Brigham Young.

The brethren through the southern settlements responded promptly and cheerfully to my calls. At Cedar City, Bishop Philip K. Smith and Elder Ira Hatch, Indian interpreter of the Santa Clara Mission, accompanied me, furnishing the necessary means of transportation and provisions for our outfit.

We arrived at Las Vegas on the 6th of May, 1856. After a day or two of rest, we visited the place where the specimens had been obtained that were sent to the President's office. After examining the strata, I came to the conclusion that it would not pay for the working.

The range bearing the mineral runs north and south, and the mineral lays in a connected horizontal sheet, closely pinched in the rock.

In our explorations through the country we learned from the Indians that there was a quantity of the same kind of ore about fifty miles south from this place. I hired a guide and set off immediately in search of it. We were safely conducted to the place. The mineral to all appearances was inexhaustible; in quantity, it was several rods wide and varying from one to four feet in thickness; in places it was much brangled [entangled] through the rock and in others considerably burnt with ochre, though in the aggregate it was an exceedingly flattering prospect.

This mineral lays from the Vegas south by west, distance 27 miles, and about four miles east from the military road leading to California, and about 25 miles west from the Colorado and is situated high in the tops of the mountains.

The nearest running water is 12 miles, though there is a small mound spring within 1 1/2 miles from the mineral that will do for camp purposes. There is plenty of timber for fuel in the mountains, but no grass for animals.

After our explorations, we returned to the Vegas. After a day or two of rest, we started to explore the country north-west from the Vegas. We penetrated the country about 400 miles in this direction and found it to be one continuous stretch of dry, burnt-up mountains and arid sand plains entirely destitute of vegetation or timber. Not feeling disposed to risk too much in an unexplored region, thereby jeopardizing the lives of men and animals, we thought it advisable to retrace our steps. During the trip we saw nothing worthy of note, except a strata of gold-bearing quartz about 70 miles north-west from the Vegas. We were gone about six days on the trip.

On the 22nd of May, 1856, we left Las Vegas on our return to Cedar City, and in four days and three hours, we arrived safely at that place; distance 300 miles. After stopping a few days, I resumed my explorations in company with Bishop Tarlton Lewis and his son, in the mountains south of the settlement on Beaver, where it has been reported there is mineral which proved to be specular, iron ore. From here I turned my course towards this city (G.S.L. City), where I arrived on the 13th of June, after an absence of two days less than two months.

Immediately on my return, I visited Prest. Young, giving him a full account of the prospects of the lead, etc.

After a few days I was called upon to take a company and proceed immediately to the working of the mines.

On the 9th of July I started in company with three others and two four-mule teams, with all the necessary tools for the speedy prosecution of the work.

We arrived at the Vegas on the 8th of August in good health and spirits. Immediately on my arrival, I sought the first opportunity to communicate my instructions to Brother William Bringhurst, the president of the place, which were not very cordially received by him, and on the day following, it being Sunday, he came out in public against the plan of operation and refused to render me any assistance whatever. It was a matter of regret that such a feeling should have occurred.

The determined course of Brother Bringhurst was such that I was driven to an extremity, either to depart from my instructions to gratify him, or force my way through, however unpleasant it might be. I accordingly called upon the men that I was instructed to, who cheerfully responded to the call and made the necessary arrangements for provisions and set off for the mines, where we commenced our operations on the 14th of August, 1856.

The difficulties attending the opening of the mines were considerable. The mineral was situated high in the mountain and the way of access exceedingly difficult for a footman and not at all practicable for pack animals until a trail was constructed.

During the months of August and September we hired the Piedes [Paiutes] to pack down the mineral, for which we fed them during the time they were at work and gave them clothes.

The material for the furnace, except the adobes, we had to haul about 7 miles and 5 of it we had to make at considerable outlay of labor. About the 10th of September we put the furnace in blast; we soon found that the material would not stand the fire. The material throughout the country being untried, and not wishing to spend the time experimenting with it, I thought best to go to G.S.L. City, and get up a bellows and construct a blast furnace which I had every reason to believe would answer the desired purpose.

The season was far advanced to think of making a trip of nearly 1100 miles, and the time that would necessarily be spent in getting the fixtures. I started back on the 15th of September and arrived in G.S.L. City on the 1st of October, made my report to the president and proceeded forthwith to the getting of the necessary machinery.

During my stay in the city, the matter between Bro. Bringhurst and myself was brought before the presidency, the result of which was that Brother Bringhurst and council should be suspended from their office and disfellowshipped until satisfaction should be made.

On the last of October I started back with all the necessary fixtures for the furnace. After a prolonged and difficult journey I arrived at the mines on the 9th of December.

During my absence there had been but little done. The work which I left the men was for the most part untouched, and a part of the men were in favor of vacating the premises. Two of them had left, my blacksmith and smelter. I, however, sent for them and fetched them back.

After much delay we set the furnace running on the 25th of the month during which we constructed a pack trail to the diggings and set the mules to packing the ore to the furnace.

I soon found that the yield of lead was not so much as I had anticipated. We continued our work until we had smelted all of the coarse ore. We then tried to smelt the fine material. We soon found that it would not pay the board of the hands in its present impure state. By far the greatest portion of the mineral taken from the mines is in this state and to smelt it to any profit it will have to be washed, which cannot be done without hauling it about 12 miles over a very rough mountain road and from there the nearest fuel that can be got for the furnace is 7 miles.

The difficulties attending the working of the mines are very great. All the provisions and forage for animals have to be hauled 230 miles over a very hard, difficult road.

During the time we were working the mines, our mules had three pints of oats per day without any grass or hay. They lived on their own dung and this scanty allowance for six weeks. There is no grass in the country. We would sometimes send them out to browse the desert weeds and sage and of a night they would eat up rawhide ropes and everything that we could tie them with, except chains.

Besides these difficulties, the Indians threatening us upon every hand. They were stealing from us every chance they could get.

Most of the Indians in the country had collected at a spring, about 3 hours' travel from us, and were making their calculations to drive off all of our stock and drive us out of the country, or kill us. This they had been talking of doing for some time past, and I had every reason to believe they would put their threats into execution.

The difficulties attending the working of the mines, together with the hostile feelings of the Indians made me not consider it wisdom to remain longer. Accordingly, on the 26th of January, 1857, we left the mines for the Vegas. When we arrived there we sent for the Indian chiefs and had a long talk with them and made them many presents. They appeared to feel better for a few days, but in a few days after, one of the chiefs came into the fort and threatened to come upon us and kill us all.

We remained here about three weeks. During this time, I visited a prospect of mineral to see if it would pay for working, but found it would not.

On the 17th of February (perhaps the 18th) we started for the City, where we arrived the 22nd of March, 1857.

Nathaniel V. Jones

The Gold Hill Record Book

Throughout the 1850s California-style placer miners worked the sandbars of a western Great Basin ravine they called Gold Canyon. By the end of the decade it appeared that they had depleted the reserves of free gold, raising the choice of leaving or finding the source of the deposits. The problem with finding the "mother lode," as they would have called it, was that deep rock mining and extensive milling would probably have been necessary, and this was more than these early miners could afford or knew how to master.

Then, in January 1859, James "Old Virginny" Finney, John Bishop, Alexander Henderson, and John Yount struck an ore body at the head of the ravine in an area they called Gold Hill. On June 8 of that year, Patrick McLaughlin and Peter O'Riley found another ore body emerging from the ground at a spot that would be known as the Ophir Digs, located near the center of what would become Virginia City. With these discoveries, the emphasis of the mining district shifted from work on extensive but scattered gold deposits to intensive excavation of highly valuable concentrated resources. Records became important, and shortly after the June discovery local miners began documenting claims in a book now known as *Gold Hill Record Book C*, housed in the Storey County Recorder's Office.

The following describes a trade of services—the building of a mill called an arras-tra—in exchange for a share of the newly discovered ore body. The participants, some of whom failed to spell their own names consistently, executed the agreement on June 22, 1859, two weeks after the discovery. J. W. Winters Jr. is particularly note-worthy as the son of a rancher from nearby Washoe Valley. Many of the miners named in the document were important in the earliest development of the district.

—Ronald M. James

Notice of an Article of Agreement. This Indenture made and entered into this the 22nd of June 1859 between Emanul Penrod, Henry Comstock, Peter O'Ri-ley, Pat McGloughlin of the first part and J. A. Osborn, J. D. Winters Jr. of the 2nd part, Witnesseth that the first part above named do agree to sell and con-vey to the second party (J. A. Osborn, J. W. Winters Jr.) two sixth of fourteen hundred (1400) feet of a certain Quartz and Surface claim lying and being lo-cated on Pleasant Hill, U.T. for and in the [unclear] considerations, to wit. The said second party (J. A. Osborn and J. Winters Jr.) do agree to build two aras-tras and furnish stock to run the same worth the sum of seventy-five dollars each and the number of horses or mules are to be two. It is further agreed by the parties that after the completion of the first arastras, the proceeds from the vein and claim shall be equally divided between the members of the com-pany after all debt settled. . . . Copartnership it is also agreed that the second arastras shall be as soon as possible after the completion of the first. It is also agreed by the first party that the second party (J. A. Osborn and J. Winters Jr.) shall have an equal interest in all the water now on the claim for the use of working said claim and arastras. It is farther agreed by the members of the company, that, if any members of this company proposed to sell, he is to give the members of the company preference in the sale. . . .

Emannuel Penrod
Patrick McGlaughlin
J. A. Osburn
Peter O'Rielly
Joseph D. Winters Jr.
Henry Comstock
V. A. Houseworth

Congressman James M. Ashley's (R-Ohio) Reasons for Nevada's Statehood, 1865

The day after the 1862 Nevada Legislative Assembly adjourned sine die, Congressman James Mitchell Ashley of Ohio, the chairman of the House Committee on Territories, introduced bills to create the states of Nevada, Nebraska, Utah, and Colorado. Ashley's bills were setting the scene for the future of Radical Reconstruction. Clement Laird Vallandigham, a Peace Democrat from Ohio, argued against the bills, insisting that Congress should work to get back the "states that were absent before we make provisions for new States."

On February 12, 1863, as Congress was in its final month, Senator James Henry Lane of Kansas introduced the bills. The act stated that the State of Nevada would have a republican form of government and that the constitution drafted and adopted would contain an ordinance clause "irrevocable without the consent of the United States and the people of the new state." The conditions were that slavery was to be prohibited forever, there would be "perfect toleration" of all religious sentiment, and the people would disclaim forever the right and title to all unclaimed public lands.

—Jeffrey M. Kintop

Mr. Ashley of Ohio. On the 24th March, 1864, the Congress of the United States passed an enabling act authorizing the people of the Territory of Colorado to form a constitution and state government prior to their admission into the Union. Enabling Acts were also passed for the Territories of Nebraska and Nevada. I drew up those enabling acts and introduced them into this House; but finding that the Committee on Territories would not be reached in time for action on them in the Senate during the second session of the Thirty-Seventh Congress, I carried them to the Senate and had them introduced there and they passed that body; but this house failed to pass them at that session. At the first session of the Thirty-Eighth Congress the same bills or enabling acts were again introduced into both the Senate and the House, and became laws. The bill authorizing the people of Colorado to form a constitution and State government became law, as I have said, on 24th March, 1864.

My object in drafting and urging passage of those enabling acts was two-fold: one to establish a new principle in the admission of states into this Union, negativing, so far as I could in the enabling acts, the idea of State rights; the other to secure the vote of three more States, in case the election of the President and Vice President in the year 1864 should come to the House of Representatives.

William M. Ormsby's Letter to Stephen Douglas

The non-Mormon settlers of the eastern Sierra Nevada valleys began agitating for a separate territory in the late 1850s. William M. Ormsby wrote the following letter to Stephen A. Douglas, chairman of the U.S. Senate Committee on Territories, requesting just that sort of action. Douglas was no ordinary senator; in fact, there would have been no Utah Territory if not for Douglas's popular sovereignty compromise idea, which allowed the creation of new western territories and states without an explicit decision on the legality of slavery. The dream of a separate government would be realized on March 2, 1861, with the creation of the Nevada Territory. Ironically, Ormsby did not live to see the moment. He died on May 12, 1860, leading the Carson City Rangers during the ill-conceived Pyramid Lake War. Ormsby County became home to Carson City in 1861. In 1969 Ormsby County disbanded so city and county governments could consolidate and reduce costs.

—Ronald M. James

Genoa Carson Valley Utah Territory
February 12th, A.D. 1858

Hon Stephen A Douglas—

Sir   Although I have not the honor of either a personal or an epistolary acquaintance with you knowing you to be chairman of the Senate Committee on Territories, and being myself, a resident of that portion of Utah, out of which with a portion of New Mexico, it is asked in a memorial already presented to Congress, that a new Territory be formed. I am induced to address you this letter to urge upon you the immediate necessity for the organization of a Territorial Government for this country.

It is supposed that there are about six thousand inhabitants residing in the proposed new Territory and many of them like myself, have their families, their homes and their all here, and have no protection for either life or property—we have commenced the settlement of a country rich in its natural resources and the protection of Government only is needed to make it the happy home of thousands—we need a government of our own, for it is impossible for us to have the necessary means of communication with any other people for a greater portion of the year—at this season of the year, we have no communication with any but Californians and have to cross the Sierra Nevadas on snow shoes, to get to California—On the east of us we have for neighbors a people that are not only our declared enemies, but also the open enemies of the General Government, and if their fast acts indicate any thing, we are liable at any time to be driven from our homes and robbed of our property, and we need protection, we are American citizens, and are we not entitled to it—Having full confidence in your knowledge of the wants of a people situated as we are, and believing you to be disposed to urge the just claims of such a people upon the general Government, we trust the matter may be favorably considered by you at an early period, and that ere long we may have the protection of the laws of our Country.

I remain your most obedient servant and fellow citizen.

Wm. M Ormsby

President Abraham Lincoln's Proclamation of Nevada Statehood, 1864

Congress and President Lincoln agreed to invite the Nevada Territory, as well as several other pro-Union territories, to become states during the Civil War. Lincoln was particularly interested in seeing Nevada's statehood confirmed before the November 1864 election, assuming that the new state would vote for his second term in the presidency.

Fierce debate gripped Nevada's first state constitutional convention in 1863, and the final document failed to win popular support. A second convention in 1864 drafted a document that the electorate embraced, and the draft constitution went to Washington, D.C., for approval so that Nevada could achieve statehood. Unfortunately, the constitution was lost somewhere in the nation's capital.

On October 24, 1864, territorial governor James Nye received word that Washington needed another copy. It was too late for the mail service to deliver the constitution for approval before the November presidential election, so Nye had it telegraphed across the country. Costing $3,416.77 and at 16,543 words, it was the longest telegraph ever sent. Washington received the document, and Lincoln signed the following proclamation of statehood on October 31, 1864.

Fulfilling Lincoln's hope, Nevada returned its electoral votes in his favor during the election the following week. Lincoln's reference to "equal footing" could be taken to have positive implications, but in fact it was an outgrowth of the new federalism in the wake of the Civil War. This reference was a way for the federal government to suggest that Nevada would have the same rights as other states and that those rights were completely subservient to the interests of Washington, D.C.

—Ronald M. James

By the President of the United States of America: A Proclamation

WHEREAS, The Congress of the United States passed an Act, which was approved on the 21st day of March last, entitled "An Act to enable the people of Nevada to form a Constitution and State Government, and for the admission of such State into the Union on an equal footing with the original States:"

And whereas, the said Constitution and State Government have been formed, pursuant to the conditions prescribed by the fifth section of the Act of Congress aforesaid, and the certificate required by the said Act, and also a copy of the Constitution and ordinances, have been submitted to the President of the United States;

Now, therefore, be it known, that I, ABRAHAM LINCOLN, President of the United States, in accordance with the duty imposed on me by the Act of Congress aforesaid, do hereby declare and proclaim that the said State of Nevada is admitted into the Union on an equal footing with the original States. In witness whereof, I have here unto set my hand, and caused the seal of the United States to be affixed.

Done at the city of Washington this thirty-first day of October, in the year of our Lord one thousand eight hundred and sixty-four, and of the independence of the United States the eighty-ninth.

(L. S.)

ABRAHAM LINCOLN

By the President:

WILLIAM H. SEWARD, Secretary of State.

The Nevada Constitution's Paramount Allegiance Clause

Throughout the Civil War, the preservation of the Union was the principal aim of President Abraham Lincoln and the Republican majority in Congress. The delegates who framed the Nevada state constitution of 1864 strongly endorsed this objective by including in the document a "paramount allegiance" clause (Article 1, Section 2). Earlier in 1864, the self-reconstructing state of Maryland had inserted into its new constitution a declaration that the citizens of the state owed "paramount allegiance to the Constitution and Government of the United States." Nevada's constitution makers went further. They asserted that the highest loyalty of *every* American citizen was to the federal government. The clause went on to deny the right of a state to secede; announce that the federal government was fully empowered to "maintain and perpetuate its existence" and authorized to use armed force to do so; and recognize the U.S. Supreme Court's power of judicial review. Pre–Civil War state constitutions contained no such wording. Nor was the paramount allegiance clause something required of Nevada by Congress; rather, it was a spontaneous and earnest expression of the state's commitment to the Union cause. Only one delegate voted against the clause. New constitutions drawn up in the southern states during Reconstruction and the constitutions of the new states of the trans-Mississippi West contained statements acknowledging federal supremacy. None, however, had the sweeping language found in the Nevada Constitution—except for Arkansas's constitution of 1868, which adopted the Nevada paramount allegiance clause almost verbatim.

—Michael J. Brodhead

Sec. 2. All political power is inherent in the people. Government is instituted for the protection, security and benefit of the people; and they have the right to alter or reform the same whenever the public good may require it. But the paramount allegiance of every citizen is due to the Federal Government, in the exercise of all its Constitutional powers as the same have been or may be defined by the Supreme Court of the United States; and no power exists in the people of this or any other State of the Federal Union to dissolve their connection therewith, or perform any act tending to impair, subvert or resist the supreme authority of the Government of the United States. The Constitution of the United States confers full power on the Federal Government to maintain and perpetuate its existence, and whatsoever any portion of the States, or the people thereof, attempt to secede from the Federal Union, or forcibly resist the execution of its laws, the Federal Government may, by warrant of the Constitution, employ armed force in compelling obedience to its authority.

4

The Comstock

Mark Twain and Gold Fever

Gold fever was epidemic in the nineteenth-century West, inspiring masses of people to flow like the tides. These "mining rushes" could suddenly swell the location of a strike, which was just as likely to dissipate with the realization that the boom was a bust. Those with experience recognized that the excitement of a mining "bonanza" was typically little more than a fraud. Such shrewd players usually relocated or bought stock only when there was certainty in the enterprise. More often, it was the novice who responded with ignorant enthusiasm to such excitement.

Samuel Clemens was taken in by just such mining excitement. Gold fever grasped him early in his stay in Nevada in 1862. For a fleeting moment, he fashioned himself to be richer than he hoped possible. He was neither the first nor the last to succumb to gold fever, but unlike many others he was able to describe it eloquently. The following is taken from *Roughing It*, Clemens's semiautobiographical recollection of his stay in Nevada and the West. Although he is more famous for his experience with Virginia City's *Territorial Enterprise*, where he took the name Mark Twain, Clemens traveled through much of the Nevada Territory. He examined prospects in Aurora on the Nevada-California border, and he did some mining in Unionville, then the county seat of Humboldt County. He failed miserably and found mining to be hard, dirty work. The experience inspired him to find an occupation that would demand less of him. He turned to writing.

—Ronald M. James

By and by I was smitten with the silver fever. "Prospecting parties" were leaving for the mountains every day, and discovering and taking possession of rich silver-bearing lodes and ledges of quartz. Plainly this was the road to fortune. The great "Gould and Curry" mine was held at three or four hundred dollars a foot when we arrived; but in two months it had sprung up to eight hundred. The "Ophir" had been worth only a mere trifle, a year gone by, and now it was selling at nearly four thousand dollars a foot! Not a mine could be named that had not experienced an astonishing advance in value within a short time. Everybody was talking about these marvels. Go where you would, you heard nothing else, from morning till far into the night. Tom So-and-So had sold out of the "Amanda Smith" for $40,000—hadn't a cent when he "took up" the ledge six months ago. John Jones had sold half his interest in the "Bald Eagle and Mary Ann" for $65,000, gold coin, and gone to the States for his family. The widow Brewster had "struck it rich" in the "Golden Fleece" and sold ten feet for $18,000—hadn't money enough to buy a crepe bonnet when Sing-Sing Tommy killed her husband at Baldy Johnson's wake last spring. The "Last Chance" had found a "clay casing" and knew they were "right on the ledge"—consequence, "feet" that went begging yesterday were worth a brick house apiece today, and seedy owners who could not get trusted for a drink at any bar in the country yesterday were roaring drunk on champagne today and had hosts of warm personal friends in a town where they had forgotten how to bow or shake hands from long-continued want of practice. Johnny Morgan, a common loafer, had gone to sleep in the gutter and waked up worth a hundred thousand dollars, in consequence of the decision in the "Lady Franklin and Rough and Ready" lawsuit. And so on—day in and day out the talk pelted our ears and the excitement waxed hotter and hotter around us.

I would have been more or less than human if I had not gone mad like the rest. Cart-loads of solid silver bricks, as large as pigs of lead, were arriving from the mills everyday, and such sights as that gave substance to the wild talk about me. I succumbed and grew as frenzied as the craziest.

Every few days, news would come of the discovery of a brand-new mining region; immediately the papers would teem with accounts of its richness, and away the surplus populations would scamper to take possession. By the time I was fairly inoculated with the disease, "Esmeralda" had just had a run and "Humboldt" was beginning to shriek for attention. "Humboldt! Humboldt!" was the new cry, and straightway Humboldt, the newest of the new, the richest of the rich, the most marvelous of the marvelous discoveries in silver-land, was occupying two columns of the public prints to "Esmeralda's" one. I was just on the point of starting to Esmeralda, but turned with the tide and got ready for Humboldt. That the reader may see what moved me, and what would as surely have moved him had he been there, I insert here one of the newspaper letters of the day. It and several other letters from the same calm hand were the main means of converting me. I shall not garble the extract, but put it in just as it appeared in the *Daily Territorial Enterprise*.

> But what about our mines? I shall be candid with you. I shall express an honest opinion, based upon a thorough examination. Humboldt County is the richest mineral region upon God's footstool. Each mountain range is gorged with the precious ores. Humboldt is the true Golconda.
>
> The other day an assay of mere *croppings* yielded exceeding *four thousand dollars to the ton*. A week or two ago an assay of just such surface developments made returns of *seven thousand* dollars to the ton. Our mountains are full of rambling prospectors. Each day and almost every hour reveals new and more startling evidences of the profuse and intensified wealth of our favored county. The metal is not silver alone. There are distinct ledges of auriferous ore. A late discovery plainly evinces cinnabar. The coarser metals are in gross abundance. Lately evidences of bituminous coal have been detected. My theory has ever been that coal is a ligneous [*sic*] formation. I told Col. Whitman, in times past, that the neighborhood of Dayton (Nevada) betrayed no present or previous manifestations of a ligneous foundation, and that hence I had no confidence in his lauded coal mines. I repeated the same doctrine to the exultant coal discoverers of Humboldt. I talked with my friend Captain Burch on the subject. My pyrhanism vanished upon his statement that in the very region referred to he had seen petrified trees of the length of two hundred feet. Then is the fact established that huge forests once cast their grim shadows over this remote section. I am firm in the coal faith. Have no fears of the mineral resources of Humboldt County. They are immense—incalculable.

Let me state one or two things, which will help the reader to better comprehend certain items in the above. At this time, our near neighbor, Gold Hill, was the most successful silver-mining locality in Nevada. It was from there that more than half the daily shipments of silver bricks came. "Very rich" (and scarce) Gold Hill ore yielded from $100 to $400 to the ton; but the usual yield was only $20 to $40 per ton—that is to say, each hundred pounds of ore yielded from one dollar to two dollars. But the reader will perceive by the above extract, that in Humboldt from one-fourth to nearly half the mass was silver! That is to say, every one hundred pounds of the ore had from *two hundred* dollars up to about *three hundred and fifty* in it. . . .

This was enough. The instant we finished reading [about the Humboldt strike], four of us decided to go to Humboldt. We commenced getting ready at once. And we also commenced upbraiding ourselves for not deciding sooner

—we were in terror lest all the rich mines would be found and secured before we got there, and we might have to put up with ledges that would not yield more than two or three hundred dollars a ton, maybe. An hour before, I would have felt opulent if I had owned ten feet in a Gold Hill mine whose ore produced twenty-five dollars to the ton; now I was annoyed at the prospect of having to put up with mines the poorest of which would be a marvel in Gold Hill.

[*After arriving in Unionville, Twain and companions began the hunt for precious metals.*]

I confess, without shame, that I expected to find masses of silver lying all about the ground. I expected to see it glittering in the sun on the mountain summits. I said nothing about this, for some instinct told me that I might possibly have an exaggerated idea about it, and so if I betrayed my thought I might bring derision upon myself. Yet I was as perfectly satisfied in my own mind as I could be of anything, that I was going to gather up, in a day or two, or at furthest a week or two, silver enough to make me satisfactorily wealthy— and so my fancy was already busy with plans for spending this money. The first opportunity that offered, I sauntered carelessly away from the cabin, keeping an eye on the other boys, and stopping and contemplating the sky when they seemed to be observing me; but as soon as the coast was manifestly clear, I fled away as guiltily as a thief might have done and never halted till I was far beyond sight and call. Then I began my search with a feverish excitement that was brimful of expectation—almost of certainty. I crawled about the ground, seizing and examining bits of stone, blowing the dust from them or rubbing them on my clothes, and then peering at them with anxious hope. Presently I found a bright fragment and my heart bounded! I hid behind a boulder and polished it and scrutinized it with a nervous eagerness and a delight that was more pronounced than absolute certainty itself could have afforded. The more I examined the fragment the more I was convinced that I had found the door to fortune. I marked the spot and carried away my specimen. Up and down the rugged mountainside I searched, with always increasing interest and always augmenting gratitude that I had come to Humboldt and come in time. Of all the experiences of my life, this secret search among the hidden treasures of silver-land was the nearest to unmarred ecstasy. It was a delirious revel. By and by, in the bed of a shallow rivulet, I found a deposit of shining yellow scales, and my breath almost forsook me! A gold mine, and in my simplicity I had been content with vulgar silver! I was so excited that I half believed my overwrought imagination was deceiving me. Then a fear came upon me that people might be observing me and would guess my secret. Moved by this thought, I made a circuit of the place, and ascended a knoll to reconnoiter. Solitude. No creature was near. Then I returned to my mine, fortifying myself against possible disappointment, but my fears were groundless—the shining scales were still there. I set about scooping them out, and for an hour I toiled down the windings of the stream and robbed its bed. But at last the descending sun warned me to give up the quest, and I turned homeward laden with wealth. As I walked along I could not help smiling at the thought of my being so excited over my fragment of silver when a nobler metal was almost under my nose. In this little time the former had so fallen in my estimation that once or twice I was on the point of throwing it away.

The boys were as hungry as usual, but I could eat nothing. Neither could I talk. I was full of dreams and far away. Their conversation interrupted the flow of my fancy somewhat, and annoyed me a little, too. I despised the sordid and commonplace things they talked about. But as they proceeded, it began to amuse me. It grew to be rare fun to hear them planning their poor little economies and sighing over possible privations and distresses when a gold mine, all our own, lay within sight of the cabin and I could point it out at any moment. Smothered hilarity began to oppress me, presently. It was hard to resist the impulse to burst out with exultation and reveal everything; but I did resist. I said within myself that I would filter the great news through my lips calmly and be serene as a summer morning while I watched its effect in their faces. I said:

"Where have you all been?"

"Prospecting."

"What did you find?"

"Nothing."

"Nothing? What do you think of the country?"

"Can't tell, yet," said Mr. Ballou, who was an old gold miner, and had likewise had considerable experience among the silver mines.

"Well, haven't you formed any sort of opinion?"

"Yes, a sort of a one. It's fair enough here, may be, but overrated. Several thousand–dollar ledges are scarce, though. That Sheba may be rich enough, but we don't own it; and besides, the rock is so full of base metals that all the science in the world can't work it. We'll not starve, here, but we'll not get rich, I'm afraid."

"So you think the prospect is pretty poor?"

"No name for it!"

"Well, we'd better go back, hadn't we?"

"Oh, not yet—of course not. We'll try it a riffle, first."

"Suppose, now—this is merely a supposition, you know—suppose you could find a ledge that would yield, say, a hundred and fifty dollars a ton—would that satisfy you?"

"Try us once!" from the whole party.

"Or suppose—merely a supposition, of course—suppose you were to find a ledge that would yield two thousand dollars a ton—would *that* satisfy you?"

"Here—what do you mean? What are you coming at? Is there some mystery behind all this?"

"Never mind. I am not saying anything. You know perfectly well there are no rich mines here—of course you do. Because you have been around and examined for yourselves. Anybody would know that, that had been around. But just for the sake of argument, suppose—in a kind of general way—suppose some person were to tell you that two-thousand-dollar ledges were simply contemptible—contemptible, understand—and that right yonder in sight of this very cabin there were piles of pure gold and pure silver—oceans of it—enough to make you all rich in twenty-four hours! Come!"

"I should say he was as crazy as a loon!" said old Ballou, but wild with excitement, nevertheless.

"Gentlemen," said I, "I don't say anything—*I* haven't been around, you know, and of course don't know anything—but all I ask of you is to cast your eye on *that,* for instance, and tell me what you think of it!" and I tossed my treasure before them.

There was an eager scramble for it, and a closing of heads together over it under the candle-light. Then old Ballou said:

"Think of it? I think it is nothing but a lot of granite rubbish and nasty glittering mica that isn't worth ten cents an acre!"

So vanished my dream. So melted my wealth away. So toppled my airy castle to the earth and left me stricken and forlorn.

Moralizing, I observed, then, that "all that glitters is not gold."

Mr. Ballou said I could go further than that, and lay it up among my treasures of knowledge, that *nothing* that glitters is gold. So I learned then, once for all, that gold in its native state is but dull, unornamental stuff, and that only low-born metals excite the admiration of the ignorant with an ostentatious glitter. However, like the rest of the world, I still go on underrating men of gold and glorifying men of mica. Commonplace human nature cannot rise above that.

The Old Corner Bar's Water Filter

The thirst for water in the midst of the American desert is the stuff of Hollywood films. It was an incredibly difficult task to establish a mining camp in a remote location, removed from life-sustaining resources, simply because nature placed an ore body inside a steeply sloped mountain. After the strikes of 1859, thousands of opportunists rushed to the Comstock Lode in the western Great Basin. They founded Virginia City and then tried to invent ways to keep the community and its inhabitants alive. One of the pressing problems the residents of the Comstock mining district faced was how to obtain a wholesome source of water.

J. Ross Browne, journalist and artist, visited Virginia City in 1860 and was forced to leave because the foul water made him sick. He wrote in *A Peep at Washoe and Washoe Revisited* that the community's water

> was certainly the worst ever used by man. Filtered through the Comstock Lead, it carried with it much of the plumbago, arsenic, copperas, and other poisonous minerals alleged to exist in that vein. The citizens of Virginia had discovered what they conceived to be an infallible way of "correcting it;" that is to say, it was their practice to mix a spoonful of water in half a tumbler of whisky, and then drink it. The whisky was supposed to neutralize the bad effects of the water. Sometimes it was considered good to mix it with gin. I was unable to see how any advantage could be gained in this way. The whisky contained strychnine, oil of tobacco, tarentula [*sic*] juice, and various effective poisons of the same general nature, including a dash of corrosive sublimate; and the gin was manufactured out of turpentine and whiskey, with a sprinkling of prussic acid to give it flavor. For my part, I preferred taking poison in its least complicated form, and therefore adhered to the water. With hot saleratus bread, beans fried in grease, and such drink as this, it was no wonder that scores were taken down sick from day to day.

In 1873, the Virginia City Water Company completed one of the engineering wonders of the century by piping Lake Tahoe Basin water down nearly two thousand feet to Washoe Valley and then using the siphoning power of the water, bringing it back up to the Virginia Range. The community celebrated the arrival of clean, pure water with cannon fire.

Historians have generally looked at the early development of Virginia City as a time without solutions for bad water, a situation not remedied until the completion of the new water line. An archaeological investigation in 1997–98 excavated approximately one hundred thousand artifacts from John Piper's Old Corner Bar, which operated in the center of town between 1861 and 1883. Included among these remnants of the past were fifty-nine stoneware fragments of a large vessel that once served the Old Corner Bar. Volunteer Dan Urriola meticulously reassembled the fragments, restoring an extremely rare artifact that sheds light on Virginia City's past.

F. H. Atkins and Company manufactured its "patent moulded carbon filters" at 62 Fleet Street, London, England, between the 1860s and 1880s. Because the need was greatest on the Comstock during the 1860s, it is safe to assume that Piper purchased this means to obtain a clean glass of water during that decade. Emblems on the filter include the royal seal, indicating that the queen had provided the company with a license to operate.

—Ronald M. James

Obtaining drinkable water in remote mining districts could be a tremendous problem. The evidence of an English-made water filter found in Virginia City's Old Corner Bar provides insight into at least one way a community in the 1860s dealt with bad water sources. Photo by Ronald M. James

Candelaria, Nevada, displaying its "camp town" phase in 1876. Wood-frame structures and streets suggest an aim towards permanence. Courtesy of Nevada State Historic Preservation Office

Nevada Architecture in the Nineteenth Century

Nevada's architecture is a study in functionality, with its historic buildings reflecting the principal activities and natural resources of the time. Early buildings were modest and transitory in nature, in keeping with the boom-and-bust cycle of mining, Nevada's main industry. Most of the state's historic buildings are vernacular and built of local materials.

In his study of Colorado mining towns, Eric Stoehr identifies three phases of mining-town development, which apply to most Nevada communities. The first is the settlement phase, consisting of log cabins and tents and a haphazard layout. The second is the camp phase, with a larger population, more permanent, wood-framed buildings, and town grids. The architectural styles of this phase are vernacular commercial, with false fronts, and modest vernacular houses, occasionally with simplified Victorian-style elements. The third is the town phase, which reflects increased mining productivity. Towns are more formally organized, having established infrastructure. Build-

The William Wilson Cabin at the Spring Mountain Ranch, Las Vegas, built ca. 1870. It is a typical Nevada vernacular cabin, making use of local materials. Courtesy of Nevada Historical Society

As towns became more established, property owners employed architectural ornamentation, as in this modest "folk Victorian" home in Paradise Valley, Nevada. Courtesy of Nevada State Historic Preservation Office

ings are more permanent and elaborate and are frequently built of stone and brick. Public buildings built from these materials incorporate high-style Italianate, Greek Revival, Queen Anne, and Second Empire architectural details.

Nevada adds a fourth phase to mining-town development, which coincides with mining's inevitable bust cycle. This phase includes abandonment, which in Nevada often involves wholesale or partial relocation of town buildings to a more profitable location. Gaming, divorce, travel, and tourism have influenced Nevada's twentieth-century commercial architecture in the state's larger communities, closing the gap between vernacular forms and more regional styles.

—Mella Rothwell Harmon

The *Virginia Evening Chronicle* Reports on Opium on the Comstock

In the *Virginia Evening Chronicle*, a July 9, 1877, article entitled "In the Cradle of Hell" profiled the pervasive prostitution on the Comstock and its relationship to the recreational use of opiates. Equally important, however, is what it suggests about the legal context of opiate use. Interestingly, the reference to Rose Benjamin's notorious

Reno was Nevada's biggest city in the 1930s, as reflected in the high-style architecture of the beaux arts courthouse and the period revival Riverside Hotel. Courtesy of Mella Rothwell Harmon private collection

"house" is recorded several times in the *Chronicle*. Also noteworthy is the appearance of her name in both the Storey County District Indictment Records (1875–85) and *The Journals of Alfred Doten*, a diary kept by a famous newspaperman on the Comstock. The portrait of opium use is further brought to life by newspaper accounts of citizens overdosing on opium, as in the case of a prostitute who had taken a lethal amount of the opiate laudanum and was found dead in her bed at "Rose's fancy brothel."

Still, public opinion regarding the use of opiates was seemingly ambiguous until the mid-1870s, when articles such as "In the Cradle of Hell" inflamed citizens of the Comstock into pressuring the Board of Aldermen in Virginia City to enact laws that not only abolished opium dens but fined anyone smoking the drug. Clearly, the prototype user was no longer restricted to the fringes of society, that is, thieves and prostitutes and non-Euro-Americans. Rather, opium use had infiltrated mainstream Comstock society, as reflected in this account in the *Virginia Evening Chronicle*. Shocked citizens now understood that not only were their children being enticed by drugs, but often they were pressured into engaging in commercial sex to pay for their habit, as in the case for thirteen-year-old Bertha Brinton.

As accounts such as "In The Cradle of Hell" increased, public outcry resulted in legislation passed by the Nevada legislature in 1877–78 that restricted opium to medical use and made it illegal to sell opium in the state except by prescription from "legally practicing physicians." Laws were also enacted making it illegal to possess not only opium but pipes and related apparatus. As would be expected, these laws were difficult to enforce, and opiate use continued through the turn of the century, which saw the demise of mining prosperity on the Comstock. Nevertheless, attitudes about opiate use were beginning to change. As part of the Progressive agenda, national legislation such as the Pure Food and Drug Act (1906) and the Harrison Narcotics Act (1914) restricted the use of opiates and expanded federal responsibility for the welfare of ordinary citizens including those of the fledging Comstock Lode.

—Sharon Lowe

IN THE CRADLE OF HELL

A Missing Girl Found in Rose Benjamin's Den of Infamy.

The Father and Mother Refused Admittance by the Old Hag—An Indignant Crowd Threaten to Tear Down the House—The Girl Finally Surrendered.

An extraordinary scene was enacted on D Street last night, the villainous aspect of which cast a shadow even over that contaminated locality. It appears that about four days ago a laboring man living near the C. and C. shaft sent his daughter to a grocery store for some soap and she did not return that night. Becoming alarmed for her safety he began a search, which was unsuccessful until last evening, when a young man conveyed to him the information that she was in the house of Rose Benjamin, a den which is ranked as the most notorious deadfall in the city. The parents of the child immediately went to the place and the father demanded admittance. Mrs. Benjamin, the harridan who runs the establishment, refused him admittance and slammed the door in his face. The mother stood on the walk weeping and wringing her hands, and the father, unable to force the door and fearing for his life if he did, was obliged to remain on the outside, while a crowd of over 100 men collected in the street.

The Crowd Roused

When the gathering crowd took in the situation the excitement became intense and cries of "Pull down the house!" "Gut the den!" "Clean out the deadfall!" and similar expressions were heard on all sides. Two citizens who had arrived in the meantime told the man to force the door and go in, and pledged themselves to see him through, even if they had to break the necks of every woman in the place. A number of men then declared their intention of forcing the door, when the woman Benjamin came to the door, and with the blandest smile possible said: "Why, gentlemen! Why do so many people come about my door?" She was greeted with groans of derision, and the father then went into the house and began searching the rooms. A young boy who was in the place told him to go upstairs. The father went upstairs and found the girl in a room fronting the street, but the blinds were shut and the curtains drawn close to prevent any light from reaching the outside. He brought his daughter out, while Rose, all smiles and politeness, remarked: "Why, certainly, if this girl is your daughter, take her home, this is no place for a young girl." The parents hurried the young girl away as soon as possible, while the excited crowd remained for some time and discussed the propriety of demolishing the building. It was rumored that another girl was detained there who was but thirteen years old, but no one seemed to take a sufficient personal interest in her to go in and take her out, and the certainty of her being there at all was not established, and the crowd gradually dispersed. Half an hour afterwards a CHRONICLE reporter called at the place to ascertain the cause of the difficulty, and the woman solemnly asserted that everything had been perfectly quiet and peaceful there for the past twelve hours. If there had been any disturbance at all it was at a place a few doors above.

An Interview with the Girl

The reporter called at the girl's house this morning and obtained additional particulars. She is a rather comely and well-developed girl, fifteen years of age. She faced the interviewer boldly and did not seem to experience the slightest sense of shame. She at first refused to answer any questions, until her mother, who was in the room, told her to come out with the whole story, which was substantially as follows:

"I was four days in the house, and was induced to go there by a girl named Frankie Norton. I first met her at Charley Summers' lodging house, on North C Street, some months ago. We smoked opium together, and she asked me to come to the house. I did so, and for the three nights I was at the house I slept with her. Rose said that I must sleep with men like the rest of the girls, but I never did. I remained up stairs in Frankie's room all of the time."

Reporter—How long have you smoked opium?

Girl—About seven months.

Here the mother threw up her hands in astonishment and burst into tears. The girl took no special notice of this, but in answer to a query of the reporter continued: I smoked in Chinatown and Gold Hill. The places are open every night. All the places are open, but I never went into but two of them.

Reporter—Into which place did you go?

Girl—I shan't tell you that.

Reporter—How many pipes did you smoke in a day?

Girl—About thirty-five, but sometimes not more than twelve. If I don't smoke it I feel sick; I want some now.

Here the girl showed signs of weariness, gaping repeatedly and leaning her head on the back of the chair in a half sleepy state.

Something for Officer Kinzle

The mother here stated that some months ago she was unable to find her daughter, and went to Judge Moses, who gave Officer Kinzle a warrant to arrest her and take her home. The officer found her at a house on E street, knowing who she was, but took no pains to return her to her parents.

This the girl denied *in toto*, but after a little questioning admitted that the officer had found her there, and knew who she was, but made no attempt to detain her, knowing she was going to Gold Hill to smoke opium.

Another Young Girl in the Place

Rep.—Are there any more girls there?

Girl—Yes; a girl named Bertha Brinton of Gold Hill. She was passing along the street the other day, when Rose called her in and said she would give her $20 a month to sweep out the rooms. Afterwards she told her she must sleep with men, but I don't know whether she did or not. She is about 13 years old.

The mother then stated that three months before the girl had been enticed into the same house and taken out, and that she had to be continually watched to prevent her stealing off to smoke opium. At the time of the interview the girl seemed stupefied with the drug and utterly indifferent to her situation.

Something about the Den

The establishment over which Mrs. Benjamin presides is a resort for thieves, prostitutes and opium-smokers. It is notorious for the number of its robberies, and men who go there are treated to drugged liquors. Each girl acts as a procuress to the place, and half a dozen pimps are generally at work furnishing women. It is a sink-hole for the dregs of the street and continually full of frouzy, emaciated and diseased women, who have been turned out of other houses or recruited from the opium dens of Chinatown. The woman has been before the Police Court dozens of times, yet she has generally managed to get off, and boasts that she can "break" any policeman on the force who interfered with her business. Her last application for a license was refused by the Board of Aldermen and the house is now run in the name of some male "friend" who holds a license.

Last night the Board of Aldermen were openly denounced for allowing such an infamous deadfall to exist, and it is to be hoped that at the next meeting the license under which the place is run will be revoked.

Dan De Quille on Woodcutting in the Sierra Nevada

Dan De Quille, also known as William Wright, worked as a reporter (with a young Samuel Clemens) for the *Territorial Enterprise* during the peak years of the Comstock Lode. In this capacity he became an expert on mining and milling, and he frequently wrote articles about the mines and other aspects of life in Virginia City. The following excerpt is from De Quille's 1877 book, *History of the Big Bonanza*, in which he collected stories and told the history of the Comstock.

De Quille's astute observations about the environment—particularly his concerns about regional warming—raise issues that resonate today. His concerns about deforestation and the loss of quicksilver may sound antibusiness, but De Quille was a firm supporter of the mines and the economy they supported. Lumber was needed to support vast underground excavations, and De Quille would have seen deforestation as a necessary evil.

Nineteenth-century deforestation of the Sierra Nevada and the Tahoe Basin in particular continues to be an issue for those who live and recreate in the area. The trees that replaced the old growth tend to be limited to a few dominant species. Lacking prehistoric diversity, the forest now responds to drought, climate extremes, and diseases in a monolithic way. While only some of the trees of the older forest may have been affected by a shortage of water, for example, now the entire forest tends to react in the same way. Although the Tahoe Basin may appear to have recovered from Comstock-era deforestation, the effects are still with us today.

De Quille also describes the loss of millions of pounds of mercury into the environment. During the 1990s the federal Environmental Protection Agency (EPA) studied the Carson River and the Dayton area as a potential Superfund site. The EPA authorized cleanup of some sites but concluded that it would not be possible to retrieve the vast majority of the lost mercury. As it turns out, most of the mercury—some of which is undoubtedly amalgamated (or combined) with gold and silver—has sunk into the depths of the Carson River bed. It would be possible to retrieve the heavy metals, but the process would inevitably return at least some toxins to the flowing river. EPA officials determined that it would be best to leave the mercury where it is, since it is for the most part inactive in the present-day ecosystem.

—Ronald M. James

The Comstock Lode may truthfully be said to be the tomb of the forests of the Sierras. Millions on millions of feet of lumber are annually buried in the mines, nevermore to be resurrected. When once it is planted in the lower levels it never again sees the light of day. The immense bodies of timber now being entombed along the Comstock will probably be discovered some thousands of years hence by the people to be born in a future age, in the shape of huge beds of coal some thousands of years hence, and the geologists of that day will probably say that this coal or lignite came from large deposits of driftwood at the bottom of a lake; that there came a grand upheaval, and Mount Davidson arose, carrying the coal with it on its eastern slope.

Not less than eighty million feet of timber and lumber are annually consumed on the Comstock Lode. In a single mine, the Consolidated Virginia, timber is being buried at the rate of six million feet per annum, and in all other mines in like proportion. At the same time about 250,000 cords of wood are consumed.

The pine forests of the Sierra Nevada are drawn upon for everything in the shape of wood or lumber, and have been thus drawn upon for many years. For a distance of fifty or sixty miles all the hills of the eastern slope of the Sierras have been to a great extent denuded of trees of every kind—those suitable only for wood as well as those fit for the manufacture of lumber for use in the mines. Already the lumbermen are not only extending their operations to a greater distance north and south along the great mountain range, but are also beginning to reach over to the western slope—over to the California side of the range.

Long since, all the forests on the lower hills of the Nevada side of the mountains that could be reached by teams were swept away, when the lumbermen began to scale the higher hills, felling the trees thereon and rolling or sliding the logs down to flats whence they could be hauled. The next movement was to erect sawmills far up in the mountains, and from these to construct large flumes leading down into the valleys, through which to float wood, lumber, and timber. Some of these flumes are over twenty miles in length and are very substantial structures, costing from $20,000 to $250,000 each. They are built on a regular grade and, in order to maintain this grade, wind round hills, pass along the sides of steep mountains, and cross deep canyons, reared, in many places, on trestle-work of great height.

These flumes are made so large that timbers sixteen inches square and twenty or thirty feet in length may be floated down in them. In a properly constructed flume, timbers of a large size are floated by a very small head of water; and not alone single logs, but long processions of them. Timbers, wood, lumber—in fact all that will float—are carried away as fast as thrown in. When a stick of timber or a plank has been placed in the flume, then ends all the expense of transportation, as without further attention it is dumped in the valley—twenty miles away, perhaps. By means of these flumes tens of thousands of acres of timber-land are made available that could never have been reached by teams.

In some places, where the ground is very steep, there are to be seen what are called gravitation flumes, down which wood is sent without the aid of water. These, however, are merely straight chutes, running from the top to the bottom of a single hill or range of hills. In places they are of great use, as through them wood may be sent down within reach of the main water-flume leading to the valley. Nearly all of the flumes have their dumps near the line of the Virginia and Truckee Railroad or some of its branches or side-tracks, and in these dumps are at times to be seen thousands upon thousands of cords of wood and millions of feet of lumber.

In some localities a kind of chute is in use made by laying down a line of heavy timbers in such shape as to form a sort of trough. Down these tracks or troughs are slid huge logs. When the troughs are steep, the logs rush down at more than railroad speed, leaving behind them a trail of fire and smoke. Such log-ways are generally to be seen about the lakes, and are so contrived that the logs leap from them into water of great depth, as otherwise they would be shivered to pieces and spoiled for use in the manufacture of lumber. Occasionally, in summer, a daring lumberman mounts a large log at the top of one of these chutes, high up the mountain, and darting down at lightning speed, with hair streaming in the breeze, takes a wild leap of twenty or thirty feet into the lake. . . .

The time is not far distant when the whole of that part of the Sierra Nevada range lying adjacent to the Nevada silver-mining region will be utterly denuded of trees of every kind. Already one bad effect of this denudation is seen in the summer failure of the water in the Carson River. The first spell of hot weather in the spring now sweeps nearly all the snow from the mountains and sends it down into the valleys in one grand flood, whereas while the mountains were thickly clad with pines the melting of the snow was gradual and there was a good volume of water in the river throughout the summer and fall months.

The prevailing breezes in Nevada are from the west—indeed the wind seldom blows from any other quarter than the west—which is directly over the Sierra Nevada Mountains. In passing over the fields of snow on the summit of the Sierras, the breezes are cooled, and the summer weather in Nevada is thus rendered delightful. But when once the mountains shall have been denuded of their timber, all the snow on both slopes will be swept away by the first warm weather of spring—as it is now swept away on the eastern slope—when a marked increase in the heat of the summers in Nevada is likely to be experienced. . . .

Just what becomes of all the quicksilver used in the reduction works of Nevada is a question that has never yet been fully satisfactorily answered. Much floats away with the water flowing from the mills, but it cannot be that the whole of the immense quantities used is lost in that way. Quicksilver in great quantities is constantly being taken into the state, and not an ounce is ever returned. When it has been used in the amalgamation of a batch of ore, it is taken to the amalgamating-pans and is used over and over again until it has disappeared. Whether it may float away with the water used in amalgamating, or is lost by evaporation while in the hot-bath of the steam-heated pans, there must be a vast amount of the metal collected somewhere, as it is a metal not easily destroyed. In case it is lost by evaporation it must condense and fall to the ground somewhere near the works in which it is used, and if it floats away in the water it must eventually find a resting-place on the bottom of the stream in which it is carried away.

It is an axiom among millmen that "wherever quicksilver is lost silver is lost"; therefore, there must be a large amount of silver lost, as we shall presently see. The amount of quicksilver used by mills working the Comstock

The Comstock mines and towns had a voracious appetite for lumber. Loggers used water, gravity, and V-shaped flumes to deliver large timber from high in the Sierra Nevada to mills in the valleys. An occasional daredevil could not resist the thrilling and dangerous ride pictured here. From Dan De Quille, *History of the Big Bonanza;* courtesy of Ronald M. James Collection

alone averages 800 flasks, of 76 1/2 pounds each; or 61,200 pounds per month. This in one year would amount to 734,400 pounds of quicksilver that go somewhere, and counting backwards for ten years shows 7,344,000 pounds that have *gone* somewhere—either up the flue or down the flume.

Fortune-Telling on the Comstock

Diverse occupations in the communities of the Comstock Lode reflected mid-nineteenth-century American culture. Fortune-tellers and spiritualists were found nationwide, and many people used their services. Numerous residents of the Comstock mining region turned to these seers for direction and insight and pondered timeless questions about life and love.

Ready to supply answers, these workaday prophets, primarily women, practiced ancient divination techniques familiar to many immigrants. In individual sessions fortune-tellers interpreted astrological charts, gazed into crystal balls, and studied palms and tea leaves. Spiritualists conducted group séances, demonstrated automatic writing and levitations, and spoke with spirits. Some audiences found the idea of communicating with spirits entertaining, while others believed in the supernatural powers of mediums.

Among the fortune-tellers and spiritualists were frauds who duped the public with fabricated messages and prank forecasts. The Comstock was no different than other communities across the country, drawing all sorts of swindlers as well as serious practitioners.

Some women found their voice in the spiritualist setting. Mediums could publicly philosophize on social topics that might have previously been addressed by men. They could offer advice based on a spirit's interpretation even if it conflicted with the conventions of society. Many women who had early roots as mediums became popular and influential lecturers for social reform.

Whether lecturing on the limited view of the Bible, conversing with spirits, or advertising their abilities to tell past, present, and future events by studying cards and the movement of planets, these women offered an alternative to existing cultural standards. Their long presence on the Comstock underscores an age-old need that has been prevalent throughout history. Fortune-tellers and spiritualists offered explanations and directions for those who were curious and uncertain about the past and the future. The following newspaper clippings (and, in one case, a journal entry) give a sense of the practices and public perceptions of spiritualists in Comstock-era Nevada.

—Bernadette C. Francke

From the *Virginia Evening Chronicle*, April 15, 1867

SPIRITUALISTS THIS EVENING—All the spiritualists of this city and their friends are notified that this evening, at the Court House, at half past 7 o'clock Mrs. Dettenrieder will deliver a lecture under the inspiration of the spirits, giving their view of the idea of forming an institute for the elevation of woman, and through her of the race. Ladies are admitted free, but gentleman are of course expected to pay toll at the door. Madame Dettenrieder is a writing medium, chosen by the spirits through whom to communicate with the lower world, and all who attend this evening will undoubtedly be much interested.

From the *Gold Hill Evening News*, November 18, 1867

SPIRITUAL MATTERS—Ada Hoyt Foye the well known rapping* and writing medium, held a séance at the District Court Room, Virginia, last evening which was very fully attended, even all the standing room being occupied. The manifestations were very numerous, and answers to questions correctly given. Much interest was demonstrated on the part of the audience. The séance was inaugurated by the recital by Lisle Lester of an excellent poem entitled "No Sect in Heaven." Mr. and Mrs. Foye left on the Pioneer stage this afternoon for Grass Valley, where a series of séances will be given. Mrs. Laura DeForce Gordon, said to be a highly gifted inspirational trance medium, will arrive at Virginia in three or four days, where she will deliver a course of lectures.

From the *Gold Hill Evening News*, July 6, 1870

LAURA DEFORCE GORDON—A letter from the above talented lady informs us that she will shortly visit this section and lecture in all the principal cities and towns upon "Spiritualism," "Woman's Rights" and kindred subjects. She is one of the best and most effective lecturers in the United States, and having numerous friends in this section, she will doubtless draw as good audiences as she did when here before.

From the *Territorial Enterprise*, December 10, 1878

"SPIRIT POWER."—Those who went to Piper's Opera house last Sunday evening to witness exhibitions of "spirit power," to be given by "Miss Graham"

---

*Presumably this means that she would knock on the table and spontaneously write, using herself as a conduit for the spiritual world to make contact.

and Anderson, the weird "wizard" of Bitter Creek, got a very thin dose of it. It was the most glaring and inartistic humbug ever peddled out on the Comstock. To travel on so small a stock of bald, third-rate tricks the pair must have the cheek (and jowl) of a hippopotamus.

From *The Journals of Alfred Doten*, Book 25, October 25, 1867

At 11 A.M. I went with Joe Goodman & Dagget & had a private sitting with Mrs. Foye—They called up the spirit of E G Page (Dow Jr)—He told when he died, correctly, & also that his death was from the too free use of Russian Arrack—& and that he used to drink it from an oil can sometimes (correct)—They also called up two other literary men & got satisfactory answers—I could not raise anybody. . . .

From the *Territorial Enterprise*, September 25, 1874

A SEERESS ON OUR MINES—Mrs. Bowers, of the Bowers' Mansion, Washoe Valley, widow of Sandy Bowers, was in this city day before yesterday on a visit to some friends. Mrs. Bowers—was born and reared in the "Land o' Cakes" and claims to have inherited the Scottish gift of second-sight. Her fathers before her were seers of great repute, far and near, in the Highlands of her native land. She has at various times foretold things that were to happen in this part of the county and along the line of the Comstock. . . .

A July 9, 1877, issue of the *Virginia Evening Chronicle* included advertisements for three fortune-tellers. Courtesy of Nevada State Library and Archives

Julia Bulette's Probate Records

On the morning of January 20, 1867, Comstock prostitute Julia Bulette was strangled for a few pieces of costume jewelry and some fancy dresses. The discovery of her body caused a sensation when Virginia City newspapers reported the details of the grisly crime scene. Then interest in the story all but disappeared until a French immigrant named John Millian was arrested, tried, and hanged for the murder over a year later. The combination of sex, violence, and a public execution inspired one of the Comstock's most enduring legends.

"Jule" Bulette began plying her trade in the booming mining district in the early 1860s. By nineteenth-century standards she was a midrange prostitute, several notches above streetwalkers and the concubines of the community's Chinatown. Bulette competed for business with the fancy brothels as well as other independent operators like herself. She lived and worked in a small rented crib on the northeast corner of D and Union Streets in the heart of Virginia City's "entertainment district." Probate records and inquest testimony indicate that Bulette was sick and in debt at the time of her death.

Later folklore would propel Bulette into the role of magnificent prostitute, brothel owner, and philanthropist. The idea that she was a grand courtesan became a cornerstone of her evolving story. One author incorrectly asserted that she rode through the streets of Virginia City "in a lacquered brougham upon whose side-panels were emblazoned her crest—an escutcheon of four aces, crowned by a lion couchant." Others have written of lavish parties that placed the demimonde at the center of Comstock culture.

Twentieth-century chroniclers perpetuated the exaggerated version of oral tradition, partly because Bulette fulfills a western archetype of the whore with a heart of gold. Her story employs the motif of an intrinsically kind, wealthy prostitute whose morals may have fallen but who still wishes to engage in good works. The altered account of Bulette's life insulates readers from the miserable reality of the sex trade. Her legend, far removed from fact, has proven more powerful than truth.

Today only a few primary sources offer a glimpse into Bulette's actual existence. The following list of property was associated with the probate of her will, the result of a failed effort to raise enough funds to cover her debts. From the document housed in the clerk's office at the Storey County Courthouse, it is clear that Bulette was a clotheshorse who invested in the finery that might have given her an edge in the competitive world of sexual commerce.

—Susan James

Appraisement of the Estate of Julia Bulette

DECEASED

February 5, 1867

No.	Item	Value
1	Double Mahogany Bedstead	$12.00
1	Red Saloon Table	1.00
7	White Lace Curtains	8.00
2	Pair Damask Curtains	5.00
1	Parlor Set: 4 Black Walnut A.C. Chair	
	1 Black Walnut A.C. Rocker	
	1 Black Walnut A.C. Sofa	Total 30.00
3	Maple C. S. Chairs	3.75
1	Dark C. S. Rocker	3.00
1	Mahogany Whatnot	7.00
1	Double Spring Mattress	13.00
1	Double Hair Mattress	14.00
1	Mahogany Bureau with Glass	14.00
1	Mahogany Parlor Table	5.00
1	Black Walnut Marble Top Table	9.00
2	Large Parlor C. O. Lamps @ 2.50	5.00
3	Pieces Brussels Carpet as is	
1	Piece Ingrain Carpet as is	Total 10.00
1	Door Rug	.50
1	Small Box Stove 7 Pipe 1 Elbow 1pc. Zinc	5.00
1	Mahogany Wash Stand enclosed	6.00
1	Large Iron Stove	8.00
1	Double Pulu Mattress	3.00
4	Buff Window Shades	1.00
3	Gilt Cornices	.50
1	B. S. Spittoon	
1	Feather Duster	Total 1.00
1	Lot Assorted Tinware	1.00
2	Washbowls	
1	Pitcher	

Appraisement of the Estate of Julia Bulette (continued)

No.	Item	Value
1	Chamber[pot]	
2	Spittoons	Total 2.00
1	Buckel	
1	Waiter	Total .25
2	Feather Pillows & Slips	5.00
		Amount Carried Forward $173.00
	Amount Brot forward	173.00
1	Bolster	1.00
2	Pair White Blankets Cal.	8.00
1	Pair White Mars. Spread	1.00
1	Fancy Bed Spread	2.00
1	Black and Striped Silk Dress	15.00
1	Brown Col. Silk Dress	15.00
1	Stone Col. Silk Dress	15.00
1	Black Fig Silk Dress	15.00
1	Solferino Skirt	5.00
1	Brown Wrapper	5.00
4	Wool Dresses @ 2.50	10.00
1	Grey Marino Suit	5.00
15	Linen Cotton and Calico Dresses @ 1.50	22.50
2	Riding Habits @ $5.00	10.00
1	Riding Skirt	4.00
2	Silk Cloaks @ 3.00	6.00
1	Red and 1 Black Velvet Coat @ 1.00	2.00
2	Cloaks	2.50
3	Assorted Sacks	1.00
1	Red Circular Cloak	2.50
1	Red and Black Wool Cloak	1.50

No.	Item	Value
1	Cashmere Shawl	2.50
1	Box Hair	.50
1	Parasol	.50
5	Pair Stockings	1.00
16	Assorted Skirts @ 1.00	16.00
15	Assorted Chemise @ 1.00	15.00
6	Assorted Flannel Skirts @ 1.00	6.00
12	Assorted Jackets @ .50	6.00
2	Corsets	.50
1	Pair Shoes & 1 Pr. Slippers	.25
4	Pillow & Bolster Cases	5.00
2	Bolster Cases 1 Tidy & 2 Pillow Cases	2.00
	Amount Carried Forward	$377.25

Amount Brot Forward		$377.25
11	Pair Assorted Drawers @ .25	2.75
1	Table Clock	.25
1	Double Sheet	1.00
1	Gilt Frame Picture	.50
1	Bandbox containing 3 Assorted Hats	2.00
1	Lot Glass ware Tea Bell, etc.	5.00
2	Baskets Books	3.00
1	Basket fancy Box Basket Fruit	1.00
3	Trunks	10.00
1	Basket & 1 Bag Calamities	.50
4	Double Sheets	4.00
14	Towels	1.50
3	Sacks @ .50	1.50
1	Chemise	1.00
1	Double White Mars. Spread	1.00
2	Handkerchiefs	.25
2	Pair Drawers	1.00

Appraisement of the Estate of Julia Bulette (continued)

No.	Item	Value
1	Small Dressing Case with Glass	1.00
1	Diamond Ring & Purse	50.00
1	Opera Glass	5.00
1	Pair Gold Bracelets	30.00
1	Gold Chain & Locket	6.00
	Coin	1.50
1	Small lot assort. Jewelry	1.50
1	Hair Dagger & Breast Pin	1.00
1	Coral Necklace	2.50
		$512.00
1	Gold Buckle and Belt	5.00
		$517.00

Mark Twain's Description of the Execution of John Millian, 1868

Before he left Nevada for the last time, Mark Twain sent two dispatches about his western travels from Virginia City to the *Chicago Republican*. Twain's second letter, dated May 2, 1868, included his eyewitness report of the hanging of John Millian (or Melanie), who the previous year had been convicted of murdering Virginia City prostitute Julia Bulette. Together, Bulette's murder and Millian's trial and execution rank among nineteenth-century Nevada's landmark events, and over the years the pair has reached mythological status, with Bulette as the prostitute with a heart of gold and Millian as the archvillain.

Remarkably, Twain scholars have paid scant attention to his May 2 letter from Virginia City, which also covered mining news and travel notes and appeared in the *Chicago Republican* on May 31, 1868.

—Guy Louis Rocha

THE CHICAGO REPUBLICAN, May 31, 1868 LETTER FROM MARK TWAIN.

CURIOUS CHANGES.

Special Correspondence of the *Chicago Republican*

Virginia, Nevada, May 2

I find some changes since I was here last. The little wildcat mines are abandoned and forgotten, and the happy millionaires in fancy (I used to be one of them) have wandered penniless to other climes, or have returned to honest labor for degrading wages. But the majority of the great silver mines on the Comstock Lode are flourishing . . .

NOVEL ENTERTAINMENT

But I am tired talking about mines. I saw a man hanged the other day, John Melanie, of France. He was the first man ever hanged in this city (or county either), where the first twenty-six graves in the cemetery were those of men who died by shots and stabs. I never had witnessed an execution before, and did not believe I could be present at this one without turning away my head at the last moment. But I did not know what fascination there was about the thing, then. I only went because I thought I ought to have a lesson, and because I believed that if ever it would be possible to see a man hanged, and derive satisfaction from the spectacle, this was the time. For John Melanie was no common murderer—else he would have gone free. He was a heartless assassin. A year ago, he secreted himself under the house of a woman of the town who lived alone, and in the dead watches of the night, he entered her room, knocked her senseless with a billet of wood as she slept, and then strangled her with his fingers. He carried off all her money, her watches, and every article of her wearing apparel, and the next day, with quiet effrontery, put some crepe on his arm and walked in her funeral procession.

Afterward he secreted himself under the bed of another woman of the town, and in the middle of the night was crawling out with a sling-shot in one hand and a butcher knife in the other, when the woman discovered him, alarmed the neighborhood with her screams, and he retreated from the house. Melanie sold dresses and jewelry here and there until some of the articles were identified as belonging to the murdered courtesan. He was arrested and then his later intended victim recognized him. After he was tried and condemned to death, he used to curse and swear at all who approached him; and he once grossly insulted some young Sisters of Charity who came to minister kindly to his wants. The morning of the execution, he joked with the barber, and told him not to cut his throat—he wanted the distinction of being hanged.

This is the man I wanted to see hung. I joined the appointed physicians, so that I might be admitted within the charmed circle and be close to Melanie. Now I never more shall be surprised at anything. That assassin got out of the closed carriage, and the first thing his eye fell upon was that awful gallows towering above a great sea of human heads, out yonder on the hill side and his cheek never blanched, and never a muscle quivered! He strode firmly away, and skipped gaily up the steps of the gallows like a happy girl. He looked around upon the people, calmly; he examined the gallows with a critical eye, and with the pleased curiosity of a man who sees for the first time a wonder he has often heard of. He swallowed frequently, but there was no evidence of trepidation about him—and not the slightest air of braggadocio whatever. He prayed with the priest, and then drew out an abusive manuscript and read from it in a clear, strong voice, without a quaver in it. It was a broad, thin sheet of paper, and he held it apart in front of him as he stood. If ever his hand trembled in even the slightest degree, it never quivered that paper. I watched him at that sickening moment when the sheriff was fitting the noose about his neck, and pushing the knot this way and that to get it nicely adjusted to the hollow under his ear—and if they had been measuring Melanie for a shirt, he could not have been more perfectly serene. I never saw anything like that before. My own suspense was almost unbearable—my blood was leaping through my veins, and my thoughts were crowding and trampling upon each other. Twenty moments to live—fifteen to live—ten to live—five—three—heaven and earth, how the time galloped! And yet that man stood there unmoved though he knew that the sheriff was reaching deliberately for the drop while the black cap descended over his quiet face! Then down through the hole in the scaffold the strap-bound figure shot like a dart! A dreadful shiver started at the shoulders, violently convulsed the whole body all the way down, and died away with a tense drawing of the toes downward, like a doubled fist—and all was over!

I saw it all. I took exact note of every detail, even to Melanie's considerately helping to fix the leather strap that bound his legs together and his quiet removal of his slippers and I never wish to see it again. I can see that stiff, straight corpse hanging there yet, with its black pillow-cased head turned rigidly to one side, and the purple streaks creeping through the hands and driving the fleshy hue of life before them. Ugh!

James Nye's Speech to the First Territorial Legislature

In 1861 the Congress of the United States issued the Nevada Organic Act, which allowed the western Utah Territory to organize as a separate territory. Two developments made this possible. First, the discovery of the Comstock Lode attracted thousands to western Utah. The population of the proposed Nevada Territory more than doubled in 1860–61, and nearly all of those people resided in the Comstock and its environs. Second, the creation of the Confederate States of America in February 1861 removed Southern opposition to a Nevada territory from Congress while simultaneously giving incentive to that Congress to create new pro-North territories and eventually pro-Republican states. Hence Nevada was truly "battle born."

In the speech excerpted below, James Nye of New York addresses the territorial legislature just days after his arrival in northern Nevada. In a second-floor room of Abe Curry's hotel in Carson City, Nye unambiguously sets the tone for that first legislative session. He proclaims Nevada's pro-Northern stance strongly (he was appointed because of his work in support of Republicans in the 1860 election in New York), and, ironically, he sets a strong moral tone for the territory that would soon head elsewhere as the Nevada mining towns embraced the "noisy amusements" that Nye condemns.

—John B. Reid

Gentlemen of the Council and House of Representatives

Your presence here in the capacity of Legislators, furnishes the highest and most satisfactory evidence of the kind parental regard and attention that our best of governments bestows upon her most distant people. Its care and protection leap over mountains, fly over seas, pass over deserts, in pursuit of its most erratic and wandering citizens, as the ever watchful mother, whatever her cares, troubles, and embarrassments at home, never fails to watch vigilantly for her absent children. A government so kind and considerate cannot fail, if properly appreciated, to attach all good and reflecting people to it. Its blessings are so apparent, that to enumerate them would impugn the intelligence of the chosen Representatives of a people engaged in an effort to form a system of laws for their guidance, in harmony with the benign example of the General Government from which they receive this authority.

It can be truly said that this Territorial organization came into existence in an hour of national embarrassment and trouble, just as the mutterings now ripened into rebellion began to be heard.

It is impossible if we would, to be less than anxious observers of these trials and tribulations of the Government from which we derive our power and existence. The natural instinct of the human heart is to make grateful returns for favors gracefully bestowed, and if instinct teaches this ennobling and lofty principle, how much more should reason, the proud boast of man, teach us to revere and honor the power that has conferred upon you and your constituents the high prerogative to discharge the responsible duties you this day assume.

The power conferred, the responsibility of your positions, the consequences attendant upon your action, not only upon the present inhabitants, but upon the countless ones that shall come after them, should serve to admonish you that your joint and several action, should be marked by discretion, wisdom, and patriotism; remembering that it is a fearful thing to have only the present in view when making laws for unborn generations.

The magnanimity of the General Government, in placing in the Organic Act speaking this Territory into existence, no restraints, shows the confidence it reposes in even its minor children. It gives free scope to our youthful energies, and relies upon our judgment to direct them aright. Fully imbued with the belief that self-government is man's Heaven-born heritage, and that he is fully possessed of sufficient capacity to husband well so rich a patrimony, it hands it over to our keeping with all the confidence of a doting parent. There is but one single restraint, if indeed that can be called a restraint, and that is, that all of our legislation, and public and private acts, shall be in accordance with the Constitution of the United States, an instrument combining more excellencies, more safeguards, more protection, than any other constitution under which any people were ever permitted to live.

The wisdom displayed by its authors in so directing the powers of the government as to make it certain that no oppression can exist under it, in making each of the three powers occupy so important a position as to operate as a check upon the others, challenges the admiration of the world. The true test of all things is the result produced. Under the benign influence of the constitution, a weak and tottering government, existing under a simple confederacy, has become strong and irresistible; its infantile limbs are robust as the giant's; its feeble steps firm with strength; its weakness has been changed into power; its expansion is unparalleled; its glory unequaled; its wide-spread Territories have been as by magic transformed into States. Civilization has kept pace with the pioneer, and enterprise, education and religion have grown up and flourished in the most distant settlements. Under it Commerce has spread her whitened wings upon the bosom of every ocean, sea, lake and navigable river in the known world. It leaves untrammeled the boundless energies of all who live under it. It adopts no form of religion, but kindly fosters and protects all. It leaves the conscience of each, aided by revelation, the monitor to point the way to a brighter and better state of existence. Here no streams of blood wash the shrines of religious bigotry. Here no restraint is placed upon the freedom of political thought or action. The sacred ballot is the chosen arbiter of an intelligent people, for the reason that it is the recorded judgment of the community, territory, state or nation, upon every question of a political character. To, and before that arbitrament, all must bow with that becoming deference which is title to the constitution that created it. An instrument so pregnant with good, and so barren of wrong, is property regarded by all loyal citizens as the paramount law of the land. Its framers so regarded it; the compeers of its framers so regarded it; the nation so regarded it; the enlightened world so regarded it. Indeed, at the time of its adoption it was regarded as the great luminary around which the smaller planets of state constitutions should revolve; and all the legislation, both in States and Territories, should be in strict accordance with its provisions; and all the state constitutions were to pale their lesser lights in the presence of the commanding majesty of the Constitution of the United States. So long as we all so regarded it, and walked in its paths, and were guided by its light and its councils, we glided swiftly upon the waves of prosperity and peace, to a national importance second to no power on the earth. In the midst of this unparalleled prosperity, we slept soundly in fancied security. Alas! While we slept the tares were sown; the seeds of discord, strife, and disunion, were scattered broadcast on the very face of the Constitution, and those who scattered them were in possession of the fruitful fold, and the weeders are now attempting to pull up the wheat, and leave the tares, alone to occupy the ground made so rich and productive of good by the hands of the founders of the government. The tares to which I alluded is the heresy that the state constitutions are paramount to, and independent of, that of the United States. A doctrine so absurd, so unnatural, and so unwise, was regarded when first broached as a dogma of a diseased brain, unworthy even of refutation; yet this subtle poison has been so insidiously infused by the wicked, designing, and, in many instances, disappointed politicians of our nation, that we now behold the startling spectacle of its adoption as a basis of a separate political and national existence by eleven States of this Union, and so far have they been carried in their madness, as to call it invasion of a State, if the national government attempts to march troops, through or across its territory, to put down rebellion or treason in another State, or to protect the citizens or the property of the nation. A doctrine so fraught with evil can never obtain, a theory so repugnant to the existence of our government will never become the judgment of an enlightened people. The innumerable blessings that have flowed in the wake of the opposite theory and doctrine will never be exchanged for the certain discomfiture and destruction attendant upon such a wild and delusive theory. As well might you look for an orderly and well conducted family where all parental restraint and authority were repudiated and disregarded by the offspring, as for a happy, prosperous, well-ordered government containing within it thirty-four independencies, each claiming superiority over the Parent government.

That a state constitution should be the power behind the throne greater than the throne itself is a theory so startling, so entirely destructive in its operations and results, that I entertain no apprehensions that it will ever be adopted by the people of this Territory, that has so much garnered up in the rich treasure-house of a nation's benevolence, and so much in the future, if we remain contented under the protecting and sheltering wings of our national constitution.

[*Later, Nye recommends legislation to the representatives.*]

The consequences attendant upon the almost universal habit or practice of carrying concealed or deadly weapons by the citizens of this Territory lead me to recommend that some law be passed making it a penal offense to carry them, fully believing that human life will be much safer by prohibiting the use than by tolerating it.

I also recommend that such laws be passed for the regulation of the sale of intoxicating liquors, as shall protect the public from the devastating influence of an unrestrained traffic, prohibiting its sale to persons under certain ages, and to persons of known intemperate habits, fully believing that the temporary gain to the vendor is a poor remuneration for the blasted hopes and crushed spirit of loving families.

It seems to me that a proper regard for the well-being of society demands that the sale on Sunday or the Sabbath of all intoxicating liquors (except for medicinal purposes) should be prohibited, so that the day may be observed as one of rest and quiet, and be enjoyed by those who desire it, by such religious observances as the habits of more than eighteen centuries have sanctioned.

I particularly recommend that you pass stringent laws to prevent gambling. Of all the seductive vices extant, I regard that of gambling as the worst. It holds out allurements hard to be resisted. It captivates and ensnares the young, blunts all the moral sensibilities and ends in utter ruin. The thousand monuments that are reared along this pathway of ruin demand at your hands all the protection the law can give.

Frances Fuller Victor's "Nevada"

Frances Fuller Victor (1826–1902) was born in New York State. Along with her sister, Metta Victoria Fuller, she gained fame as a writer in the 1840s. She lived in Ohio, Michigan, and Nebraska before she moved west in 1863 with her second husband, settling first in San Francisco and then in Portland, Oregon, where she published *The River of the West* in 1870. Separated from her husband in 1868, she supported herself as a writer and traveled throughout the West in search of material. In addition to publishing numerous books about the West, she wrote poetry and fiction. She contributed to the *Overland Monthly* (from which this selection comes) and to newspapers in Oregon and California, including the Portland women's rights advocate, the *New Northwest*.

Beginning in 1878, Victor was on the staff of Hubert Howe Bancroft, famous compiler of nineteenth-century western histories. She wrote most of several volumes, including the one that covered Nevada. Victor stopped working for Bancroft in 1889, after producing perhaps 15 percent of the *Works* published under his name, but she continued to write tirelessly, her work including popular fiction. In honor of her prodigious output, she was elected an honorary member of the Oregon Historical Society in 1900. Her last published work, *Poems*, appeared in the same year.

In her 1869 poem "Nevada," she depicts a place that she finds difficult and mysterious. The state's silences, and its constant disappointment of human hopes, defy understanding.

—C. Elizabeth Raymond

NEVADA

Sphinx, down whose rugged face
The sliding centuries their furrows cleave
By sun, and frost, and cloud-burst; scarce to leave
   Perceptible a trace
   Of age or sorrow;
Faint hints of yesterdays with no tomorrow;—
My mind regards thee with a questioning eye,
   To know thy secret, high.

   If Theban mystery,
With head of woman, soaring, bird-like wings,
And serpent's tail on lion's trunk, were things
   Puzzling in history;
   And men invented
For it an origin which represented
Chimera and a monster double-headed,
   By myths Phenician wedded—

   Their issue being this—
This most chimerical and wondrous thing
From whose dumb mouth not even the gods could wring
   Truth, nor antithesis:
   Then, what I think is,
This creature—being chief among men's sphinxes—
Is eloquent, and overflows with story,
   Beside thy silence hoary!

   Nevada—desert, waste,
Mighty, and inhospitable, and stern;
Hiding a meaning over which we yearn
   In eager, panting haste
   Grasping and losing,
Still being deluded ever by our choosing—
Answer us, Sphinx: What is thy meaning double
   But endless toil and trouble?

Inscrutable, men strive
To rend thy secret from thy rocky breast;
Breaking their hearts, and periling heaven's rest
    For hope that can not thrive;
    Whilst unrelenting,
Upon thy mountain throne, and unrepenting,
Thou sittest, basking in a fervid sun,
    Seeing or hearing none.

    I sit beneath thy stars—
The shallop moon beached on a bank of clouds—
And see thy mountains wrapped in shadowy shrouds,
    Glad that the darkness bars
    The day's suggestion—
The endless repetition on one question;
Glad that thy stony face I can not see,
    Nevada—Mystery!

5

Nineteenth-Century Social History

Letters to Wovoka

Wovoka, also known as Jack Wilson, was born about 1856 in the Mason Valley near modern-day Yerington in northern Nevada. He was the son of a Northern Paiute shaman. In 1889 Wovoka experienced a series of visions that instructed him to revive the Ghost Dance religion of the 1870s. He preached living in peace with whites, loving one another, and dancing the Ghost Dance, so that all who practiced the faith would be reunited with their loved ones in the "afterlife," and there would be no more illnesses. Almost immediately, Wovoka's vision spread to tribes on the plains, including the Arapahos, Cheyennes, Kiowas, Assiniboines, and Sioux, and to the Shoshones and Bannocks in Idaho. Wovoka even traveled to Oklahoma twice to visit devotees of the Ghost Dance. One reason the news spread so quickly was that the railroad had arrived in the American West. Railroad companies let Native Americans ride free of charge, giving them a far-reaching, modern mode of transportation that enabled them to travel to Nevada to meet the "Prophet" Wovoka, and learn the Ghost Dance from him directly. Also, Plains tribes were spiritually devastated by the Indian Wars that culminated at Wounded Knee in South Dakota in 1890 and needed the spiritual rejuvenation that they found in the Ghost Dance. Certain devotees from the plains wrote letters to Wovoka, requesting that he send "medicine" to them, such as red ochre paint and eagle feathers blessed by him. Often, they would send money or gifts such as beaded moccasins or belts. The letters to Jack Wilson (Wovoka) that follow were part of a group of letters to him found in an earthen structure after his death.

The Northern Paiutes practiced the Ghost Dance for a short time only, but distant tribes followed the movement and sought Wovoka's counsel until his death in 1932. A modified version of the Ghost Dance is practiced today by Utes, Eastern and Northern Shoshones, and some Southern Paiute groups in Utah.

—Terri McBride

Allen, South Dakota

April 27th 1911

Mr. Jack Wilson.

Nordyke, Nevada

Dear father

I send you five dollars from Allen P.O. for P.O. money order that time I think you were at Colorado state but the money order return to me at Allen S. Dak. and I sent you another five dollars cash and I never heard from you. If you receive the five dollars or not so I want to know all about it. And tell me all about it the news is that we are people all sick, sick all time the little folks but now it all over by this spring and do you know what kind medicine best? These sickness cough, and lungs sick and measles and how we pray it, our god may mistake and tell me all about it these things.

Yours, poor son

John. Short Bull

Answer soon as possible.

Porcupine Tail Creek

August 10 1908

Dear Father Jack Wilson

Today I was doing and was very sorry and I was going to send you $6. I want to know that some medicine good for your peoples—I like to see those medicine soon as you could and I want you to send those. I send 4 bead belts working. I like you to send me those medicine for myself. How much it cost? Those medicine makes those pills them it and send it to me. When I was there and you give me some medicine give me some of those for the belt. That is all want to say for you. I am glad to shake hand with you that is me your son

Bear Comes Out.

Arapahoe Wyoming

Fremont co. April 30–11

Dear Father in christ. Jack Wilson,

Today I am thinking of you and I would like to write you a few lines to you this morning and to let you know that I am well with my folks and also my wife was very sickness for along time. But she go round now days and she go down River to take a cold bath in water and she said she feels much better after she take bath. And rest of Indians are well. Some of Indians are farming for oats and wheat and some are working for shearing time. Now I want to ask you something. My brother came from Oklahoma and he want me to go with him to your country to visit you. He would like to see you very much. So I wish you please tell us if is alright to visit you. My brother he is waiting for his money from Oklahoma. But we would like to hear from you before we start off to your place. And I wish you please send us little Painted if you got to spare and tell us some that is if any new from this spring. Or anything go on. Let us hear from you by return mail.

I am yours truly.

F. W. Antelope

Pine Ridge, So. Dak.

April 29, 1911

Jack Wilson,

Nordyke, Nev.

Dear Father: Why do you not write to me. I sit with you and I write to you this letter. I hope I will come to see you. I send you a dollar bill. Why don't you answer me?

When you get this letter answer soon, Father. This man writing a letter for me but he lives far and this man write for me this letter.

This man a good man write for me this letter. I sit with Cloud horse and we write this letter.

Your living son, I shake hands with you. Answer quick when you get this letter.

Cloud horse

Address answer to Red star

Pine Ridge, So. Dak.

Lodge Pole, Mont.

March 31—1910

My Dear Father,

I am so capable to answer your welcome letter. I was very glad to hear from you again. My Post Office from my plow is about a quarter of a mile, I received the medicines you send me some time ago. When I got I make a pray meeting with a good—men who have respect of you and also we have a fest over it. I give the medicines and paints to the fellows crew of 13 and also give some to those who have ask me after I got the point. I always have my own son to write letters for me but he has been out working about two week he have just come home and he write this letter for me again. Samon First Shoot is also a good young man he some times writes for me my wife is The Girl. . . . I can not Trust no other man so this is reason I always [have them] write for me. The older Indians are still praying for what you now send. I am so anxious to know how to used the medicines and would like to have advice in regards to the medicine. The Arapahoe Indians some here about two years ago Their names are Sherman Sage and The Gun. These two men claim to see you at your place when they come here they told me lot of news about what you have said. I stayed with the two about seven days They made me one hand game stick. Both of the men are my best friends they like me very well. I like to know if you will send the medicine rest of the medicines what we ordered in our letter. It was hard to get the money this winter that was the reason I . . . send you.

[*Note: No signature, probably an Assiniboine or Arapahoe correspondent; letter badly fragmented and stained.*]

Wovoka's lodge in Mason Valley, as photographed by ethnographer Robert Lowie in 1912. Numerous handwritten letters to Wovoka were found inside the lodge after his death in 1932. Photo by Robert H. Lowie; courtesy of the Nevada State Historic Preservation Office

The *Reno Evening Gazette* Reports on Coxey's Army in Nevada

In 1893, thirty-six years before the better-known Great Depression, the newly triumphant industrial capitalism of the United States faced its second great crisis—a stock-
market collapse followed by a downward spiral of business failures, unemployment,
and labor unrest. Unemployment reached 25 percent among industrial workers, and
unemployed and poor people wandered America's back roads and sometimes rode
the railroad freight cars that crisscrossed the country. In rural areas, poor families
sometimes died of starvation. This crisis generated anger and fear, and Reno residents experienced a small taste of both from Coxey's Army.

A wealthy quarry owner from Ohio, James S. Coxey, led one of the most dramatic
responses to this crisis. Frustrated by the lack of relief measures from the federal government, Coxey organized several hundred unemployed workers and led them on a
protest march from Ohio to Washington, D.C. Sympathizers joined the march along the
route, and a group was organized in California with the intention of meeting Coxey in
the capital for the protest. Given that the nation had experienced a number of violent
conflicts between unhappy workers and authorities (the Homestead strike of 1892, for
example, had resulted in several deaths), the specter of an "army" of disgruntled men
marching into one's town generated concern and some fear.

Reno residents had reason to be concerned about this group of disaffected marchers as its plans to travel through the middle of Reno became known. Nevada was in
desperate straits in the 1890s—the Comstock mines had ceased producing, removing
the economic foundation on which Nevada had been built. People left Nevada for
greener pastures by the thousands; in fact, 32 percent—nearly one-third—of Nevada's
residents left the state between 1880 and 1900. In this context, authorities worried
that the message of the marchers might connect with those Nevadans suffering particular economic hardship and lead to disruptive protests or even violence. The following articles from the *Reno Evening Gazette* convey the apprehension of Renoites
as the army approached and passed through.

—John B. Reid

THE INDUSTRIAL ARMY
Special to Gazette.
Oakland (Cal.), April 4.—After breakfast this morning, at which each man was
given half a loaf of bread and a cup of coffee, the Industrial Army held a meet-

ing. Mrs. Dr. Kellogg Lane, Mrs. Teats and Mrs. Bowen, lady missionaries, addressed them on the advisability of keeping straight.

W. S. Parsonage was appointed chaplain and H. A. Gregg, the Populist, made an address, telling the men to assert their rights, and said if they wanted to stay in town till tomorrow they could do so. His speech was rather inflammatory.

The army then paraded outside the tabernacle and at 10 o'clock formed in line and marched to the Sixteenth street station, where they are endeavoring to obtain transportation to Sacramento. They say if they cannot get it peaceably they will take it by force. They struck a snag anyhow, for the railroad company refused to take them, and after some haranguing, it was agreed to confer with the Mayor at 2 p.m. and endeavor to arrange the matter peaceably. There are 498 men in the army this morning.

Oakland (Cal.), April 5.—The regiment of the Industrial Army, which arrived on Tuesday from San Francisco is stranded here. Efforts to secure transportation eastward for the men have proved futile, and they appear to be in no humor for a walk to Sacramento or anywhere else. The Southern Pacific Company remains obdurate and refuses transportation to any point unless the customary rate charged is forthcoming.

COXEY'S ARMY
One Thousand Men Said to Be Headed for Reno.

Oakland's action in procuring transportation for the San Francisco contingent of Coxey's "Industrial Army" to Sacramento, and Sacramento's proposed action to send them to Reno brings the problem right home. In all probability they will be here in a day or two, and the citizens may just as well take one horn or the other of the dilemma first as last. Steps must be at once taken to prevent them crossing the State line, or the people must provide for them when they come.

A Gazette reporter was detailed to interview the citizens generally this morning on the question, and found them, as a rule, opposed to feeding them or offering them any relief; and many were in favor of calling out the State militia and stopping them on our western border.

Commissioner McLaughlin said that he, as a County Commissioner, did not feel competent to act in the matter, and suggested calling a public meeting to see what disposition could be made of them.

Chairman Alt said the Board was powerless to act without publishing a call for a meeting of the Board for one week, but that he was opposed to going to the County Treasury for money to assist them in any way. He said he would certainly oppose any suggestion of the kind. As a private individual he was opposed to the movement and was not in any way in sympathy with it.

The Gazette sent the following dispatch this morning:

Reno, April 6.

Govenor R. K. Colcard, Carson: It is said that Sacramento will send 1,000 members of Coxey's army to Reno in a day or two. What can you do to stop them at State Line, or what idea have you regarding their disposition? Answer immediately.

Allen C. Bragg

The following telegram the Gazette sent to Sacramento:

Reno, April 6.

Bee, Sacramento: What does Sacramento propose doing with Industrial Army? It is rumored here that Sacramento will provide them with transportation to Reno.

Allen C. Bragg, Gazette.

Colcord's Reply:

Carson, April 6, 1894.

A. C. Bragg, Reno: I doubt the statement, but if true we have no law preventing their coming. It would be madness for such an army to attempt to subsist while marching through this sparsely settled State. If the railroad company dumps them here they will be compelled by force of circumstances to take them through the State.

R. K. Colcord, Governor

What the "BEE" says:

Sacramento, April 6.

Allen C. Bragg, Reno: Mayor Steinman has completed arrangements to ship the army east at 4 P.M. today. They will probably make a stop at Reno. The "BEE."

The Gazette received the following dispatch at 4 o'clock this afternoon:

Sacramento, April 6.

Allen C. Bragg, Reno: Ten cars will leave here at 4 o'clock with a thousand men.

They will be delivered at Reno. The "BEE."

Later.—Superintendent Whited of this division received orders late this after-noon from the railroad authorities at San Francisco to rush the Industrial Army over his division as rapidly as possible.

Mr. Whited figures that they will arrive here about 1 o'clock tomorrow morning, and will be sent over the road as rapidly as possible.

THE INDUSTRIAL ARMY

Special to Gazette.

Oakland, April 6.—Because the 640 men from San Francisco to join Coxey's army refused to leave here the populace was on the streets all night. The riot alarm was sounded, extra police and deputy sheriffs were sworn in and the Governor was asked to call out the militia. When the army arrived the men were fed by the Oakland people, and refused to proceed because the railroad would let them ride only in box cars. Then the anxiety began; two local compa-nies of militia assembled ready to move at command of the Governor; the Ga-tling gun was loaded and placed in front of the city hall; armed police, firemen and citizens moved to the camp of the army and made the men leave the city.

About 4 o'clock this morning eight box cars were drawn out of Oakland des-tined for Sacramento. In these cars were huddled six hundred of the Industrial Army, which for the past two days have caused the good people of Oakland so much uneasiness. It was decided by Mayor Pardee that this army must move. About 3 o'clock this morning a force of police, firemen armed with axe-han-dles and armed citizens proceeded to the Tabernacle where the army was sleeping. Some riotous proceedings ensued and for a time things looked omi-nous. Finally, however, the army consented to move peacefully. At 3:30 they formed in line and escorted by 200 armed police marched to the Sixteenth Street Station where they entered box cars and shortly after 4 the train pulled out, and Oakland heaved a big sigh of relief and went back to bed.

THE INDUSTRIAL ARMY

[April 7]. The man styling himself Major-General of the Industrial Army and his Lieutenant, who arrived on this morning's train from Sacramento, started in to canvass the town for recruits and money to pay for transportation to Ogden.

They established headquarters beneath an American flag which they hoisted at the Palace Hotel corner. At 3:30 o'clock the recruits were formed in line and with the stars and stripes marched to the Plaza and were addressed by the "Major General," who said the object of their journey was to demand of the Government work for the vast number of unemployed throughout the United States.

He was followed by his lieutenant, who read the constitution of the army telling the recruits what was expected of them. He said he thought the people of Reno should be willing to furnish them enough provisions to last 24 hours, and that they expected to leave Reno on a freight train as soon as they learned what transportation would cost.

He said that when they arrive at Washington they will demand of the Government the free and unlimited coinage of silver and the restriction of immigration. A committee was appointed to solicit provisions.

THE RENO REGIMENT INCREASING IN NUMBERS

[April 9]. One of the Industrial Army agitators who is here trying to get followers to go to Washington with him made a demand of Director W. O. H. Martin of the Agricultural Society Saturday night for the Pavilion to accommodate his "army." Mr. Martin said he was without authority and declined to give his consent.

Captain Kelly of the Industrial Army passed through on this morning's east bound train en route to Ogden. He told Major General Houbert to accept all recruits wishing to join the regiment at Reno and get them through to Ogden as soon as possible. He said he would hold the main division of the army there or at Salt Lake until their arrival.

Lieutenant General White returned on today's local from Carson, where he had an interview with the Governor, who told him that as an official he could not act without breaking the law, but as an individual would help all he could toward securing transportation from Reno to Ogden.

Continuing, the Lieutenant reported the Governor as having said that he is in sympathy with the laboring class and realizes their sad condition; that he does not wish any citizen of Nevada to leave, as the population of the State is small enough, and if any are in need the State will assist them; that he does not recommend the movement, but is in sympathy with those who compose it.

Lieutenant White told the reporter that he wished to give thanks for the sympathy shown by Governor Colcord, and that if every Governor was as sincere at heart in his wishes for the welfare of the laboring class there would be no need of an Industrial Army. He concluded by saying he hoped to see Governor Colcord occupying the next Presidential chair.

The operators along the line say recruits are leaving every town to join the Reno contingent of the Industrial Army.

The railroad company absolutely refuses to contract for carrying the members of the army to Ogden unless they pay the regular fare of about $20 a piece.

A meeting of the citizens has been called for this evening at 4 o'clock to see what disposition to make of those men here and those who are expected.

The Industrial Army paraded the streets with 48 men in line, and the leaders say there are 110 that have enlisted and that they intend getting out of here to-night. When asked by a Gazette reporter how they could pay the $20 each demanded by the railroad company the reply was that he thought they would be able to go. At any rate we are on the road to Washington and intend going there.

In front of the Opera House a meeting was held, where the constitution was read for the benefit of the new members. The Major-General and Lieutenant delivered addresses, in which they stated that they were law-abiding citizens, and if they had broken any law of this county or State it had been unintentional, and they would like to know what it was. They said that for the benefit of the citizens of this community they would ask the members of the army who were in favor of such sentiments to hold up their hands. All hands went up. The speaker said they would leave the town peacefully and thanked the Lord that the Governor of the State had promised them his protection.

Two Voices for Civil Rights in the Nineteenth Century— W. H. Hall and Alexander W. Baldwin

The issue of civil rights—the rights of people not to be discriminated against in various ways based on the color of their skin—has been a part of Nevada's political/legal system since the late 1950s. However, this was not the first time the issue was raised in the state's history. For a brief period during the 1860s, the civil rights issue was central to the law and politics of Nevada.

The background for this early conflict was very different, however, from the circumstances of the 1950s. When Nevada became a separate territory and then a state, by constitution and law all persons who were not white were excluded from voting, being officeholders, testifying against white people in civil or criminal cases (with a minor exception), marrying white people, or attending public schools (unless separate schools for nonwhite children were established), to list the most important areas of discrimination.

This condition was unfortunately common in the Northern states at the time, but the Civil War made some changes. The only formal constitutional changes at the federal level resulting from the maelstrom of the war abolished slavery, tried to provide due process of law and equal protection to the freed slaves, and gave black men the right to vote. Many states then abolished racial laws, though incompletely, as was the case in Nevada.

In the state of Nevada, pressure to expand rights came from two sources. First, the small African American population of the state did not hesitate to demand an end to most forms of racial discrimination. For example, as early as January 1, 1864, a meeting of black residents of the Comstock hailed the first anniversary of the Emancipation Proclamation and demanded for African Americans "the rights . . . which properly belong to every member of the human family. . . . We demand for ourselves and for our posterity only that liberty which is our God-given inalienable right."

Black men could vote in Nevada for the first time in 1870, although the state constitution was not amended to this effect for ten more years. In Virginia City in April of that year, an extensive celebration of the adoption of the Fifteenth Amendment produced enlightening oratory and a parade. One of the addresses delivered at this gathering was given by W. H. Hall, an excerpt of which is the first document presented here. While he was then a resident of California, Hall had lived and worked in the Treasure Hill area of eastern Nevada. His address has its florid elements, but he was following the oratorical style of the time. The following excerpt gives the flavor of black views on equality in Nevada at that time.

A second force for change came from a number of the most important elected leaders in Nevada in the 1860s. At that time almost all elected officials were Republicans (sometimes calling themselves Unionists). A few outstanding leaders of this party embraced what would today be called advocacy for civil rights, although these views were rare among white Nevadans at the time. James W. Nye, the territorial governor and one of Nevada's first two U.S. senators, was one of them. Nye consistently urged the legislature to allow black persons to testify against whites; in 1865 it did so for African Americans in criminal trials, though not yet for Indians and Chinese. William M. Stewart, the other first Nevada senator, also advocated repealing racist laws at the time.

One of the most ardent members of this almost entirely Republican contingent for civil rights was Alexander W. (Sandy) Baldwin, the first federal judge in the state's history. In 1868 Baldwin gave an impassioned speech that explains how the Civil War had shaped his view on the civil-rights issue. Part of his speech is the second document included here. Again, the language is somewhat florid by contemporary standards.

Judge Baldwin meant what he said in this speech. For example, he asked the federal grand jury to examine the laws of Nevada to determine whether any of them were in conflict with the Civil Rights Act adopted by a Reconstruction Congress in 1866. Judge Baldwin noted that "those Negro Slaves throughout the Struggle were, almost to a man, on the side of the Nation. They rendered it signal service. When the Cause was won, they were not forgotten, a debt was due to them. . . . To complete their enfranchisement it was necessary by amendment of the Constitution and by Congressional enactment to place them squarely upon the footing of equal citizen-ship." The failure of the grand jury to find violations of this act, although they were flagrant, and the failure in 1869 of an attempt by Judge Baldwin to secure convictions after the Chinese residents of Unionville were forcibly ejected from that camp, do not weaken the evident strength of his commitment against racism. Judge Baldwin was killed in a train wreck in California later in 1869. If he had lived, Nevada law might have been very different.

—Elmer R. Rusco

Address of W. H. Hall at the Celebration in Virginia City of Ratification of the Fifteenth Amendment to the United States Constitution. Published in the *Virginia City Territorial Enterprise*, April 9, 1870.

We meet here today for the first time in the history of our country to occupy a new position before the American people—for the time has come when the colored Americans of the whole country must assume the duties and respon-sibilities of their changed condition, by confronting the unrelenting prejudice engendered in the past, with clear conception and full capacities to equal the considerations imposed upon them. . . . An unseen and higher power decreed the fiat, that the conquest of equal rights which loyalty has won should first be realized in the Senate of the United States, in the person of the black man's ex-ponent, Hiram Revels. What a grand realization of Republican freedom, dem-onstrating the truth of our forefathers' dream—that this should be a govern-ment for all men alike. Witness the admiration of the votaries of liberty, scan the origin and defeat of the adherers of the white man's government as they surrounded Revels, the type of a degraded people, standing in the presence of the most august assembly ever congregated in the world, with his right arm uplifted towards the throne of God, swearing by his hope of heaven to support the amended Constitution of his country. . . .

I am here in your presence today, through the partiality of valued friends, to represent the colored Americans of Nevada, and through them the whole race upon the Pacific Coast, and it seems incumbent that I should indicate their views upon the policy involved between the two great parties who now divide the nation. This is essential in consequence of the equivocal position occupied by thousands of my race through coercion in the Southern States at the last Presidential election, and from the apprehension manifested that many more will cast their votes in the same way at the subsequent elections. I do not pretend to be a political adept nor to be able to foreshadow the probable reconstructed Democracy to be marshalled under the guidance of that consummate statesman and jurist, Salmon P. Chase, so long the advocate and true friend of the black man's rights, but from what has transpired with that party and from all we can glean from their future intentions we feel justified in asserting that every colored man, from the frozen-bound confines of Maine to the genial borders of redeemed Florida, is under a never-to-be forgotten debt of respect and gratitude toward the great Republican party from the auspicious time they enunciated the dogma of no more extension of slave territory to the completion of the grand event we are commemorating here to-day. . . .

I appeal by the bleeding bones and emaciated limbs of the millions of our brethren in the South; I appeal for the hopes that you cherish for the coming generation; I appeal to the aspersions that [the Democratic] party has always vented upon the negro's inferiority; I appeal to the truth of impartial history all through the war, which never reported one black traitor, to never be untrue to the triumphant party that stooped down from their lofty position from motives of humanity and lifted up the poor negro race to freedom and manhood. Guard well and zealously the great right imparted to you because to use it for personal aggrandizement against those who have always stood by us, will be to endanger the possibility at some future time of having the great right wrested from our grasp. In conclusion we ask all classes of men—the native-born and generous Americans, the impetuous and misguided Irishmen, the toiling and liberty-loving Germans who, from the foundation of the Government, have been exercising the great right of franchise of which we are today made a part and parcel, to meet the new element in the pathway of our country's greatness with impartial frankness—because, if they prove false to the lessons of liberty, we can with the ballot in our hands oppose all invidious distinctions, and if our race hereafter suffer wrong and injustice, it will be their own fault.

Let us combine as one people all our energies in augmenting the power and shaping the destinies of our country's progress, so that she may for countless years to come escape that fate which has plunged so many millions of the past in a wreck of mouldering ruins.

Address by Alexander W. Baldwin, July 4, 1868. Published in the *Virginia City Territorial Enterprise*, July 8, 1868.

Fellow Citizens: This day is the anniversary of American independence. It is not merely for that reason and on grounds of narrow and selfish patriotism that we celebrate it by imposing concourse with pomp and pageant, banners and music. But because we reverently claim for it the highest and holiest place in the calendar of civilization and freedom. On the fourth day of July, 1776, the Declaration of American Independence was uttered at Philadelphia. The brave men who put their names to it, well knew that they were signing their death warrant, on their country's title to freedom. Heroic hearts! But the history of our race is the history of heroes. And this day holds the place in our hearts and in the world's esteem, not merely for its commemoration of a high-hearted and daring deed, but because it witnessed the laying of the corner-stone of a system of government which declares and protects the rights of man. . . . We can never forget that day in April 1861, when the news came of the bombardment of Fort Sumter. On every pale face, on every sparkling eye, in every surging heart, was written an inflexible determination, at every cost and hazard, to preserve unsullied the honor and unbroken the boundaries of the United States. That determination never wavered during the years of war which followed. It grew sterner and more resolute in the face of disaster and defeat. It quailed not before the taunts and undisguised enmity of England and France. Its embodiment was Lincoln, the hero and martyr of the war. It gave us the inflexible and unconquerable Grant. . . . It was vindicated when Lee surrendered to Grant—when the rebel flag was torn down from the high places of the Confederacy and chief priests and scribes scattered in base and ignominious flight.

Splendid as was our victory, it was achieved at a cost which nothing could have warranted but the requirements of so sacred a cause. Many a manly life was given in sacrifice. Many a young heart, beating high with the holy impulses of patriotism and the quick energies of youth, was stilled in death. Many a mother has been made to mourn for her children even as Rachel mourned of old. Many a widow weeps over her little children for him who will return to her no more.

But the great struggle, beginning with the birth of the Government in an unreconcilable antagonism between right and wrong, and ending finally in drenching a continent in blood, is past. The battle, never to be renewed, has been fought and won. . . .

Incalculable has been the cost, yet let us not dwarf the mission of the patriotic hosts who perished in the fight, by doubting that from the soil which their blood has sanctified will blossom blessings commensurate with the sacrifice. From the Potomac to the Rio Grande, hill and valley are billowed with the graves of our dead. The cypress droops from the mantels of half a million homes, and limbless men and weeded willows tell us the terrors of the past. The South is still a desolation, over which walks pinch-faced famine and glares the demon of discord. But stop! These things are of the past, for even while we speak some strange enchantment is smoothing down the rough track of war, making glad the waste places, and exorcising from the heart of malice the spirit of anarchy which plumed it to rebellion and still prompts it to revenge. It is building churches and schoolhouses, clothing the naked, feeding the famished, and arching the sky of the downcast and sorrowing with the bow of hope and promise. And what is this strange enchantment lighting up the face of the South with this golden glow? Read the Constitutions of the States just readmitted. They are thoroughly republican. "Life, Liberty and the pursuit of happiness" are guaranteed to all; the principles of the immortal Declaration are engraved at last upon the brass of the Constitutions of the South, never to be effaced; and the genius of republican freedom is breathing into the redeemed and reconstructed tabernacle the spirit of a grander and purer life.

Like the low voice of the retreating thunder, the echoes of the terrible struggle are still reverberating through the valleys of the South, and the blue wreath of battle lingers yet along the track of our armies. The shoulders of our heroes are still callous with the harness of war, and the campfires have scarcely died out along the banks of the James and Chickahominy; yet we know that all is well, and from the Atlantic to the Pacific are the people singing the paeans of a lasting peace today.

In the blood of our sons and fathers, in the prayers of our mothers, in the tears of our children, has this deliverance been wrought, and the great sacrifice will last for all coming time. The altar upon which it was offered has been made a corner stone of the Republic, and the prayers which ascended to God as an incense with it, have become a vital principle of the Government—a part of the political religion of the people—a part of the people themselves.

PART 3 | **Rolling the Dice**

6

Turn-of-the-Century Mining Booms

Mrs. Hugh Brown on Tonopah Housekeeping

"Tonopah? Where's Tonopah?" With these words, Marjorie Anne Brown began the story of her eighteen years in that mining boomtown. Her husband's answer explained its significance: "It's a mining camp in southern Nevada," he said. "They've discovered ore there—gold and silver. A boom's on." Like her fellow San Franciscans and the rest of America at that time, Brown had not heard of the dusty, treeless municipality 250 miles southwest of Reno. There was no reason to have heard of Tonopah—it did not exist until part-time miner Jim Butler discovered silver and gold ore there in May 1900. The subsequent mining and associated economic boom restored Nevada's fortunes, pulling the state out of a twenty-year depression and contributing (with its close neighbor Goldfield) to the growth of the city of Reno. But Brown's stories of her life in Tonopah are not the usual tales of a rough-and-tumble mining town. Rather, they tell the story of a middle-class housewife striving for gentility in the spare city of Tonopah. In the selected excerpt, Brown struggles with already difficult turn-of-the-century housekeeping tasks in the booming mining town.

—John B. Reid

When my thoughts return to the women of Tonopah, I recall how my sympathy went out to the brides. As soon as a young man made a stake, he invariably went back for the girl he had left behind. Many were entirely unfitted for the life of a mining camp. The older women, wives of engineers, mine officials, and tradesmen, seemed adequate, but you could almost tell by looking at the brides whether they would be able to stick it out.

The problems of housekeeping on the desert were very real. During the bitter cold winters the wind moaned and whistled through the cracks in the board-and-batten houses. In the terrific summer heat, you had to cook over a wood stove with one eye always watchful for insects. Have you ever inadvertently crushed a stinkbug and lived with that stench for days? Have you ever turned suddenly to look at your baby on the floor and found a scorpion on his arm? Have you ever found a bedbug on your pillow and faced the task of getting rid of the pests? The women used to say it was no disgrace to get bedbugs, but it was certainly a disgrace to keep them.

We were successors to that wonderful race of pioneer women who have been scattered over the West since the western trek began, women who brought their babies into the world in lonely places, women who cooked for their sick neighbors. These were women who washed the dead and laid them out, and rode horseback for miles to help a beleaguered home.

Jen Stock and her mother belonged to that race of women. Jen became my most intimate friend. She had a keen mind and a grand sense of humor. She did much to smooth that first year when I wrestled with new problems. She taught me to darn, to make soap, to wet paper and sprinkle the bits over the floor before I swept so that the fine talc-like dust would be kept down; and best of all, she taught me to make bread. But there was one thing she didn't teach me. She didn't teach me how to wash clothes, because I was ashamed to confess my ignorance to my more experienced neighbor.

Once I had called in Annie, an Indian woman, who looked a thousand years old though she was probably not as old as my own mother, but things were in such disorder by the time she was through that I could not think of having her in my neat little kitchen again. I watched Jen and other neighbors hang out sheets, tablecloths, pajamas, shirts, until every bit of linen I owned had been used up in an effort to postpone the evil day. At last I tackled it. If other women could do the washing, I could.

The water, remember, was in a big barrel in the kitchen. Once a week a man came up the hill behind a team of mules struggling against the weight of a wagon loaded with six huge barrels full of water. He'd stop as close to the front of the house as the uneven ground would allow, prop the back wheels with a wooden wedge, and empty one of the barrels through a bunghole into buckets. Then he came teetering into my kitchen, carrying two buckets at a time, from which water spilled across the floor, but ultimately most went into my barrel. Each week I paid him a silver dollar.

Every bit of water we used was lifted out of the barrel. Bathing was not too difficult, for we had two oversize tea kettles. One of these, heated to boiling, then poured into the big galvanized iron tub on the floor and cooled with more water, was not too hard to handle. But for laundering I had to lift the kettle from the stove to a tub balanced between two kitchen chairs, scrub the clothes as I had seen Annie do, then dip the water out with a pitcher until the tub was light enough to drag along the floor and empty out the back door. I repeated the effort of getting them hung on the line, and then mopped up the water that had splashed on the floor! This was more than I had ever bargained for.

The task was not half complete before I had rubbed the skin off the backs of my fingers, and when the job was done, my body ached in every joint.

When Hugh came home, I cried in his arms, poor man, he didn't know what to do with me; but that night, when I lay in bed, my hands throbbing with pain, I made a vow: I would never try it again! Tomorrow I'd go down to the little cubbyhole on Main Street that passed for a dry goods store and buy bed linen. My husband (as if it were his fault) would have to get his shirts washed in the same way he had managed before I arrived, and everything else would go to a Reno laundry and back by stage.

Reno was two hundred miles away. It took two days for the laundry to get there and a little less than three weeks for it to return, but I've never been ashamed to confess I didn't do my washing myself. After I maneuvered Hugh into carrying the package down to the stage office, he decided to send his own linen to Reno, too. For the next two years the arrangement was a great comfort to both of us.

Washing my windows was the next source of humiliation for me though without quite serious repercussions. I had been reared by a Victorian mother who insisted that no lady should ever be seen doing menial labor. I had no hesitancy about doing the necessary scrubbing and polishing indoors—in fact I loved it—but it did give me a sense of degradation to realize I would have to go out on the porch in full sight of the whole town to wash those windows. Should I hire old Annie? Unthinkable. I'd have to do it.

So I went at it, making myself as small as possible and hoping no one would notice me. But alas for foolish wishes, that afternoon a lady knocked at the door. She was the wife of the bank cashier, and, I had been told, the granddaughter of a Virginia City millionaire. That day she was elegantly dressed in soft brown wool under a sealskin coat.

"Oh, Mrs. Brown," she announced gaily, "I've wanted to come to see you ever since you arrived, and when I saw you out washing your windows this morning, I said to myself, 'There now, I'll go this very afternoon.'"

I'm sure she washed her own windows, and I was relieved to think she didn't know how mortified I was. But gradually I learned it was not the doing of the menial labor that was "déclassé," but the *not* doing it. I learned to discount the toll on my complexion and the awful things that happened to my fingernails (Hugh never did get over regretting the condition of my hands), and never since have I been able to recapture the importance of such things. There is very little in the way of physical labor I haven't done, even chopping wood for the cook stove. I *love* to swing an ax!

Theodore Roosevelt's Admonition of Governor John T. Sparks

Radical unionism emerged in the late nineteenth and early twentieth centuries in the United States, and a major showdown between one of these unions and its enemies occurred in Nevada in 1907 in Goldfield, Nevada. This was just one of thousands of conflicts that erupted in this era as workers united to resist the powerful consolidation of economic power in the hands of owners of industrial enterprises. For example, the Bureau of Labor Statistics recorded 1,432 labor strikes and 140 lockouts involving 610,025 workers in 1886 alone.

These labor-management conflicts came to the mining districts of the West in the 1890s as workers resisted the increasing demands of mine owners. Many involved the Western Federation of Miners (WFM), an openly socialist labor organization that formed one of the largest segments of the famous International Workers of the World (IWW). Violence erupted during miner strikes in Coeur d'Alene, Idaho, in 1892; Cripple Creek, Colorado, in 1894; Leadville, Colorado, in 1896; and Coeur d'Alene again in 1899.

Labor strikes in this era tended to conform to a general pattern. A strike would occur, and workers would join with local residents to prevent replacement workers from reopening the factory or mine. To fight back, employers turned to outside authorities to break the strike. They called on a state militia or, in some cases, federal troops, ostensibly to keep order. In reality this outside force allowed the hiring of nonunion replacement workers, creating a situation that would eventually break the strike. This pattern emerged in several states as early as 1877 during railroad strikes.

Goldfield, Nevada, became the center of the broader conflict in 1907, as mine owners used a strike to attempt to remove the WFM from the Goldfield mines. Events followed the typical pattern. The mine owners, seeking to insert replacement workers by force under the guise of "keeping the peace," requested assistance from the state government through an appeal to Nevada governor John T. Sparks. With no state militia to assist the mine owners, Sparks appealed to President Theodore Roosevelt to send federal troops. Ultimately, federal troops arrived and allowed the reopening of the mines with nonunion workers.

The following documents are Roosevelt's responses to Sparks's request. They reveal aspects of Roosevelt's opinions of organized labor and the federal government's appropriate role in labor-management conflicts.

—John B. Reid

THE WESTERN UNION TELEGRAPH COMPANY

RECEIVED at 17 Q. JM350 Paid GOVT
The White House, Washington DC Dec 28, 1907

Hon John Sparks, Governor, CARSON CITY NEV

Your telegram December 26 is received. It in effect declares that you have failed to call the legislature together because in your judgment the legislature would not call upon the Government of the United States for the use of troops although in your opinion it ought to do so.

The constitution of the United States imposes, not upon you, but upon the Legislature if it can be convened the duty of calling upon the Government of the United States to protect the state of Nevada against domestic violence. You now request me to use the armed forces of the United States in violation of the constitution because in your judgment the legislature would fail to perform its duty under the constitution.

The state Government certainly does not appear to have made any serious effort to do its duty by the effective enforcement of its police functions. I repeat again what I have already said to you several times, th[at] under the circumstances now existing in the State of Nevada as made known to me, an application from the legislature of The State is an essential condition to the indefinite continuance of the troops at Goldfield.

Circumstances may change and if they do I will take whatever action the needs of the situation require so far as my constitutional powers permit, but the first need is that the state authorities should do their duty and the first step towards this is the assembling of the legislature.

It is apparent from your telegram that the legislature of Nevada can readily be convened, [and] you have fixed the period of three weeks as the time necessary to convene and organize a special session. If within five days from the receipt of this telegram you shall have issued the necessary notice to convene the legislature of Nevada, I shall continue the station of the troops at Gold-field during such period of three weeks if within the time of five days such notice has not been issued the troops will be immediately returned to the former station.

Theodore Roosevelt. 1:33 P.M.

THE WHITE HOUSE.
WASHINGTON.
January 4, 1908.
Sir:

I have received the copy of your proclamation, dated December 30, 1907, summoning the legislature. As I have notified you, the troops will stay for three weeks from the date of this call, so that the legislature can meet and opportunity be given the State authorities to take efficient action for the preservation of the public peace in the exercise of the police powers of the State. I call your especial attention to the telegram sent to you on December 14th by the Secretary of State. This sets out what must be shown as a matter of actual fact to exist in order to warrant the President in acting on the request of the State authorities. The action must be either to suppress an insurrection, which the State authorities are unable to suppress, or to secure to some portion or class of the people of the State the equal protection of the laws to which they are entitled under the Constitution of the United States, and which is denied them. Action under this or any other section requires the production of evidence sufficient to sustain a judgment by the President that the condition described in the statute exists. A mere statement of domestic disturbance, still less a mere statement of apprehension of domestic disturbance, is not sufficient, even though it comes from as high and unimpeachable a source as the Governor of a State. Such a communication from the Governor or from the legislature warrants the President in taking immediate steps to put himself in readiness to act, in view of the probability of conditions arising which will require his action. I accordingly sent the troops to Nevada on your request, and I have now directed that they be kept there pending the assembling of the legislature. Meanwhile, I sent out Assistant Secretary of Commerce and Labor Lawrence O. Murray, Commissioner of Corporations Herbert Knox Smith, and Commissioner of Labor Charles P. Neill to investigate and report to me the actual condition of affairs in Goldfield. I have just received a report from these three gentlemen, which set forth in the most emphatic language their belief, after a careful investigation on the ground, that there was no warrant whatever for calling upon the President for troops, and that the troops should not be kept indefinitely at Goldfield. The report further states that there was no insurrection against the power of the State at the time the troops were called for, that nobody supposed that there was such an insurrection and that none of the conditions described in sections 5297-8-9 of the Revised Statutes as warranting interference by the Federal Government existed, and that the effort was and is plainly an effort by the State of Nevada to secure the performance by the United States of the ordinary police duties which should, as a matter of course, be performed by Nevada herself. The report further says:

"There is absolutely no question that if the State of Nevada and the County of Esmerelda exercise the powers at their disposal they can maintain satisfactory order in Goldfield; that so far these authorities have done nothing but are relying upon Federal aid, and their attitude now is expressly that of refusing to do anything and desiring to throw their own burdens upon the Federal Government for the maintenance of those elementary conditions of order for which they, and they only, are responsible."

The signers of the report express their conviction that the troops should remain in Nevada until the assembling of the legislature, so as to preserve the status quo in order that the legislature may deal with the situation as it exists; but that shortly thereafter the troops should be removed.

I agree with the recommendations of this report, of which I enclose a copy, and shall act accordingly. Unless it can be shown that the statements of the report are not in accordance with the facts, it will be incumbent upon the legislature of Nevada, when it convenes, itself to provide for enforcing the laws of the State. The State of Nevada must itself make a resolute effort in good faith to perform the police duties incident to the existence of a State.

Sincerely yours,
Theodore Roosevelt
Hon. John Sparks,
Governor of Nevada,
Carson City, Nevada
Enclosure

The *Sacramento Bee* on George Wingfield

Hollywood wanted to make a movie about his life. The eastern press gave him the romantic moniker "the cowboy who refused a toga" when he rejected an offer to become a U.S. senator. In a less flattering allusion to Roman emperors, one of his opponents labeled him the "Sagebrush Caesar." Few people in Nevada history are as storied, controversial, and enigmatic as George Wingfield. In the eyes of some, he was a respectable and benevolent leader who invested his millions in Nevada; for others, his name is associated with avarice, political manipulation, and the support of vice.

Born in Arkansas and raised in Oregon, Wingfield made a living as a ranch hand, a saloon keeper, and even as a professional gambler before moving to central Nevada just after the discovery of gold and silver there. In partnership with George Nixon, Wingfield acquired several Goldfield claims that earned him a $20 million fortune by the age of thirty. He moved to Reno and began to build an economic empire that included twelve banks, hotels (including the Riverside Hotel in Reno), and substantial landholdings.

This wealth gave Wingfield enormous power in the sparsely populated Nevada of the early twentieth century. When the Depression led to the failure of Wingfield's banks, he vividly exhibited the extent of his economic power. Bank closures forced the Nevada state government to shut down temporarily because Wingfield banks controlled 60 percent of all the assets in the state. A historical controversy concerns Wingfield's use of this power. The fact that Wingfield did not hold political office complicates matters. He exercised his power behind the scenes and left little documentation that could confirm some of the less savory allegations of his activities. The following article from the *Sacramento Bee* for October 19, 1928, and the accompanying political cartoon are examples of the anti-Wingfield sentiment during Wingfield's heyday.

—John B. Reid

Wingfield Uses Strangle Hold on Nevada to Secure Votes for Herbert Hoover. Sagebrush Caesar Lines Up with the "Bond Drys" and Bootleggers to Ballyhoo For Republican Ticket; Free Thought Crushed by Silver State Octopus

Reno (Nev.), Oct. 19. George Wingfield, the Nevada Caesar and multi-millionaire boss of the Nevada Republican organization.

"Jimmy" McKay and "Bill" Graham, brigadiers of a reeking crew of gamblers and bootleggers and owners of record of Reno's "red-light" district.

The "bone-dry" forces of the Women's Christian Temperance Union and the "100 per cent Americans" of the Ku Klux Klan.

Such is the strange line-up that is now sounding the tocsins for Herbert Hoover and the Republican ticket in the State of Nevada. And the most powerful of these, backed by the octopus-like influence of his enormous wealth and the stranglehold he has on the political and financial life of Nevada, is Wingfield.

SPEAK IN WHISPERS. Of Wingfield's place in the lineup they speak only in whispers in Reno. For the Wingfield influence stretches far a field, reaching over the desert, through his chain of banks, into the mortgage-ridden homes of cattle and sheep men and filtering into the cash registers of merchants and realtors through other loans and mortgages.

Churches, institutions of learning, uplift organizations and semi-charitable bottles are not exempt from the Wingfield influence. Gifts and donations, discreetly placed, have served to still the voices that might have been raised against Wingfield dictatorship, and protests of the righteous have been smothered by the weight of the Wingfield pocketbook.

ISSUES STATEMENT. It was a short time before the Ku Klux Klan burned its fiery cross near Reno for Hoover that Nevada's multi-millionaire Mussolini issued his first ukase on the political situation.

It was a mild sort of document in the form of a letter directly from the Wingfield offices and was sent to practically every one of Nevada's 34,000 voters. In this document, addressed to "The People of Nevada," Wingfield discussed the tariff question at length, pointing out that Nevada's heavy output of wool, meat and metals needed protection. He alluded to several business depressions following Democratic Administrations, conveniently forgetting, however, to mention the disastrous depression of 1907 during a Republican administration.

ASKS HOOVER SUPPORT. He closed with an appeal for the support of the entire Republican ticket including Sam Platt, who is apposing the veteran, United States Senator Key Pittman, running for re-election on the Democratic ticket.

A couple of weeks later came a significant statement from the capitalist that served to remove Smith buttons from the lapel of many a timorous Reno business man and to tell the chamber of commerce and kindred organizations what was what.

HE SCARES 'EM. "I have been considering a development program of my Reno properties and particularly an enlargement of my Riverside Hotel." Said Wingfield in substance. "This work, however, will wait until I know the outcome of the presidential election."

Thus, indirectly, did Wingfield inform the business men interested in Reno's development what he expects them to do.

AN OLD TRICK. This method of indirect intimidation is not new in the Wingfield bag of tricks, however. On two previous occasions, once when the women's suffrage amendment was up and again when a proposal to pass a state prohibition enforcement law was pending, the capitalist threatened to sell his holdings and leave the state if either proposal were passed. But the latent fire of the old Nevada spirit was still present. The voters crossed him both times. Wingfield stayed on.

CHARGE BOOTLEG RING. The Wingfield statement was hardly off the press until James C. McKay and William J. Graham, owner of records of Reno's "tenderloin," went into the towns of the Nevada hinterland in what James. T. Boyd, Democratic leader, charged was an open attempt to form a gigantic bootleggers' ring under the guise of a Hoover club.

Behind them came two members of the Reno Women's Christian Temperance Union organizing the women voters for Hoover.

IN IRON CLUTCH. The iron clutch in which Wingfield holds the political and financial life of the state of Nevada may best be understood by a study of the peculiar conditions and circumstances that created it.

Although Nevada is the fifth largest state in the Union in size, the actual population of its seventeen counties is only about 78,000 or considerably less for the entire state than for the city of Sacramento. Its voting population, roughly, this year is 34,000 persons, 19,000 Republicans and 15,000 Democrats.

VOTES ARE SCATTERED. About one-third of them are in Washoe County, in which Reno is located. The remainder are scattered over a vast area of desert and mountains spotted here and there with a sheep or cattle ranch, a prospector's cabin or a struggling mining town.

This has endangered a peculiar political condition in many of these isolated counties. The scarcity of votes frequently has resulted in important contests for members in the legislature and other important posts being decided by one or two ballots.

Politics touch the intimate, personal lives of these Nevadans. The smallness of numbers and the large numbers of offices to be filled means that nearly every citizen is personally involved at some time or another. Indeed, it is said to be hard to find a voter in some of the counties who has not been a candidate for office at some time.

Contests decided by such close margins often mean bitter factional quarrels, jockeying for votes, and an occasional district election riot. Demands for recounts are frequent.

There is a saying that you can start a fight easier in Nevada on Election Day than at a pugilists' convention and that Nevadans take their liquor straight and their politics seriously.

It is obvious that the secret ballot does not always afford the mortgage-harassed farmer or miner the protection he should have in casting his ballot according to the dictates of his conscience, under these conditions. For in these sparsely settled districts, where so few votes are cast, it is a comparatively simple matter to check results after election day and guess who has obeyed orders and who has not.

UNLUCKY FOR HIM. And woe betide the luckless mine employee or operator or debt-ridden sheep man, at the coming election, who shoves aside the honeyed dose of Hoover physic so thoughtfully prepared for him by the joint chemists of the Wingfield faction, the McKay-Graham bootlegging ring, the W.C.T.U. and the Ku Klux Klan!

Nevada's mining towns were not the dispirited, depopulated places they are to-day when George Wingfield made his appearance in Winnemucca and Tonopah a quarter of a century ago, after finding the life of a buckaroo on a Humboldt cattle ranch too tame for his adventurous spirit.

Prosperity in capital letters sat astride the state when he made his first loan from George S. Nixon and embarked on the career that was to make him Nevada's future dictator. Virginia City, now a ghost town of a few hundred people, was a booming, rollicking camp of 40,000 eager souls, Goldfield was five times as big, Carson City, Winnemucca, Tonopah and a dozen other towns were teaming with hope and reeking with wealth.

Into this happy-go-lucky maelstrom of unlimited money, flowing liquor, unrestricted "ladies of joy" and wide-open gambling, came Wingfield.

The magic of Midas was his. All that he touched turned to gold. Fearless and ruthless in his business deals but generous and democratic with his friends, Wingfield went from his success with Goldfield Consolidated to one venture after another, pyramiding his fortune to a figure now estimated all the way from $20,000,000 to $50,000,000.

Now Wingfield's vast interests stretch across the state, controlling the financial destinies of thousands. Governors and gamblers, preachers and parasites, dance alike to the tune of the Wingfield music.

Of late he has centered his attention to the control of Nevada's banks, although his activities in other fields are legion. In Reno Wingfield owns the Reno National, the Reno Trust and Savings and the Riverside Banks. And he owns or controls the Henderson Bank of Elko, the First National Bank in Winnemucca, the Carson Valley Bank in Carson City, the Churchill County Bank in Fallon, the Tonopah Banking Corporation in Tonopah and the Virginia City Bank in Virginia City.

He owns the Riverside and Golden, Reno's two leading hotels. He has vast holdings in real estate in Reno and other parts of the state. His banks are said to hold mortgages on most of Reno's important business houses.

He is directly or indirectly interested in a score or more of mining projects scattered all over the state. Hundreds of farmers in the hinterland are directly obligated to him through bank loans.

This cartoon from the *Sacramento Bee* expresses the power of George Wingfield in Nevada as well as the concerns of many about his seemingly imperial desire for power. Courtesy of Nevada State Library and Archives

Small wonder, then, that when the Wingfield whip is cracked for Hoover and the Republican ticket, there is a general scurrying to get on the band wagon. It now remains to be seen whether The People of Nevada are willing to forget that George Wingfield is the man who put over the famous "compromise bill" in the Nevada legislature that saddled a burden of some $362,000 on the taxpayers to relieve his Carson City bank of paying back funds taken from it through the joint manipulation of the cashier, the state treasurer and the state controller.

The state's funds had been entrusted to this bank. But when a shortage of $516,000 was discovered Wingfield prevailed on his friend, Governor Balzar, to call a special session. For weeks before the session, Wingfield's agents were busy all over the state. And when the legislators met, so great was the power of the Wingfield dictatorship that only a few voices were raised when his bill, compromising with the payment of $154,000 for a shortage of $516,000, was brought up for passage.

7

Twentieth-Century Social History

The Baskets of Dat-so-la-lee

Washoes are native inhabitants of the Great Basin, their traditional territory stretching between the crest of the Sierra Nevada and the Pine Nut Mountains and from Honey Lake, in California, south to Antelope Valley (near Bridgeport, California). Until the early twentieth century they summered in the mountains and occupied five of the most abundant valleys along the eastern Sierra Nevada during the winter.

Washoe women once wove baskets to cook and store food, winnow seeds, and carry infants. Louisa Keyser, also known as Dat-so-la-lee, is the most famous Washoe basket weaver. Dat-so-la-lee was born in the Woodfords area in the first half of the nineteenth century, before Euro-Americans settled Nevada. She moved to Carson City at about sixty years of age, in 1895, offering small baskets for sale to the owner of an emporium there. From that time until her death in 1925, Abe and Amy Cohn supported Dat-so-la-lee so that she could concentrate on making her superb baskets to sell to tourists and collectors. Even during her lifetime, her baskets sold for thousands of dollars, a large sum for the early twentieth century. Dat-so-la-lee was the undisputed master of a craft that was dying in her culture at the time. Steel pots and pans had virtually replaced baskets, and the younger Washoe women never learned how to weave. Dat-so-la-lee was an inspiration to young women and girls in her time who wanted to learn the ancient art of basket weaving, and she is still important to modern Washoes and other Native American weavers today. She is the only Native American basket maker to achieve international recognition for her weaving.

Dat-so-la-lee transformed Native American woven baskets from domestic craft objects into objects of artistic expression, making them a collectible art form. Her baskets can be seen at the Smithsonian Institution in Washington, D.C., and in the Nevada State Museum in Carson City, among other distinguished institutions. Dat-so-la-lee's baskets, with their simple, repetitive geometric designs and intricate stitching, have a lasting, classic quality.

—Terri McBride

Untitled, 1901. Made of willow and bracken fern; eighteen stitches to the inch. This basket took Dat so-la-lee thirty-five days to complete. Photo by Scott Klette; courtesy of the Nevada State Museum

Carvings and Structures of Nevada's Basque Sheepherders

Mainstream historians tend to overlook the sheepherding industry, which for over a century played a fundamental role in the development of the state of Nevada and the American West. The sheep industry provided meat and wool, a strategic material protected by the government, yet people tend to associate Nevada ranching only with cattle and cowboys. Nevertheless, there were 33,000 sheep in Nevada in 1870, 260,000 in 1880, and 2.5 million in 1900. The numbers increased somewhat further until they leveled off in the 1920s and were dramatically reduced during the Depression. But these figures are probably too low; after all, who counted sheep? In the 1960s and 1970s new federal guidelines, ecological awareness, and cheap imports conspired to make sheepherding unprofitable and insignificant. In 2002 Nevada had just 100,000 ewes and lambs.

For a hundred years sheepherding in the American West was dominated by a small group of immigrants from the Pyrenees Mountains, the Basques, who were so essential that in the 1950s the U.S. Congress passed a special law—the McCarran-Omnibus Bill—to allow additional herders into the country.

In addition to their sheepherding, the Basques deserve recognition for the thousands of aspen carvings, or aborglyphs, they left in the high country—a true historical record of their lonely summer days. "To kill time," as one herder put it, they scratched the bark of trees with their knives and carved primarily their names and dates of residence in the mountains, sometimes followed by stark messages about loneliness, homesickness, erotic fantasies, predators, weather, politics, life in America, and dozens of other topics. Their favorite images were human figures, self-portraits, women (usually nude), animals, Basque farmsteads, and various symbols, the cross and stars being the most common.

Other evidence of sheepherder material culture includes cabins, bread ovens, and stone cellars that are still found in remote sheep camps. But more alluring are the *harri mutilak*, or crude stone cairns, which the Basques erected on high ridges to mark range boundaries and perhaps as a reminder of their own solitary lives.

—Joxe Mallea-Olaetxe

Nevada's Basque sheepherders often passed the time and expressed themselves by carving images on trees. Here, a sheep is carved into an aspen tree in Washoe County. Photo by J. Mallea-Olaetxe; courtesy of the J. Mallea-Olaetxe private collection

Inazio Arrupe herded sheep from 1959 to 1964. Here he was pondering his future—should I move to town and buy an American house? He decided to return to Europe. Photo by J. Mallea-Olaetxe; courtesy of the J. Mallea-Olaetxe private collection

The sheepherders erected stone cairns, or *harri mutilak*, on strategic high peaks to serve as range boundaries or trail markers. This one is located in Elko County, Nevada. Photo by J. Mallea-Olaetxe; courtesy of the J. Mallea-Olaetxe private collection

C. L. R. James's Letters from Nevada

C. L. R. James (1901–89) must certainly count as one of Reno's most singular visitors during the time when it was the divorce capital of America. James was a playwright, historian, literary critic, journalist, revolutionary Marxist, and pan-Africanist. Born and educated in Trinidad, he spent significant periods of time in Britain, the United States, and Ghana in addition to returning to Trinidad in the early 1960s at the time of its independence. James came to Reno in August 1948 to divorce his first wife, Juanita, a Trinidadian from whom he had been estranged since 1932, when he emigrated to England. He needed the divorce so that he could marry Constance Webb, an attractive blonde less than half his age; an actress, model, writer, and socialist. James ended up at the Pyramid Lake Divorce Ranch, where he wrote a book on the philosopher Hegel. Long hours of work on the manuscript were interrupted only by trips to town to play and lose on the slot machines.

The following selection is drawn from three of the numerous letters that James wrote to Webb while he was living in northern Nevada. His description of racial segregation and discrimination is among the very few surviving accounts of what it meant to be black in Nevada at the time. As a black Trinidadian, James felt himself to be different from African Americans, yet he felt a common bond with them as well, for while living in the United States he was treated by the dominant culture as a "Negro."

—Dennis Dworkin

New York Central System
En route

[August 2, 1948]
Sunday a.m.

When I came to R [Reno], I consulted the Red Cap. He gave me an address at once. I went to eat first—not a bad lunch, giblets, rice, etc., 70 cents. Then I took a taxi—a white man and I asked him if *he* knew anywhere. He took me to a black parson's place. They are just completing the rooms—a kind of annex. $10.00 a week. The room is about 9 ft. square and private. There is a bath and shower upstairs, but no hot water. There is hot water in the house though. I drove over to see the other women, probably curious, about the place. I preferred the other one, and took it. For the time being, the lady here tells me to buy my meals and she will cook them. That will stop soon, however, as she is going away. I hope the real mistress of the house will continue. If not I shall eat in restaurants. The Jim Crow here in restaurants is powerful. But there are 2 or 3 places set aside for Negroes—one joint, the Chinese restaurant, and a Negro place. However, one can eat.

After this I went to the Greyhound Station and "accosted" the Negro porter. He knew somewhere I could go if I wanted a room. Boy, the solidarity among Negroes is something. He asked if I was here for long. I said 6 weeks or so. He said Oh! Divorce. I said I wanted to see a Negro lawyer if there were any. He said there were none yet but one fellow was going to be soon, and I would find him at the Y.M.C.A. Off I went and sho'nuff at the Y.M.C.A. was a Negro, Mayfield, who takes his finals on Monday. I told him what I wanted. He recommended me to a woman, a friend of his from law school in Oakland. He said she was a good lawyer and would not gouge my eyes out. I was a bit nervous. I asked him if her sex and my race would not prejudice matters. He said not at all. He called her and I am to see her on Monday at 3. I would prefer a man, but I may need a friend—and Mayfield is willing to be. I have to say if not today, perhaps to-morrow, certain things and I think here is a safe place. To-morrow I will see. So, sweetie, so far, so good. We'll hope for the best. But, for better or for worse, we go through. And honey, that was the packingest bag that was ever packed. If you had come out of it at the end I would not have been surprised.

[August 2, 1948]

. . . It began in the morning. The landlady introduced me to a young fellow 29, in dark glasses. Very good-looking, particularly a neat figure about 5 ft 8. I was saying that I wanted to go to some seaside place or lake—if any. He then said he would take me, and when I asked frankly about cost, he said it would not cost me a penny. He asked if I minded whether he and his friends stopped for some highballs every now and then. I answered. He said I perhaps was religious. I said not very much. He told me afterwards that he did not want me to find myself in company whose procedures or conversation might embarrass me. He liked to get these things clear in advance. At about 10:30 he knocked at my door. We went out to a large car—Chev. '41 with a mulatto girl sitting in front—neat, short, and with a very large Negroid mouth. We went to pick up someone else, dark fellow who had a hangover, and who lived with two other Negro couples in a fairly nice house. One of the women had a brother, an orchestra leader who made records. But *the* thing about the house was a baby—a white baby, yellow-haired, blue-eyes, about a year old.

The parents had given him to this young woman to keep. *All* these Negroes loved him. They played with him and fondled him and just loved him. If he had been Nob he couldn't have been more secure. Paul, the mechanic in reply to a delicate enquiry from me, held forth while playing with the baby.

"Plenty of these whites do this. Many of the so-called white liberals grow up like this. After they grow up they can't forget where they come from and they don't go along with the rest of the whites. You see, he don't know anything about prejudice. If some of his own people came in here now, he wouldn't notice them. But when he grows up, you never know how they will turn out."

All the time playing most lovingly with the kid. Not one of them showed the slightest, the faintest hint of ill-feeling. I think they loved the kid more than usual because it was white and there could be warm feeling without prejudice. They overflowed. It was worth the whole day.

We set off.

The black fellow moaned for 20 minutes. He wanted a girl to go with him, but couldn't think up one who was available. I watched him. He said that there was no fun if he didn't have a girl to talk to.

We started to climb, 10,000 feet up, then 4,000 feet down. A superb lake. All we did was to drive round it—about 80 miles. We stopped 3 or 4 times for whiskey and coke. They had brought half-a-bottle. The only lack of harmony was a period of jokes. I have to think this out but they made some extraordinarily stupid, dull, and vulgar jokes, and laughed uproariously. I distinguish between my prejudices and the jokes as jokes. None of our friends would have been other than very embarrassed. They felt *from the start* that I was not one to like these jokes. I said I was not good at that sort of thing and they told me another. Otherwise, they and I got on wonderfully. I was a "killer." They liked my jokes so that there was no distance between us.

The lake was lovely, the drive splendid. It should have been a perfect outing. Yet it wasn't. For there were no colored people in sight. We were excluded. All round were houses, people, cabins, cars, people bathing. But Negroes were out. The exclusion was always present. It did not ruin the day but it poisoned it. You and Dick between you have taught me much about the Negro question.

The girl worked behind the bar at the Dixie Club—a Negro club—a horrible joint. But she was a lady and very self-possessed, calm and sure of herself. She and Paul sat in front, saying pleasant things to one another. Paul is a peculiar man. He was making love to her all day—Jimmy, isn't she sweet? Honey talk to me, tell me something. Thelma, you liking this? Every minute. Very warm. But he was a tyrant. Darling, I want you to come in here with me. Come on, darling, I want you to come—you don't want breakfast? But I want some and I want you to have some with me. You must—talk to me, darling, tell me something, make me feel good. She was quiet but acquiescent. Swift was a notoriously savage man with his women, too, but was capable of great tenderness at times. A woman once told Thackeray that she would put up with all his savagery for the sake of his tenderness. Maybe that's why old-fashioned women loved to be beaten.

. . . In this town, I can't find anything to do. As soon as I finish work I leave it and drive into the country—anywhere, I love it, and I want to get away. I feel I am going mad if I stay in it or go to the alley for all I can do there is to get drunk. Sometimes I don't even stop to eat. . . .

Postmark November 9, 1948

Honey, I see a chance of getting a letter off, an inoffensive one, i.e., not too private. I therefore scribble this to tell you that I love you. I dreamt of you last night, vague and shadowy but calm and peaceful—almost I saw you coming into my little cabin at one stage. It has been cold down here at times. When I go out to the football match, D [Harry Drackert] lends me a coat.

Whom do I go out with? Nobody. Sad but true, for all I care. The guests, or some of them go. We have seats that D has reserved. They are—guests, and I am a kind of nondescript. The formalities are observed, but even in walking from the carpark to the seats for the game, our isolation from each other stands out. I am not hostile, but I am not over-friendly. As soon as we reach Reno from Pyramid I go my way, library, Negro restaurant, drugstore to play the machine. I drop in sometimes to my attorney's office. I have not been to her house for months. I am not boasting about it but I simply live my own life. I talk to the servants, the help a bit. There are women around but I don't see them—a pleasant word or two. Barbara, about 3, is my genuine friend and now and then asks me if she still is my cutiepie. . . .

Warden Dickerson's Account of the Execution of Gee Jon, 1924

Gee Jon was the first person in the United States to be executed by lethal gas. He was executed at the Nevada State Prison on February 8, 1924, for the crime of murder. Gee and Hughie Sing were convicted for killing Tom Quong Kee in Mina, Nevada, on August 27, 1921. The murder was one of many that occurred throughout the West in 1921 because of wars between business groups known as Tongs. Gee Jon was convicted of being the trigger man, and Hughie Sing, because of his youth and the fact that Gee did the actual shooting, had his death sentence commuted to life in prison. Gee Jon was twenty-nine when he died. He was born in China, but had spent most of his life in San Francisco's Chinatown. He was a member of the Hop Sing Tong.

Nevada State Prison warden Denver S. Dickerson witnessed Gee's execution and described it and his feelings in his report to the governor and the state legislature. Although lethal gas was promoted as being the most humane form of execution, Dickerson thought its use impractical and preferred shooting as the best means of execution.

—Jeffrey M. Kintop

Carson City, Nevada, January 1, 1925

EXECUTION BY LETHAL GAS

Under the provisions of chapter 246, Statutes 1921, the judgment of death in this state must be inflicted by the administration of lethal gas. But one execution has taken place in Nevada since the enactment of this law. Gee Jon, a Chinese Tong-man, convicted of the murder of another Chinese in the District Court of Mineral County and sentenced to death, was executed in the Prison yard February 8, 1924, by the injection of four pounds of hydrocyanic acid gas into a chamber eleven feet long, ten feet wide and eight feet high, in which the condemned man had been strapped to a chair.

Death resulted in six minutes from the time the gas was first turned on. The man appeared unconscious after five seconds, but continued to move his head for six minutes. There was no struggle and the expression on his face gave no evidence of the presence of pain. He had the appearance, after the first five seconds, of being overcome with extreme languor and weariness and, except that his eyes remained open, seemed to have fallen asleep.

The gas is injected in a spray from a pump and if the temperature of the chamber is proper, seventy-five degrees, it immediately volatilizes; but the electric heater failed to work properly and we were unable to get the temperature of the chamber above fifty-two degrees, with the result that a liquid pool was formed on the floor, which had to evaporate before it was safe to enter the chamber to remove the body. A wait of two hours and forty-five minutes was the consequence.

Method Impracticable

This method of execution, while no doubt painless, is not, in my judgment, practicable. The presence of an expert in handling this gas is necessary. Prison officials should be capable, at all times of conducting an execution without outside help, as that help might fail at the critical moment. The gas is highly explosive and must be kept at a low temperature to prevent explosion. It must be carried by private conveyance, as express companies refuse to handle it. Los Angeles is the nearest, if not the only, point on the Pacific Coast where it is manufactured, and it would be a hazardous undertaking to transport this gas from Los Angeles to Carson City by automobile during the summer months, and its rapid deterioration makes it impracticable to keep a supply on hand.

Real Suffering Before Penalty Inflicted. The real suffering of the condemned, regardless of the manner of inflicting the death penalty, is endured before the actual infliction of the penalty. I have been a reluctant witness to executions by hanging, shooting and asphyxiation; and in each instance the condemned was unconscious, to all appearances, immediately after the trap was sprung, the rifle fired, or the gas released. Execution by shooting is the most humane, because death by this method is instantaneous, while life remains for some little time when the other methods are employed.

Billy Murray's "I'm On My Way to Reno"

In 1910, when Billy Murray (1877–1954) released a recording titled "I'm On My Way to Reno," the town was not yet famous as a divorce capital. Murray was an Irish tenor who was well known for his popular ragtime and vaudeville songs. "I'm On My Way to Reno" fit the comedic style of many of the songs recorded in the first decades of the twentieth century. The lyrics poked fun at the annoyances of marriage and an overbearing, suffragette wife who ate crackers in bed and insisted her husband learn to knit. The song was popular in Nevada. The *Tonopah Daily Bonanza* issue of May 7,

1910, noted that the song, as sung at the Nevada Theater by Miss Hoffinan, was such a success that two more performances had been scheduled.

Just four years before this recording, Reno and divorce were linked nationally when Laura Corey, the wife of U.S. Steel president W. Ellis Corey, came to Reno for a divorce. It was headline news in part because Laura Corey's philandering husband was publicly romancing a dancer and showgirl, Mabelle Gilman. The Corey case helped put Reno divorce on the national map, and "I'm On My Way to Reno" put to music the more lighthearted aspects of the essentially somber business of marital dissolution.

—Anita Ernst Watson

I'M ON MY WAY TO RENO
(sung by Billy Murray—Victor Record, #16475-B)

My wife and I don't get along, we simply fight and fight
I married her to win a bet, it really serves me right,
The love she once declared was mine has simply turned to hate
So I've made up my mind to visit old Nevada State.

> I'm on my way to Reno, I'm leaving town today,
> Give my regard to all the boys and girls along Broadway
> Once I get my liberty, no more wedding bells for me
> Shouting the Battle Cry of Freedom.

I've stood an awful lot from her and never said a word,
But on the level, as a wife she simply was a bird.
At night when I came home from work, all tired out and dead
I always found her eating soda crackers in the bed.

> I'm on my way to Reno, I'm leaving town today
> It's liberty or death with me my hair is turning grey
> Reno life is simply great, they grant divorces while you wait
> Shouting the Battle Cry of Freedom.

It's awful when you tie yourself up to a suffragette
And suffer, suffer, suffer till your brains are all to let.
She has the sign on me all right, I really will admit
She used to make me stay at home and try and learn to knit.

I'm on my way to Reno, I'm never coming back
And if I do I surely hope the train runs off the track
Life in Reno must be grand, husbands marching hand in hand
Shouting the Battle Cry of Freedom.

There was a time when South Dakota was the proper place
But when compared to Reno, it was never in the race.
The only real Arcadia from Frisco east to Maine
Just think of it, the judge and jury meet you at the train.

I'm on my way to Reno, to break the marriage knot
You just get off the train and drop a nickel in the slot
You just get off the train and then turn around and jump right on again
Shouting the Battle Cry of Freedom.

Prohibition Legislation in Nevada

Prohibition is not too difficult for modern Americans to understand; our twenty-first-century United States has its own battles between those who consume mind-altering substances and those who define those substances as unhealthy, immoral, and illegal. In the nineteenth and early twentieth centuries, alcohol was the substance in question, and when this battle came to Nevada, it proceeded with difficulty and some unexpected consequences.

Evangelical Christianity drove the early movement against the use of alcoholic beverages, and the American Temperance Society (founded in 1826) turned this into a national issue, with traveling speakers who preached the evils of alcohol. They produced voluminous writings on the subject and printed many of these in one of the eleven journals devoted exclusively to anti-alcohol literature. In the 1890s Prohibition was an important component of the Progressive movement, as reformers—particularly women reformers—sought to improve the conditions of life through the elimination of alcohol. Scientists of the day claimed that alcohol consumption led to heart disease, cirrhosis of the liver, and even insanity. In addition, social workers observed a relationship between the consumption of alcohol and broader social problems such as prostitution, unemployment, and deteriorating families. As cities grew and became more crowded, saloons seemed to multiply. Drunkenness was a phenomenon easily observable in any major city, and it became a central target of the reform movement.

Despite the wide-open reputation of Nevada, advocates for the prohibition of alcohol made inroads there in the early 1900s. In 1911 the Nevada legislature passed a law that allowed taxpayers to close rural saloons if 10 percent of the local taxpayers signed a petition and if the petitioners could prove that the saloon damaged public health or community morals. Several saloons in rural Elko County were closed using this law. In 1916 Prohibitionists forced the issue by filing initiative petitions containing enough votes to force the 1917 legislature either to pass the legislation or to refer it to the voters in November 1918. After defeat in the legislature, the Nevada voters passed Prohibition with a vote of 13,248 to 9,060, the majority of every county voting for Prohibition with two exceptions: Esmeralda and Storey Counties. As seen in the excerpts below, the original law passed by voters prohibited "all liquids, mixtures or preparations" containing "one-half of one per centum of alcohol by volume." These phrasings had unexpected consequences; vanilla and perfumes were technically illegal until the legislature passed an act to exempt them several months later.

The story of Prohibition in Nevada did not end there. As in most other parts of the nation, it proceeded bumpily through the 1920s, as authorities enforced the Prohibition statutes inconsistently or not at all. According to U.S. district attorney William Woodburn, in many of Nevada's counties one could not find evidence that Prohibition existed, and in one case the sheriff operated the only local still and allowed no others to function. By 1925 jails in Washoe, Ormsby, and Churchill Counties were full, with a large number of the inmates facing liquor law–violation charges.

By the end of the 1920s, Nevadans began to openly express a desire to repeal the Prohibition amendment. In 1926 Nevadans voted four to one for a resolution asking the U.S. Congress to amend the Eighteenth Amendment to allow states to create their own definitions of intoxicating liquor. This request went unheeded, but anti-Prohibition sentiment continued to build across the United States. The nationwide Prohibition experiment officially ended with the ratification of the Twenty-first Amendment on December 5, 1933.

—John B. Reid

LAWS OF THE STATE OF NEVADA
PASSED AT THE
TWENTY-NINTH SESSION OF THE LEGISLATURE
1919

CHAPTER I—*An Act to prohibit the manufacture, sale, keeping for sale, and gift, of malt vinous and spiritous liquors, and other intoxicating drinks, mixtures or preparations, making the superintendent of the Nevada state police ex officio*

commissioner of prohibition, and defining his duties; and providing for the en-
forcement of this act, and prescribing penalties for the violation thereof.

[*Enacted pursuant to direct vote of the people, General Election, November 5, 1918.*]

The People of the State of Nevada do enact as follows:

SECTION 1. The word "liquors" as used in this act shall be construed to embrace all malt, vinous or spirituous liquors, wine, porter, ale, beer or any other intoxicating drink, mixture or preparation of like nature; and all malt or brewed drinks, whether intoxicating or not, shall be deemed malt liquors within the meaning of this act; and all liquids, mixtures or preparations, whether patented or not, which will produce intoxication, and all beverages containing so much as one-half of one per centum of alcohol by volume, shall be deemed spirituous liquors, and all shall be embraced in the word "liquors," as hereinafter used in this act.

SEC. 2. Except as hereinafter provided, the manufacture, sale, keeping or storing for sale in this state, or offering or exposing for sale of liquors or absinthe or any drink compounded with absinthe are forever prohibited in this state, except liquors manufactured prior to July first, one thousand nine hundred and sixteen, and stored in United States bonded warehouses in the custody of the United States collector of internal revenue, and the said liquors when tax paid and in transit from such warehouses to points outside of this state. . . .

SEC. 4. The provisions of this act shall not be construed to prevent any one from manufacturing, for his own domestic consumption wine or cider; or to prevent the manufacture from fruit grown exclusively within this state of vinegar and nonintoxicating cider for use or sale; or to prevent the manufacture and sale at wholesale to druggists only of pure grain alcohol for medicinal, pharmaceutical, scientific and mechanical purposes, or wine for sacramental purposes by religious bodies; or to prevent the sale and keeping and storing for sale by druggists of pure grain alcohol for mechanical, pharmaceutical, medicinal and scientific purposes, or of wine for sacramental purposes, by religious bodies, or any United States pharmaeopcoia or national formulary preparation in conformity with the Nevada pharmacy law, or any preparation which is exempted by the provisions of the national pure food law, and the sale of which does not require the payment of a United States liquor dealer's tax. But no druggist shall sell any such grain alcohol except for medicinal, scientific, pharmaceutical and mechanical purposes, or wine for sacramental purposes, except as hereinafter provided, and the same shall not be sold by such druggist for medicinal purposes, except upon a written prescription of a physician of good standing in his profession and not of intemperate habits, or addicted to the use of any narcotic drug, prescribing the amount of alcohol, the disease or malady for which it is prescribed, and how it is to be used, the name of the person for whom prescribed, the number of previous prescriptions given by such physician to such person within the year next preceding the date of such prescription, and stating that the same is absolutely necessary for medicine and not to be used as a beverage, and that such physician, at the time such prescription was given, made a personal examination of such person, and that such person is known to such physician to be of temperate habits and not addicted to the use of any narcotic drug, and only one sale shall be made upon such prescription, and such prescription shall be at all times kept on file by such druggist and open to the inspection of all state, county and municipal officers. It shall be the duty of such druggist to register in a book kept for that purpose all prescriptions from physicians mentioned in this section, stating the name of the party for whom prescribed, the date of the prescription, the name of the physician by whom the prescription is issued, the quantity of such alcohol and the use for which prescribed, and such record shall at all times be open to the same inspection as such prescriptions. . . .

SEC. 6. Every person who shall directly or indirectly keep or maintain by himself or by associating with others, or who shall in any manner aid, assist or abet in keeping or maintaining any club house, or other place in which any liquor is received or kept for the purpose of use, gift, barter or sold as a beverage, or for distribution or division among the members of any club or association by any means whatsoever; and every person who shall use, barter, sell or give away, or assist or abet in bartering, selling or giving away any liquors so received or kept, shall be deemed guilty of a misdemeanor and upon conviction thereof be punished by a fine of not less than one hundred nor more than one thousand dollars and by imprisonment in the county jail not less than thirty days nor more than twelve months; and in all cases the members, shareholders or associates in any club or association mentioned in this section, shall be competent witness to prove any violations of the provisions of this section, or of this net, or of any fact tending thereto; and no person shall be excused from testifying as to any offense committed by another against any of the provisions of this act by reason of his testimony tending to criminate himself, but the testimony given by such person shall in no case be used against him.

CHAP. 116—*An Act to amend an act entitled "An act to prohibit the manufacture, sale, keeping for sale, and gift, of malt, vinous and spirituous liquors, and other intoxicating drinks, mixtures or preparations; making the superintendent of the Nevada state police ex officio commissioner of prohibition, and defining his duties; and providing for the enforcement of this act; and prescribing penalties for the violation thereof," enacted by the people of the State of Nevada by referendum at the general election in the year 1918.*

[Approved March 26, 1919.]

The People of the State of Nevada, represented in Senate and Assembly, do enact as follows:

SECTION 1. Section one of the act entitled "An act to prohibit the manufacture, sale, keeping for sale, and gift, of malt, vinous and spirituous liquors, and other intoxicating drinks, mixtures or preparations; making the superintendent of the Nevada state police ex officio commissioner of prohibition, and defining his duties; and providing for the enforcement of this act, and prescribing penalties for the violation thereof," enacted by the people of the State of Nevada by referendum at the general election in the year 1918, is hereby amended so as to read as follows:

Section 1. The word "liquors" as used in this act shall be construed to embrace all malt, vinous or spirituous liquors, wine, porter, ale, beer or any other intoxicating drink, mixture or preparation of like nature; and all liquids, mixtures or preparations, whether patented or not, which will produce intoxication, and all beverages containing more than one-half of one per centum of alcohol by volume shall be deemed spirituous liquors, and all shall be embraced in the word "liquors," as, hereinafter used in this act; *provided*, nothing in this section shall be deemed as prohibiting the manufacture or sale of malt drinks, or so-called near beer or other similar beverage of whatever name which does not contain to exceed one-half of one per centum of alcohol by volume, nor to prohibit the manufacture or sale of vanilla, lemon or other similar extracts now in common use for culinary purposes, or perfumes or other similar articles used exclusively for toilet purposes.

The Lincoln Highway opened up Nevada to the vacationing American public and set in motion the tourism industry that Nevada relies on today. Courtesy of Michael A. "Bert" Bedeau private collection

Before motels, automobile travelers could stay in auto camps, which offered amenities ranging from flat spots on which to pitch a tent to comfortable cabins. In the 1940s motels replaced auto camps for highway travelers. Courtesy of Michael A. "Bert" Bedeau private collection

Postcards Promoting Automobile Tourism in Nevada

Automobile tourism is nearly as old as the automobile itself. It did not take long for people with wheels to get wanderlust. The horseless carriage may have excluded the horse, but horse roads are what they had to drive on. Ruts, dust, mud, and any number of wild or domestic beasts made early motoring an uncomfortable yet exhilarating experience.

Postcards like this helped promote Nevada's roadside attractions to the growing number of automobile tourists. Courtesy of Mella Rothwell Harmon private collection

Driving on a gravel road seemed luxurious to motorists in 1912, the year Carl Fisher of Indianapolis, Indiana, conceived the notion of a coast-to-coast rock highway. This idea was the birth of the Lincoln Highway and the transcontinental highway concept. Ultimately there would be four of these roads passing through Nevada by 1930. The Lincoln and Victory Highways crossed the center of the state from east to west, roughly following the routes of modern-day Highway 50 and Highway 80, respectively. The Midland Trail crossed from east to west, dropping south through Tonopah and Goldfield, and the Arrowhead Trail traveled west from Salt Lake City through Las Vegas to Los Angeles, ultimately becoming U.S. Interstate 15.

At first, motorists crossing Nevada could stop at ranches along the way for gasoline, food, lodging, and mechanical assistance. As more and more miles of roads were paved and organized national highways were developed, gasoline stations, garages, roadway diners, and auto courts sprang up both in towns and along the open road. Following World War II, the American public was raring for recreation, and Nevada's gaming industry catered to that burgeoning market. First to market Nevada casino gaming to the motoring public was Harold's Club in Reno, which initiated a roadside sign campaign declaring "Harold's Club or Bust." This early marriage of automobile tourism and gaming laid the groundwork for the economic supremacy of Nevada's present-day gaming industry.

—Mella Rothwell Harmon

8

Depression and New Deal

Nevada's New Deal Buildings

Nevada did not feel the full effects of the Great Depression until 1931, when a devastating drought, coupled with a downturn in mineral production, began to cause hardships. Federal assistance was meager and slow to arrive. The Nevada legislature took matters into its own hands by passing a more lenient divorce law and the Wide-open Gambling Law to help spur the economy.

When President Franklin Roosevelt took office in March 1933, he instituted an alphabet-soup list of federal relief agencies to assist states with their relief efforts. General relief, or welfare, was provided through the Federal Emergency Relief Administration, but Roosevelt believed that the unemployed needed to work in order to bolster their pride and self-respect. The majority of the federal relief programs that functioned in Nevada were work projects. The Civilian Conservation Corps (CCC), the Civil Works Administration (CWA), the Emergency Work Relief Program (EWRP), the Works Progress Administration (WPA), and the Public Works Administration (PWA) all employed Nevada workers. The fruits of their labors can be found in almost all Nevada communities. Other New Deal agencies that operated in Nevada during the Depression were the Rural Electrification Administration, bringing electricity to rural communities and ranches; the Resettlement Administration, which sought to put unemployed urban dwellers onto farms and ranches; the Home Owners Loan Corporation; and the Federal Housing Authority.

—Mella Rothwell Harmon

(*Facing page*)

The Public Works Administration (PWA) employed labor from the relief rolls, but the projects were larger than those of the Works Progress Administration (WPA). In Nevada the PWA built the Las Vegas Grammar School in Las Vegas (*top*), the Materials Research Laboratory in Carson City (*center*), and the Supreme Court building in Carson City (*bottom*). Top photo by Dorothy Wright, courtesy of the Nevada State Historic Preservation Office; center photo by Ronald M. James; bottom photo courtesy the Nevada State Library and Archives

A popular WPA project was the Nevada Fly-proof Privy Program, which offered sanitary outhouses to rural towns and ranches in Nevada. The concrete floors and seat risers eliminated the vermin problem, and screened vents provided welcome air circulation. Photo by Mella Rothwell Harmon; courtesy of Mella Rothwell Harmon private collection

Paul Hutchinson on Nevada Gambling in *The Christian Century*

Nevada's sin solutions of legalized gambling, tolerated prostitution, prizefighting, and quickie divorces and marriages helped it through the boom-and-bust cycles of its base economies of mining and agriculture. In 1930 Reno's mayor, E. E. Roberts, summed up Nevada's legislative attitude:

> You cannot legislate morals into people, any more than you can legislate love into the hearts of some professed Christians. You can't stop gambling, so let's put it in the open. Divorce is

the only solution when marriages are unhappy. And if I had my way in this prohibition year, I as mayor of Reno would place a barrel of whisky on every corner, with a dipper, and a sign saying: "Help yourself, but don't be a hog."

Someone else said, "If you can't do it at home, go to Nevada."

Although Nevada's sin solutions were lucrative, many roundly criticized them. Paul Hutchinson, in a series of articles in *The Christian Century*, called Nevada a prostitute state, employing the dictionary definition of prostitution as "openly devoted to lewdness, especially for gain." In spite of the national moral outrage expressed against it, the Nevada legislature continued to legalize vice for the economic good of the state.

—Mella Rothwell Harmon

Nevada—a Prostitute State

by Paul Hutchinson

The Standard dictionary defines the adjective "prostitute" as "1. Openly devoted to lewdness, especially for gain. 2. Surrendered to base or unworthy purposes." Webster's definition is "Openly lewd; devoted to base purposes; infamous; mercenary." Nevada is a prostitute state. Her citizens will, of course, resent such a designation. One finds them, in conversation, rather bristlingly defensive of their state's "good name." But if language has any meaning, the definition fits Nevada as exactly as a definition can be required to fit. The state has devoted itself to base purposes for gain.

It has done so deliberately. Talk with a dozen men of Reno and you will not find one who says that the state has legalized its present "wide open" condition because the people of Nevada desire to indulge themselves in vice. But they will tell you that the new laws have been framed with one purpose—to entice into the state people from outside who want to take a fling. The new laws are, according to the citizens of the state, a lure for tourists. "Dozens of places on the coast live entirely on the tourist trade; why not Reno?" I was asked that question again and again. But how deflect this tourist tide into this barren, sparsely settled state? Legalized vice is the present answer.

Mr. Lippmann's Philosophy. I do not want to be too harsh in judging Nevada. The prostitute is often more victim than despoiler. And there is not wanting high intellectual dispensation for the course which the state has chosen to follow. It was only last spring, for example, that Mr. Walter Lippmann entered the pages of the Forum to explain that vice is merely a catering to the undercover desires of virtue; that it is the business of supplying the disreputable desires of reputable people that produces the underworld, and that the way to wipe out the vice problem is to place the gratification of what are now generally forbidden desires easily and legally within the reach of all. Mr. Lippmann specifically mentioned drink, gambling and sexual promiscuity as three matters that might be removed from the list of social problems by legalizing them.

Had not Nevada adopted her "wide open" policy before Mr. Lippmann's articles appeared it might be concluded that the state was but putting into effect the precepts of this distinguished political philosopher. At any rate, the Lippmann theory and the Nevada practice walk hand in hand. It is the belief of Nevada that the nation is full of people who, in the secret of their own hearts, are eager to escape from the social regulations of their own communities in order to indulge in forms of relaxation there taboo. And Nevada is out to cash in on this supposed desire of virtue for vice. . . .

A Dissenting Minority. Of course, I do not mean to suggest that every citizen of the state of Nevada is a convert to the "wide open" policy. There is a strong minority in the state which is opposed to the open gambling and prostitution, and would like to see the divorce laws drastically changed. There are ministers in the state, for example, who fought the inauguration of the present policy, and will fight its continuation at every opportunity. There are churches which will throw the influence of their membership against at least the most flagrant of the present abuses. There are educators who are alarmed as to the outlook, and will do all in their power to change things.

But one is still forced to believe that the majority favors the "wide open" state. At least, any majority that can be mustered at the polls. As you circulate about and talk with the people privately, letting them know that you will not betray their confidence, you find a surprising number who question the wisdom of the present policy. However, they themselves admit that the chances of bringing the full force of this opposition into the open are not large. Behind the new laws stand powerful banks and even more powerful political interests. Men are convinced that it would mean social and economic suicide to buck the present order openly. They writhe, many of them, under the reputation which their state is coming to bear. But they writhe in secret.

A certain sort of moralist might, I imagine, advance the theory that Nevada's present condition as a purveyor of legalized vice to the rest of the nation is only a recompense for the political immorality which brought the state into the union in the first place. A territory gained as one result of the bludgeoning of Mexico in the treaty of Guadalupe Hidalgo, this huge expanse of almost uninhabited desert was given statehood in 1864 simply in order to provide the stalwart republicans, then girding for the battle with Lincoln—which fate forced them to fight with Johnson—with two more votes in the senate. If now the state shows little moral sensitivity, may this not be a natural working of its political heritage?

Economic Factors. To this day the state, although sixth in territorial size among the commonwealths, holds less than a hundred thousand inhabitants. Most of these, moreover, live on widely scattered ranches. More than three-fifths of the area of the state is regarded as too worthless to own. It is easy to understand, therefore, how the single city, Reno, with its population of 18,000—plus a suburb, Sparks, of 4,000—can dominate the state. Las Vegas, next in size, with 5,000 inhabitants, may, during the building of the Hoover dam, acquire a new importance. But up to the present, the manipulations at Washington in the 'sixties have succeeded in putting the state largely under the control of Reno.

But this is probably altogether too romantic an interpretation of Nevada's present policy. Rather than a lesson in morals, or political heredity, many observers will find in the state an example of the economic control underlying political action. The state has gone "wide open" because it has lost most of its other means of support. This, as I have already said, is the explanation that Nevadans themselves advance. They point out that their state has had, in recent years, only two sources of income that amounted to much. One of these was raising cattle and the other was mining silver. The state's tax income was especially dependent on the mining. Well, the silver mining industry is practically out of existence today, while cattle raising is in almost as depressed a condition as agriculture. Nevada is already full of ghost towns; to escape becoming a ghost state its citizens will tell you that it has set the traps of its divorce mills and gambling halls to lure money back within its borders.

But all these theories as to why Nevada has adopted her present policy are, after all, of minor importance so far as my present purpose is concerned. The bald fact is that this state has suddenly "liberalized" its laws to a degree never before approached by an American commonwealth. Gambling is now a legal occupation; prostitution is licensed; divorce is made available on extremely lax grounds after a residence of only six weeks. It is this state of affairs which has brought Nevada, and especially Reno, so conspicuously into the public eye. The nation wonders whether the facts as to what is going on in this state are as sensational as they have been rumored to be. It is the principal purpose of these articles to give the readers of *The Christian Century* a dependable account of the situation as it actually is. . . .

Reno's Divorce Mill

by Paul Hutchinson

On my way to Reno I became interested in a pair of husky young fellows in the same car. They proved to be mechanics from Bridgeport, also Reno-bound. I wondered what their mission might be, for they did not seem the type that would be drawn across the continent to share in the gambling and still less did they look like prospects for the Nevada divorce mill. Meeting them on Virginia Street, the day after our arrival, their mission came out. "If you see a Dodge from Connecticut," they said, "please let us know." They were looking for a girl who was the wife of one and the sister of the other. Lured by the promise of easy divorce, she had taken the family car and headed west. The two men had followed to bring her home.

I suspect that is a common enough story in Reno. For the little city has become a national mecca for divorce-seekers, and many light-headed freedom-seekers must rush to the place without ever stopping to inquire about the rules which govern the granting of these separations. As you walk about the town you are sure to be impressed with the variety of the license tags on the automobiles. Lined against the curbs they present mute evidence of the part which the Washoe County court of Nevada is playing in the national life.

Size of the Divorce Traffic. Reno is now granting an average of somewhere around a hundred divorces a week. There were 639 granted in August; 572 in September. No explanation is given for this drop; perhaps the economic conditions that are reducing divorce rates in other parts of the country have now begun to make their effect felt even in Nevada. As I have said before, my own visit to Reno fell in July. It was midsummer, and a scorching stretch of days. One would have thought that if the divorce business of the town was ever to fall off it would have been then. But on the Monday of that week one of the judges of the county court granted 48 divorces, and the other 41. Even on Tuesday there were 27 decrees granted, and 28 cases filed. Practically all decrees are granted on those two days of the week, for reasons which will presently be explained.

The proportions of this traffic in family disaster are due, as everyone knows, to the fact that it requires a nominal residence of only six weeks in the state of Nevada to make one eligible for divorce there. That, plus the fact that divorce is granted on charges of "cruelty," which may be made to cover almost anything under the sun, keeps the stream flowing toward Reno. Indeed, if both parties to the suit are in the state, and the action on which the suit rests has occurred there, even the six weeks' residence requirement is waived. Under such circumstances, the suit may be filed and the decree granted within a day.

Yet I do not wish to give the impression that the actual business of granting divorces is conducted in Reno in an atmosphere of anything other than the most rigid decorum. Outside the courthouse, to be sure, you will find the stores selling souvenir trinkets which try to make "the Reno cure" a subject for jest. And the town knows many tales of wild celebration parties held by wealthy divorcees, both before and after receiving their decrees. But inside the courts presided over by Judge Moran and Judge Curler there is the most rigid adherence to high standards of courtroom propriety. One day while I was in Reno one of these judges committed to jail a tourist whom he detected, while sitting among the spectators, in the act of taking a picture of the court with a small hand camera. The unfortunate spectator was held in jail all day.

Courtroom Decorum. What is the procedure in these courts? On the day set for the hearing of the case, the plaintiff arrives in court with his or her attorney. The other party to the case is represented by counsel holding power of attorney. If the plaintiff desires, the courtroom is cleared, and in by far the majority of cases the plaintiff so desires. The grinding of the Reno divorce mill is in no sense a public spectacle. Practically the whole time before the court is taken up with establishing residence. For this purpose the plaintiff has to produce a witness who will swear that the six weeks' requirement has been fulfilled. This process takes somewhere between three and five minutes, if all goes on schedule. If the judge is satisfied that the papers are in order the decree may be entered within five minutes of the calling of the case. Sometimes it takes longer, but twenty minutes is an exceptionally long time.

Uncontested Cases. Such cases are, of course, uncontested. And in studying the Reno divorce mill it needs to be borne in mind that it deals almost entirely with uncontested cases. These are the cases heard on Monday—"wash day" in the slang of Reno—and Tuesday. Contested cases come up on other days of the week, along with the usual routine of a county court, and they are no more easily disposed of in Reno than in other parts of the country. In fact, competent lawyers tell me that it is harder to get a divorce in a contested case in Nevada than in many other states. While I was in Reno an example of this difficulty came to light in the refusal of a divorce to Mr. Charles Sabin, Jr., of New York. Mr. Sabin is the son of the wealthy Sabins who have been so conspicuous in their opposition to the Eighteenth Amendment, and is himself officer of the Crusaders, the organization that is supposed to represent the younger generation in attacking prohibition. I do not know what the details of the Sabin divorce case were, but some refusal of the wife to accept the arrangements proposed by the husband led her to contest his suit, which was accordingly rejected. Later the wife sued, the case was uncontested, and the decree was granted. And this leads to the observation that, while practically all Nevada divorces involve some sort of arrangements made between the parties before coming into court, these are never incorporated in the actual decrees. The Reno courts do not assess alimony; neither do they award custody of children. The judges are cognizant of the terms of the agreements that have been made outside court, and if they do not consider these terms proper they can of course refuse to grant the decree. But the Nevada decree, in and of itself, is always simply a dissolution of the marriage tie—that and nothing more.

[*Section edited.*]

Blind to Ethical Issues. There are plenty of people who will discuss the ethical issues involved in wide-open gambling and other vice. But they apparently have a blind spot when it comes to suggesting that there may be ethical issues connected with free and easy divorce. The Roman Catholics have just conferred on Reno the honor of becoming head of a diocese, which may mean that the rigid attitude of that church on the divorce question will eventually make it something more than a dollars-and-cents issue in the city. But to the present, it is just that and nothing more.

Yet I do not wish to be understood as condemning Reno, and Nevada, too unrestrainedly for their course in this matter. In one sense, I feel that all the states have been contributory factors in the setting up of the Reno divorce mill. By resisting the movement in favor of uniform marriage and divorce laws throughout the nation, by setting up divorce regulations of necessary severity, these states have made it almost certain that some state would attempt to capitalize on the situation to its own advantage. The chaos of laws governing divorce in the United States still leaves one state refusing to grant divorces under any circumstances whatever, and another—our most populous commonwealth—granting them only in cases of adultery. The conditions imposed in many of the states have produced a widespread resort to sharp practice and deceit. It is not to be wondered at that many a person, whose marriage has plainly gone on the rocks but who revolts at conditions surrounding the local divorce courts, should say, "Isn't there some place where I can gain my freedom without stigmatizing myself, and even more my children, with lifelong scandal?" To the extent to which the other states have made it impossible for such persons to obtain divorces at home, they are responsible for Reno. But Reno herself must bear the responsibility for the notoriety that attaches to her courts. Having discovered the economic possibilities in divorce, it has been Reno's own choice that has made the residential requirements farcical. Here, too, as in the case of her legalized vice, she has shown that what counts with her is the chance of making money.

Postcards Promoting Gambling in Nevada

Gambling has followed a rocky road in Nevada, but whether outlawed or legal, it has been an activity long associated with the state. From territorial-period mining boomtown to the relative sophistication of early-twentieth-century Reno, gambling has been present either under cover or in plain sight. By the 1920s, Nevada had gained a reputation for nonconformity because of its liberal divorce laws, its apparent tolerance of illegal gambling, and its lax enforcement of the Volstead Act. Many in the state believed that rather than ignore the abuses involved in developing gambling, it might as well be legalized and controlled. On March 19, 1931, the Wide-open Gambling Law was passed. In spite of the eagerness with which the new law was received, gambling made relatively slow gains during the 1930s. Many were afraid that if gambling grew uncontrolled it would again be prohibited, so a policy of restrictive licensing was adopted in both Reno and Las Vegas. Even with this fear, few control policies were instituted and licensing authority was turned over to the counties. Little thought was given to the potential for gambling syndicates, and in 1933, upon hearing that Al

Nevada profited from activities that were illegal in other states. Gambling, quickie divorces and marriages, prostitution, prizefighting, and other generally naughty businesses were important aspects of Nevada's economy. Courtesy of Mella Rothwell Harmon private collection

Not only did Nevada allow it, Nevada advertised it. Courtesy of Mella Rothwell Harmon private collection

Nevada expanded legal gaming in 1931. Hundreds of gamblers crowded Reno's gambling halls waiting for the law to go into effect on March 20, 1931. Courtesy of Michael A. "Bert" Bedeau private collection

Reno's Harold's Club was the first gambling establishment to advertise. This postcard announces Harold's Club's move to Virginia Street, but later the ad campaign would include billboards along America's highways announcing "Reno or Bust." Courtesy of Mella Rothwell Harmon private collection

Capone was in California, Reno's sheriff said, "Al Capone is welcome in Reno as long as he behaves himself."

By the 1930s, Nevada had a fairly grim reputation as a purveyor of immorality. It was suggested at a Methodist Church conference held in Washington, D.C., in 1931 that the federal government should intervene in the sorry state of Nevada affairs. This never happened, and Nevada continued to enact more legislation that fed its tarnished image.

—Mella Rothwell Harmon

Images of Nevada Prostitution

Prostitution, like gambling, was part of Nevada's boomtown history. When Nevada was admitted to the Union in 1864 and the state constitution was written, prostitution was never outlawed, but its regulation and control were given over to county jurisdictions. Though not legalized until the 1970s, prostitution was tolerated in a number of counties and towns. Las Vegas had Block 16, and Reno's houses, also known as "cribs," were nestled among the cottonwood trees along the Truckee River. When World War II began, Reno had the largest concentration of officially sanctioned prostitutes in America, situated in three compounds known as the Green Lantern, the Mohawk, and the Alamo.

Reno and Las Vegas shut down their brothels in 1942 at the behest of the military, which argued that open prostitution was a distraction for the servicemen at Stead Air Force Base and the Las Vegas Gunnery Range. A 1971 state statute further prohibited prostitution in counties with populations greater than two hundred thousand. (The law was later amended to increase population to four hundred thousand to apply only to Clark County without mentioning it by name.) At the present time, twelve of Nevada's seventeen counties have legal prostitution. Specific local zoning regulations differ, however. For example, in Elko and White Pine Counties prostitution is only allowed within incorporated city limits, which include Elko, Wells, and Ely, respectively. On the other hand, Churchill County specifically prohibits the activity within city limits. Churchill County's only incorporated city, to date, is Fallon.

—Mella Rothwell Harmon

Currently, twelve of Nevada's seventeen counties have legal prostitution. One of the most famous brothels in Nevada's past was Reno's Stockade, which was located along the Truckee River. It closed in 1942, when the army petitioned city fathers to outlaw prostitution due to the proximity of the army air base in Lemmon Valley (later Stead Air Force Base). Courtesy of Nevada Historical Society

To protect its legality, Nevada prostitution has generally operated under strict health regulations. Brothel girls were required to have weekly health checks, and they were forbidden to make "business arrangements" off premises. Courtesy of Nevada Historical Society

Images from the Johnson-Jeffries Fight

Nevada has always been willing to exploit ways of improving its economy. The chance came again in 1897. By the end of the nineteenth century, prizefighting stood in ill-repute in the United States and Europe because of its brutality. During that time, Nevada was also experiencing one of its cyclical economic downturns and was seeking ways to attract an infusion of capital. A golden opportunity presented itself, when there was a last-moment cancellation of a scheduled heavyweight championship fight to be held in San Francisco between titleholder Gentleman Jim Corbett and challenger Bob Fitzsimmons. The Nevada legislature hurriedly enacted legislation legalizing prizefighting and offered to hold the bout in Nevada's tiny capital, Carson City. In a flurry of activity and civic involvement, the town prepared for the fight and the on-slaught of boxing fans. The event was a huge economic success, and it opened the door to future title fights in the state, filling the void created by the sport's controversial status elsewhere. Between 1897 and 1910, several prizefights held in various locations garnered national and international attention for Nevada. In 1910 a title

In keeping with its already notorious reputation, Nevada stepped in when prizefighting fell into disfavor in other parts of the country. It was a lucrative enterprise for the state for a number of years. Here, Jim Jeffries prepares for the big fight. Courtesy of Nevada Historical Society

bout between Jim Jeffries and Jack Johnson, the first black to hold the heavyweight title, was held in Reno. The fight was publicized around the world, and all available
rooms in Reno were filled. The younger and stronger Johnson beat Jeffries soundly, to
the consternation of boxing fans. Although there was no violence in Reno, at least
seven people died in rioting in other cities. Reno hosted other high-profile bouts over
the years, and several notable fighters set up training camps in the area.

Las Vegas hosted title fights in the 1930s, but the opening of the Las Vegas Convention Center in 1959 marked the beginning of big-time boxing in town. At the time
Las Vegas was usurping Reno's claim to the title "Sin City," and to enhance that image Las Vegas made a concerted effort to bring boxing matches to the convention
center. Hotels and the Convention and Visitors Authority sponsored title bouts and
other fights, because they brought high rollers to town. By the 1980s Las Vegas had
become so popular as a boxing venue that it outgrew the eight thousand–seat convention center, and several of the larger hotel/casinos began hosting fights.

—Mella Rothwell Harmon

The Johnson-Jeffries fight, held in Reno on July 4, 1910, was particularly controversial because
Jack Johnson was not only black but was also married to a white woman. Many considered this a
violation of racial etiquette in the early twentieth century. This photo shows Johnson (*left*)
training for his bout with Jeffries. Courtesy of Nevada Historical Society

The cure referred to divorce, and Reno ruled the migratory divorce trade through the first half of the twentieth century. Courtesy of Mella Rothwell Harmon private collection

Postcards Advertising Nevada Divorce

Nevada's divorce laws, like its other "sin solutions," were enacted for economic rather than social reasons. During the early 1900s, Nevada was competing for a spot in the quick-and-easy divorce trade that was developing across the country. Several states, including Florida, Idaho, Arkansas, and Wyoming, had instituted liberal divorce laws in order to entice the migratory divorce business. Competition and publicity from several high-profile divorces suggested to lawmakers that lowering the residency requirements in Nevada would increase state revenues during the bleak economic environment of the Great Depression.

In 1931 the Nevada legislature reduced the residency requirement for divorce from a liberal three-month period to an unheard-of six weeks. This, and the fact that Nevada did not require substantiation for any of the grounds except insanity, gave the state the edge in the divorce-trade competition and garnered for Reno the title of Divorce Capital of the World. The influx of divorce seekers after May 1, 1931, was so great that accommodations were hard to find. Tent cities popped up along Reno's

When the residency requirement for a Nevada divorce was reduced to six weeks in 1931, cowboys as well as Nevada's economy benefited. Courtesy of Mella Rothwell Harmon private collection

main streets, and divorce seekers camped along the Truckee River. New industries developed and others grew as a result of the crowd of divorce seekers. A number of local ranchers turned their working stock operations into divorce ranches, catering to wealthy (mostly eastern) women by offering a healthy outdoor experience and the company of handsome cowboys. The Riverside Hotel had an international reputation as a sophisticated spot to while away the hours until the final decree came, and human nature being what it is, weddings quickly became lucrative businesses in their own right.

—Mella Rothwell Harmon

Postcards Promoting Marriage in Nevada

In addition to its reputation for quick and easy divorces, Reno was a popular destination for marriages. In 1928 California had instituted a law, known as the "Gin Law," which required a three-day waiting period between obtaining a marriage license and holding the ceremony. Nevada had no such law, which provided an opportunity for yet another economic activity linked to current legislation. Once Californians discovered that they could slip over the border and get married in one day, the wedding trade took off. Even at the peak of Nevada's divorce trade, weddings outpaced divorces three to one. It was not uncommon for a divorce seeker to be married by the judge who had just granted her a divorce decree.

Postcards like this advertised Nevada's burgeoning divorce business. This one implies that the catch of the day could be a trout, a discarded wedding ring, or a divorcée. Courtesy of Mella Rothwell Harmon private collection

Most states required blood tests and a waiting period before a marriage could be performed. Nevada required nothing but payment of a license fee, so quickie marriages became big business. Where else would Cupid be dressed as a cowboy? Courtesy of Mella Rothwell Harmon private collection

Once Las Vegas became a divorce destination in its own right in the 1940s, it also jumped on the wedding bandwagon. The idea of the wedding chapel came about in Reno in the 1950s. Offering all the trappings of a wedding (artificial flowers, rented bridal gown, electroplated wedding band intended to last three months, and canned organ music), wedding chapels catered to impetuous couples. Las Vegas took the chapel idea to new heights, however, with its latest wedding innovation, the drive-through wedding chapel.

—Mella Rothwell Harmon

The concept of the wedding chapel developed in Reno in the 1950s. Courtesy of Michael A. "Bert" Bedeau private collection

Erma O. Godbey on the Construction of Hoover Dam

The construction of Hoover Dam was one of humanity's great efforts of the twentieth century, if not of all time. Thousands of the unemployed converged on the desolate, furnacelike region of Black Canyon to find work in the midst of the Great Depression. Construction began in 1932 and lasted until the dedication of the facility in 1935.

Erma Godbey was one of many people who attempted to create a normal existence out of the most challenging of conditions. Recollections about many aspects of Nevada history are preserved in the vast collection of the Oral History Program at the University of Nevada, Reno. Copies are available in libraries throughout the state, and within the dozens of volumes are insights about the state's past that might not otherwise be available in published sources. There are many oral histories of those who worked on Hoover Dam, but Godbey's memories are particularly important because they give us the point of view of a wife trying to keep a family fed, clothed, and—most importantly—cool while her husband tried to earn a living.

—Ronald M. James

We lived in a tent in the river bottom. We bought this tent from a widow whose husband had been disemboweled by a shovel handle when he had gone in to muck out after a blast that hadn't completely blown yet. There was a delayed shot, you might call it, or dynamite blast, and it hit just as he was putting his shovel down and it killed him. . . .

We also had to get another tent. That tent was the one I cooked and we ate in. Then, we got another tent to sleep in. Between the tents, we spread blankets fastened to clothesline ropes with horse blanket pins so as to make a little shade for the children, because it was so hot down there.

We bathed in the river. Of course, that meant that everybody had to wear some kind of apron or a little shift or something, and bathe the best they could. They dug some wells a little ways back from the river, but I saw that dirty looking utensils were being dipped into the wells until I was afraid to use the water. Of course, people had to use their utensils on campfires to cook.

I told my husband that I just couldn't see drinking the water out of the wells. The water from the river, although it was pure, was so full of silt that you'd have to leave it to settle before you could drink it. He would get water from the mess halls for the road crew camp.

There was an old man that had come with us from Oatman, Arizona—Scotty Grants was his name—and he had a 1909 Model Ford truck. This poor, old truck was so old that he couldn't get any parts for it. Whenever he'd need a new tappet, he'd find out where the ranger had had target practice last, and he'd use the .45 shells to make a tappet. Finally, the steel rods that hold the engine in place cracked and gave way, so he went and found some number nine wire and twisted it. The poor old engine was just slung in on this number nine wire, but it stayed.

Of course, everybody that did have any kind of a car, it had wooden wheels, because wooden wheels were the style those days. But wooden wheels were not a good thing in this country because they dried out so badly. If you wanted to go in to Vegas to get some groceries or something, you'd have to set your car in the river to let the wheels soak up before you could make the trip, because the roads were just under construction and they were very rough. Even then, by the time the trip was made, the spokes were dry again and rattling.

So, anyway, I cooked on a campfire and we hauled water from the tent mess halls. They were all tents. Everything was tents. And this water had to be hauled in from Las Vegas by train to Boulder City and then hauled by truck to the different construction companies' mess halls in the area.

When we lived in the river bottom at Williamsville or Ragtown, as we called camp, Murl Emery and his wife ran the little store. They would receive their groceries, and people needed them so badly. Oftentimes the truck with the groceries came in a day or two before the bill of lading came. Even if the bill of lading did come, they were so busy they didn't have time to check it and mark the prices, so they used just what you might call an honor system for the prices. People paid what they were used to paying for the same item from whatever area of the United States they had come from. . . .

Then, on July twenty-sixth, there were three women who died in the camp right around me there. I began to get scared. There was no way to get a doctor. I had had a very bad case of sunburn, although it was partly campfire burn and windburn, too. It was on my face, and the skin dried out completely. I thought I had caught some kind of disease from bathing in the river or something, so I was putting pure Listerine on my face. This was just drying it up more, but I was bound I wasn't going to let my children catch anything I had caught. Finally, it got so bad that my husband took me up to the Six Companies' camp, which was in Boulder City. They had a doctor who examined the men before they went to work to see that they would be able to work. But he said he had no time for women or children, so we had to drive into Las Vegas. The very first doctor's sign I saw I went in to him. I got some ointment and some kind of wash he prescribed to use on my face. When I put it on it just felt like heaven, because my face had stung so for days and weeks that I could hardly stand it, and it was just as red as fire.

When these women died on the twenty-sixth of July, they had taken two of them into Las Vegas to the mortuary, but there wasn't any transportation available to take the third woman in. Before they could get her moved, the heat had already began to work on her body, so I told my husband we had to move. We had to get in where we could get a doctor.

9

Modern Nevada

H. M. Peterson's Letter about Japanese Railroad Workers during World War II

A 1941 letter found in the Nevada Northern Collection at the East Ely Railroad Depot Museum supported the claims of hundreds of Japanese Americans for millions of dollars in reparation funds from the federal government. Fumie Shimada, a Sacramento schoolteacher who was born in Sparks, Nevada, remembered that her father, Kametaro Ishii, was fired from his job on the Southern Pacific Railway on February 11, 1942, after twenty-two years of employment. He was rehired one day after the war ended and continued to work for the railroad until his retirement. Shimada saw a connection between the date of her father's termination and the federal decision that same month to evacuate and intern Japanese Americans in the West. When Congress passed the 1988 Civil Liberties Act, which provided twenty thousand dollars in reparations to Japanese internees and others whose civil rights had been violated during World War II, Shimada applied for reparations. When she was denied because the railroad—not the federal government—had fired her father, she began a mission to search for the truth even though her father had died in 1976.

Shimada made fifteen trips to Nevada to search for evidence that her father had been fired because he was a Japanese alien (by federal law, no Japanese immigrant could ever become a U.S. citizen). Eventually she contacted Andrew Russell, who had written his thesis on Japanese Americans in eastern Nevada. He had found a letter by H. M. Peterson, a Nevada Northern Railway official in eastern Nevada, dated December 11, 1941, that proved an FBI directive had been responsible for Ishii's dismissal. Ms. Shimada sent copies of the letter and Russell's thesis to the Office of Redress Administration, and it became evidence for more than 250 claims.

—Jeffrey M. Kintop

December 11, 1941

Mr. W. Howard Gray and representative F.B.I. gave me the following instructions:

1. All Japanese, German and Italian aliens in our service must receive no pay after today in any form until we are so advised by Mr. Gray.
2. Check all personal records of all employees to get list of those born in above countries with which we are at war.
3. Contact each party born in such countries and get following information:
    (a) Are they naturalized citizens.
    (b) If so, what city were they naturalized in.
    Give list of all aliens to Mr. Gray.
4. All such aliens are to be removed from work today and asked to remain at home until the situation is clarified.
5. Notify Mr. Armstrong on line to get word to such employees today sure.

H. M. Peterson

Hank Greenspun Challenges Senator Joe McCarthy

"Nobody has ever accused me of being shy or humble." With these words, Herman (Hank) Greenspun (1909–89) begins the aptly titled 1966 memoir *Where I Stand: The Record of a Reckless Man*. His recklessness, willingness to draw attention to himself, and competitiveness, combined with his genuine journalistic talent and a fierce belief in justice, made Greenspun one of the most influential Nevadans of the twentieth century. With his blunt and often controversial editorials on the front page of the Las Vegas *Sun*, written in "primitive, pungent, and unpredictable prose," Greenspun challenged two of the most powerful men in the United States—Senators Pat McCarran and Joe McCarthy—in battles that left none of the combatants unscathed.

The grandson of a Jewish cantor and the son of a Talmudic scholar, Greenspun was exposed to anti-Semitism in New Haven, Connecticut, from a young age. Greenspun learned to fight when challenged early on as well; he claims his mother attacked a neighborhood man who had made anti-Semitic remarks to him. In his memoirs, Greenspun writes that "The episode taught me a lesson I would never forget: cowards generally avoid a target that hits back." This became a motto of sorts—as an adult, Greenspun responded in kind to behavior that he perceived as bullying. For example, when the fledgling state of Israel's struggling volunteer army was under attack from its neighbors, Greenspun conspired to send six thousand tons of contraband weapons to them (and was convicted of violating the United States Neutrality Act for doing so). The newspaper business gave him a large audience for his attacks, and Greenspun did not shy away from using this power.

Some of Greenspun's most vitriolic attacks against supposed bullies were reserved for Senators McCarran and McCarthy. In McCarran, Greenspun saw a figure analogous to the reviled machine bosses of the late nineteenth and early twentieth centuries. According to Greenspun, "I saw in McCarran what my old mentor, Fiorello La Guardia, had seen in Tammany Hall: a political machine bent on throttling all opposition, destroying democratic process, dictating policy, and thriving on the proceeds." In 1952, after Greenspun had written a series of columns that were particularly critical of McCarran and his associates, a number of local businesses began to remove their advertising from the *Sun* in what appeared to be a retaliatory boycott. Always willing to stand up to bullying, Greenspun responded with a civil suit charging McCarran, his assistant, and a large number of hotel executives with conspiracy to bankrupt the *Sun*. Greenspun was convinced that McCarran had instigated the boycott, and, according to McCarran's biographer, a great deal of circumstantial evidence points to that conclusion. The suit was settled for eighty thousand dollars—paid by the casino operators— and an agreement for the casinos to continue advertising in the *Sun*. The results saddened and discouraged McCarran and can be seen as one of the first indications of his declining power and influence.

Greenspun's most vicious attacks were reserved for Joe McCarthy. Once again, Greenspun saw bullying and responded in kind. In October 1952, McCarthy spoke in Las Vegas. McCarthy was at the height of his fame at the time and was riding high on the issue of supposed Communist infiltration of the United States. During the speech, McCarthy attacked Greenspun as a Communist mouthpiece and, incorrectly, as an "admitted ex-communist." Greenspun did not remain silent. First, he seized the microphone and unleashed a vitriolic response. Then, over the next two years, he unleashed a series of increasingly vicious anti-McCarthy columns in the *Sun*. The following article, which is one of those attacks, is of interest for two reasons. First, it contains attacks on both McCarran and McCarthy and thus shows the relationship of those two men in Greenspun's mind. Second, this article led to a federal indictment of Greenspun for allegedly sending material designed to incite murder through the U.S. Mail. Greenspun was acquitted of these charges. McCarthy's star dimmed soon afterward. His conduct during the televised Army-McCarthy hearings hurt his reputation, and he was censured by his Senate colleagues in 1954 for his unbecoming behavior.

With his reputation shattered, McCarthy gradually disappeared from the American political scene, and he died in 1957.

Greenspun also became as powerful, in the minds of many Nevadans, as the senators he attacked. His newspaper wielded political influence, and Greenspun continued as an influential newspaperman into the 1980s. The *Sun* still exists, although, as
of 1999, its circulation runs far behind that of the *Review-Journal.* Greenspun himself
bought a great deal of land, which he and his family developed into Green Valley, part
of Henderson near Las Vegas. He also owned a local television station and later became the owner of the local cable-television company, which proved to be a financial
boon for his family. In his later years Greenspun became a major benefactor to the
University of Nevada, Las Vegas, and two institutions there bear his name: the Greenspun College of Urban Affairs and the Hank Greenspun School of Communications.

—John B. Reid

I've never been one to make predictions but when a thing is inevitable, even I
can foresee the future.

Sen. Joe McCarthy has to come to a violent end. Huey Long's death will be
serene and peaceful compared with the demise of the sadistic bum from Wisconsin.

Live by the sword and you die by the sword! Destroy people and they in
turn must destroy you! The chances are that McCarthy will eventually be laid
to rest at the hands of some poor innocent slob whose reputation and life he
has destroyed through his well-established smear technique.

The poor victim will feel he has little left to live for, so he'll get a gun and
blast Joe to Hades. It might be a bit messy, but Joe is used to messiness. He has
created enough of it.

Really, I'm against Joe getting his head blown off, not because I do not believe in capital punishment or because he does not have it coming, but I
would hate to see some simpleton get the chair for such a public service as
getting rid of McCarthy.

It would be more befitting the dignity of Joe's position in society if he
leaped from a 29-story building as one of his predecessors, Marion A. Zion-
chek, did two decades ago. The insane congressman from the state of Washington, and the Mad senator from the state of Wisconsin had a great deal in
common—namely, softening of the brain.

Joe's Republican buddies plus some Democratic opponents have decided to cut his appropriations off if he doesn't get out of the Red-hunting racket. They object to his stealing the headlines at the expense of other investigating phonies in the congress.

Even his comrade in pilfering the United States treasury, Sen. Pat McCarran thinks it's time Joe was cut down to size. Most likely, the McCarran statement will earn a retort from McCarthy, and if I can add any fuel to the fire, I would like to suggest that the ideal situation would be for McCarran and McCarthy to investigate each other. The results must end in a dead heat. Both must wind up in the penitentiary.

Information from Washington from a source very close to McCarthy—in fact one of his investigators—has tipped me off to a possible investigation that McCarthy intends to conduct and in which he thinks I can be involved.

I would like to save the senator from Wisconsin some effort and money, purely in the interests of the taxpayer who must foot the bills for these personal investigations.

I am as innocent as a new born lamb; and if I were not, I would be the first to admit it, because there is nothing bad he can say about me that others haven't already said and more forcefully. I'm ready to plead guilty to anything, but does this excuse the disreputable pervert from answering for his crimes against society?

I would like to refer McCarthy to his colleague, Sen. Pat McCarran, for advice before he starts his probe. McCarran investigated me until his senile old brain turned to jelly, and he couldn't come up with anything. I've been interrogated by the Post Office department, Internal Revenue bureau, F.B.I., P.D.Q., O.G.P.U., and all the other alphabetical agencies of government, and they all left talking to themselves.

Even Westbrook (I see snakes in my typewriter) Pegler, thinks I am a model citizen; that is, compared to some of the other figures he writes about; like Franklin Delano Roosevelt, Harry Truman and Ike Eisenhower.

Westbrook was supposed to do a job on me on orders from McCarran. In fact, Pat had one of his senatorial colleagues insert one of Pegler's columns in the Congressional Record, telling what a snake I am and what a fine man McCarran is.

In senate circles, the Pegler column about McCarran is known as Pegler's fable. The Pegler strategy backfired because my column on him was also inserted in the Congressional Record and if I admit it myself, I out-Peglered "Poison Pen" himself.

McCarran also fared badly because his efforts to link me with the underworld only showed up his own affiliations with the criminal element; and his deposition, taken in connection with *The Sun*'s anti-trust suit, forever on file with the Federal court, tells the whole sordid story.

Save your strength, McCarthy, for someone much more vulnerable than I. Nevertheless, a summons from any of your committees will bring me post-haste to Washington. I wouldn't mind traveling at government expense every time I visit friends the way the McCarrans and McCarthys do.

The only condition I make is that the hearings be televised so the world can know the type of immoral scoundrel who represents the state of Wisconsin. I have the facts to expose you, which is more than the McCarthy investigators can boast they have against me.

You even can dispense with serving a subpoena, Joe! Just send airplane fare. I'd even pay my own expenses, if I had a crack at the federal treasury for as many years as you have had.

This challenge is being air-mailed to you today!

Testimony from the Kefauver Hearings in Las Vegas

In November 1950, four men from the Senate Special Committee on Organized Crime in Interstate Commerce arrived in Las Vegas to investigate the role of organized crime in the gambling industry. More commonly know as the Kefauver Committee, this group had been formed to investigate crime and vice after the April 1950 assassination of a prominent figure in Kansas City's illegal gambling rackets. Comprised of U.S. senators Estes Kefauver, Alexander Wiley, and Charles Tobey, with counsel Rudy Halley, the Kefauver Committee included Las Vegas in its fourteen-city, eight hundred–witness investigation. In the committee transcripts from the Las Vegas hearings excerpted below, the committee interrogates Moe Sedway, an alleged functionary of crime boss Meyer Lansky.

After extensive questioning of the sometimes uncooperative witnesses, the Kefauver Committee uncovered little that was unknown in Las Vegas at the time: many owners and operators of Las Vegas casinos had extensive criminal records or suspected associations with major crime syndicates. In the committee's final report, the senators condemned the close association of gambling businesses, persons with questionable backgrounds, and Nevada state government. They concluded that legalized gambling not only failed to regulate these operations successfully but gave dubious business practices the appearance of respectability by providing the illusion of regulation.

Ironically, the Kefauver Committee's investigation fueled Las Vegas's rise as the gambling capital of the United States. The committee's investigation and subsequent intensification of gambling prosecutions in other states encouraged potential gamblers and gambling entrepreneurs, some with unsavory reputations, to flee to the more welcoming atmosphere of Nevada. By the time Nevada began to lose its exclusive hold on legalized gambling in the 1970s, its reputation as an entertainment resort was firmly established in the American mind.

—John B. Reid

TESTIMONY OF MOE SEDWAY, VICE PRESIDENT, FLAMINGO HOTEL, LAS VEGAS, NEV.

The CHAIRMAN. Mr. Sedway, do you solemnly swear that the testimony you will give this committee will be the truth, the whole truth, and nothing but the truth, so help you God?

Mr. SEDWAY. I do.

The CHAIRMAN. You have been sick. What is the matter with you?

Mr. SEDWAY. I have had three major coronary thromboses, and I have had diarrhea for 6 weeks, and I have an ulcer, hemorrhoids, and an abscess on my upper intestines. I just got out of bed and I am loaded with drugs.

Mr. HALLEY. I will ask you some questions, Mr. Sedway, and if at any point you feel that you are under too great a physical strain, you just speak up.

Mr. SEDWAY. I will be all right. Thank you.

Mr. HALLEY. How old are you, Mr. Sedway?

Mr. SEDWAY. Fifty-seven.

Mr. HALLEY. What is your address?

Mr. SEDWAY. Flamingo Hotel.

Mr. HALLEY. How long have you lived at the Flamingo Hotel?

Mr. SEDWAY. Since 1947.

Mr. HALLEY. What is your business?

Mr. SEDWAY. I am vice president of the Flamingo Hotel.

Mr. HALLEY. Where were you born?

Mr. SEDWAY. I was born in Poland.

Mr. HALLEY. When did you come to the United States?

Mr. SEDWAY. 1901.

Mr. HALLEY. Are you a citizen?

Mr. SEDWAY. Yes, sir.

Mr. HALLEY. When did you become a citizen?

Mr. SEDWAY. I became a citizen on July 16, 1914, by virtue of my father's papers.

Mr. HALLEY. When you came to the United States, where did you go first?

Mr. SEDWAY. New York City.

Mr. HALLEY. How long did you live in New York City?

Mr. SEDWAY. I lived in New York City until 1938.

Mr. HALLEY. Until 1938?

Mr. SEDWAY. Yes, sir.

Mr. HALLEY. Then from New York City where did you go?

Mr. SEDWAY. I went to California.

Mr. HALLEY. To Los Angeles?

Mr. SEDWAY. Yes, sir.

Mr. HALLEY. How long did you live in Los Angeles?

Mr. SEDWAY. I lived in Los Angeles a little over 2 years. In fact, my family is in— lives in Los Angeles now.

Mr. HALLEY. From Los Angeles did you come to Las Vegas?

Mr. SEDWAY. Yes, sir.

Mr. HALLEY. And you have lived here ever since?

Mr. SEDWAY. Yes, sir.

Mr. HALLEY. That would be since 1940?

Mr. SEDWAY. About 1941, the latter part of 1941.

Mr. HALLEY. If I am going too fast, you just tell me. We want to show proper respect for your health and don't want to hurt you in any way physically.

Mr. SEDWAY. It is all right.

Mr. HALLEY. Were you ever arrested?

Mr. SEDWAY. Yes, sir.

Mr. HALLEY. When were you arrested? If you were arrested on more than one occasion—

Mr. SEDWAY. I was never convicted of a felony, if that is what you want to know.

Mr. HALLEY. I want to know, first, about arrests, and then about convictions.

Mr. SEDWAY. I was arrested in 1919.

Mr. HALLEY. On what charge?

Mr. SEDWAY. The charge was unlawful entry.

Senator TOBEY. Is that an immigration case, or breaking and entering?

Mr. SEDWAY. No, sir; it was on a Saturday afternoon and we were running a crap game in the loft up in the twenties. I don't remember what street it was. And it was raided, and I was arrested with one other man, charged with unlawful entry.

Mr. HALLEY. Were you convicted?

Mr. SEDWAY. Yes, sir.

Mr. HALLEY. Did you go to prison?

Mr. SEDWAY. Yes, sir.

Mr. HALLEY. For how long?

Mr. SEDWAY. I went to the reformatory for 3 months to 3 years. I did a little less than a year.

Mr. HALLEY. How old were you at the time, Mr. Sedway?

Mr. SEDWAY. I was 22 years old, I think.

Mr. HALLEY. Were you ever arrested on any other occasion?

Mr. SEDWAY. Yes.

Mr. HALLEY. When were you next arrested?

Mr. SEDWAY. I was arrested in 1935.

Mr. HALLEY. On what charge?

Mr. SEDWAY. Conspiracy.

Mr. HALLEY. Were you convicted?

Mr. SEDWAY. No, sir.

Mr. HALLEY. What were the facts leading to the arrest, do you know?

Mr. SEDWAY. Well—

Mr. HALLEY. Specifically with what kind of conspiracy?

Mr. SEDWAY. Conspiracy to—it was a bond case.

Mr. HALLEY. Was it a bond case?

Mr. SEDWAY. Bond.

Mr. HALLEY. Bail bond?

Mr. SEDWAY. No, security bonds.

Mr. HALLEY. You were discharged?

Mr. SEDWAY. Yes, I was acquitted by a jury.

Mr. HALLEY. What other arrests have you had? Perhaps I will go through the record with you and we can save a little time.

Mr. SEDWAY. I was arrested in 1940 in San Diego for gambling.

Mr. HALLEY. On what charge?

Mr. SEDWAY. Gambling.

Mr. HALLEY. You were convicted?

Mr. SEDWAY. No, sir.

Mr. HALLEY. In 1942, that is, isn't it?

Mr. SEDWAY. Was it 1942?

Mr. HALLEY. Yes.

Mr. SEDWAY. Around that.

Mr. HALLEY. What happened to that charge?

Mr. SEDWAY. Nothing happened to it at all. I wasn't convicted.

Mr. HALLEY. Were you ever arrested on any other occasion?

Mr. SEDWAY. It was changed to what do you call it?

Mr. HALLEY. Disorderly conduct?

Mr. SEDWAY. No; vagrancy.

Mr. HALLEY. You were convicted for vagrancy?

Mr. SEDWAY. No, I wasn't.

Mr. HALLEY. You were arrested for vagrancy in Albany, too, weren't you?

Mr. SEDWAY. Yes.

Mr. HALLEY. Were you ever arrested for assault and robbery?

Mr. SEDWAY. Not that I know of. They may have charged me with it.

Mr. HALLEY. Didn't you stay in jail overnight for assault and robbery in 1928 in New York?

Mr. SEDWAY. But I was arrested in an office on Broadway, and they charged me with assault and robbery of a person and the person was called in and failed to identify, and I was released. That is one of those things. You are Mr. Halley, aren't you? In order to hold you in New York City, they fix—they put a charge on you regardless of what it is, to keep you overnight, to bring you into court.

Mr. HALLEY. As early as 1917 you were charged with grand larceny, isn't that right, and then discharged?

Mr. SEDWAY. Yes.

Mr. HALLEY. In 1920 you were charged with burglary and discharged, is that right?

Mr. SEDWAY. I was discharged—no, I wasn't discharged. That was the unlawful entry.

Mr. HALLEY. Was that changed?

Mr. SEDWAY. Yes.

Mr. HALLEY. Reduced to unlawful entry?

Mr. SEDWAY. Yes, sir.

Mr. HALLEY. Then in 1935 you were arrested for vagrancy, is that right?

Mr. SEDWAY. No, conspiracy.

Mr. HALLEY. And discharged?

Mr. SEDWAY. Yes, sir.

Mr. HALLEY. Was your name originally Sedwits? S-e-d-w-i-t-s?

Mr. SEDWAY. Yes.

Mr. HALLEY. Is Sedway now your legal name?

Mr. SEDWAY. What do you mean "legal"? I have used it for—since 1924.

Mr. HALLEY. Is it the only name you use?

Mr. SEDWAY. Yes.

Mr. HALLEY. Then it is your legal name?

Mr. SEDWAY. Yes. I use it and my children use it in school.

Mr. HALLEY. What was your business in New York? You came to New York in 1901, is that right?

Mr. SEDWAY. Yes.

Mr. HALLEY. At that time how old were you?

Mr. SEDWAY. Seven years.

Mr. HALLEY. Did you go to school in New York?

Mr. SEDWAY. Yes.

Mr. HALLEY. Did you go through a public school?

Mr. SEDWAY. Yes.

Mr. HALLEY. Did you go through high school?

Mr. SEDWAY. No. I went to high school. I didn't finish.

Mr. HALLEY. Then what business did you go into?

Mr. SEDWAY. Well, I worked around New York in the garment industry.

Mr. HALLEY. What other businesses were you in during the time that you were in New York? That would be from 1901 to 1938, is that right?

Mr. SEDWAY. Yes.

Mr. HALLEY. Until you were 45 years old?

Mr. SEDWAY. I used to frequent racetracks, bet on horses.

Mr. HALLEY. When did you last have a regular job?

Mr. SEDWAY. I don't remember; a long time.

Mr. HALLEY. You gave up working and you became a gambler, is that right?

Mr. SEDWAY. That is right.

Mr. HALLEY. And you also got into various well, at least one other scrape for which you went to jail, is that right?

Mr. SEDWAY. Yes.

[*Section edited.*]

Mr. HALLEY. What did you do when you went to Los Angeles in 1938? What business were you in there?

Mr. SEDWAY. Bookmaker.

Mr. HALLEY. Were you associated there with Bugsy Siegel?

Mr. SEDWAY. No, sir.

Mr. HALLEY. With whom were you associated in the bookmaking business?

Mr. SEDWAY. Myself. I used to go to the racetrack and take commissions and bet for people and book.

Mr. HALLEY. How long have you known Bugsy Siegel?

Mr. SEDWAY. Twenty-five years.

Mr. HALLEY. You knew him in New York?

Mr. SEDWAY. Yes.

Mr. HALLEY. How long have you known Meyer Lansky?

Mr. SEDWAY. About the same.

Mr. HALLEY. Jack Lansky?

Mr. SEDWAY. The same.

Mr. HALLEY. Little Augie Casanno, do you know him?

Mr. SEDWAY. Yes.

Mr. HALLEY. How long have you known him?

Mr. SEDWAY. The same, 20 years, maybe a little less, about 20.

Mr. HALLEY. Do you know Frank Costello?

Mr. SEDWAY. Yes, sir.

Mr. HALLEY. How long have you known him?

Mr. SEDWAY. Twenty-five years.

Mr. HALLEY. When have you last seen Frank Costello?

Mr. SEDWAY. I have seen him about 6 weeks ago.

Mr. HALLEY. Where?

Mr. SEDWAY. In New York.

Mr. HALLEY. Where in New York?

Mr. SEDWAY. I happened to run into him accidentally in the Plaza Cocktail Bar.

Mr. HALLEY. Did you talk to him?

Mr. SEDWAY. I was sitting with some people. He came over and said "hello," and that was the extent of our conversation. He says, "How do you feel?" I says, "How are you, Frank?" and that was it.

Mr. HALLEY. When did you last see Joe Adonis?

Mr. SEDWAY. Joe Adonis I saw a year ago, at the World Series.

Mr. HALLEY. Did you know Nate Rutkin?

Mr. SEDWAY. Yes, I did.

Mr. HALLEY. When did you last see him?

Mr. SEDWAY. The last time I saw Nate Rutkin was when I was on my way to see my sister this last trip, about 6, 7 weeks ago, during the World Series, and I was in the Pennsylvania Station, and I saw him but he didn't see me. And I didn't stop to see him.

Mr. HALLEY. When did you last talk to him?

Mr. SEDWAY. The last time I talked to him was the previous year, and I met him in Gallagher's Restaurant.

Mr. HALLEY. That is where the most of the fellows eat, isn't that right?

Mr. SEDWAY. Gallagher's, Moore's.

Mr. HALLEY. Do you know Frank Erickson?

Mr. SEDWAY. Yes.

Mr. HALLEY. How long have you known him?

Mr. SEDWAY. About 20 years.

Mr. HALLEY. Have you ever had any business relationship with any of them? Bookmaking or any other business?

Mr. SEDWAY. No.

Mr. HALLEY. Have you ever had any kind of financial transaction with any of them?

Mr. SEDWAY. No.

Mr. HALLEY. Do you know "Longie" Zwillman?

Mr. SEDWAY. Yes.

Mr. HALLEY. How long have you known him?

Mr. SEDWAY. About 20 years.

Mr. HALLEY. Have you ever had any business with him?

Mr. SEDWAY. No, sir.

Mr. HALLEY. Did you ever place a bet with him?

Mr. SEDWAY. No.

Mr. HALLEY. Did he ever place one with you?

Mr. SEDWAY. No, sir.

[*Section edited.*]

Mr. SEDWAY. I have known all these fellows. They were all on the East Side. We were all brought up together.

Mr. HALLEY. You all went into various gambling businesses, isn't that right?

Mr. SEDWAY. Yes.

Mr. HALLEY. Were you ever in the liquor business during prohibition?

Mr. SEDWAY. No; very small way—nothing.

Mr. HALLEY. Did you know Charlie "Lucky" Luciano?

Mr. SEDWAY. Yes, sir; I did.

Mr. HALLEY. How long have you known him?

Mr. SEDWAY. I have known him as long as I have known the others. I think I knew him longer than the others.

[*Section edited.*]

Mr. HALLEY. Now, when you came to Las Vegas, what was your business activity? What was your business activity in Las Vegas when you came here in 1940 or 1941?

Mr. SEDWAY. I came here and I had a part interest in the Northern Club book. I came here at the request of Ben Siegel. He had bought in with Dave Stearns in the Northern Club and he asked me to come down here, and he gave me a piece of the book to look out for his interests.

Mr. HALLEY. He had been in Los Angeles in the meantime, is that right?

Mr. SEDWAY. Yes, sir.

Mr. HALLEY. Were you in any business with him in Los Angeles?

Mr. SEDWAY. No, sir.

Mr. HALLEY. Were you all by yourself? No partner?

Mr. SEDWAY. Well, I don't know, mostly by myself; sometimes you make a bet with somebody. Would you call it a partner?

Mr. HALLEY. Did you lay off your bets with somebody?

Mr. SEDWAY. If they were high, I would.

Mr. HALLEY. With whom would you lay off?

Mr. SEDWAY. Various bookmakers. I don't remember whom, exactly.

Mr. HALLEY. Name one.

Mr. SEDWAY. Irving Moss, but he has been out of business a long time.

Mr. HALLEY. Did you do any business with Bugsy Siegel at that time?

Mr. SEDWAY. I was around with him. He did a lot of betting, but I didn't do any business with him.

Mr. HALLEY. Did he have the race wire at that time?

Mr. SEDWAY. Where is that?

Mr. HALLEY. In Los Angeles.

Mr. SEDWAY. I don't know.

Mr. HALLEY. You don't know?

Mr. SEDWAY. No.

[*Section edited.*]

Mr. HALLEY. Why do you think they were trying to put you out of business after Siegel died?

Mr. SEDWAY. I will tell you.

Mr. HALLEY. Was Siegel the boy they were afraid of?

Mr. SEDWAY. I think so.

Mr. HALLEY. Could you give us some details on that, that Siegel was the boy they were afraid of?

Mr. SEDWAY. I will tell you what happened. There was only one they could get us out of the Golden Nugget or the Frontier Club, because Mr. McAfee although we didn't have a lease, but we had a man's word, which goes a long way in our business.

Mr. HALLEY. You had the wire, though?

Mr. SEDWAY. And Mr. McAfee said that, as long as he had anything with the Golden Nugget, we will have a book. That was after we made the deal for the $50,000.

Mr. HALLEY. No; I am talking about before you made it, while you had Bugsy Siegel with you.

Mr. SEDWAY. We had no difficulty when he was alive.

Mr. HALLEY. You had no difficulty at all?

Mr. SEDWAY. No, sir.

Mr. WILEY. Why were they afraid of Siegel?

Mr. SEDWAY. I don't know.

Mr. WILEY. Who was afraid of Siegel?

Mr. SEDWAY. They wasn't afraid. They just got along. Whenever he made a deal and he kept his word and they went along with him.

Mr. HALLEY. Siegel represented a certain amount of muscle from Los Angeles, didn't he?

Senator TOBEY. He was a rat, wasn't he?

Mr. SEDWAY. A rap?

Senator TOBEY. R-a-t.

Mr. SEDWAY. Maybe—I don't know.

Senator TOBEY. He got what was coming to him, didn't he? Good thing wasn't it?

Mr. SEDWAY. I wouldn't comment on it.

Senator TOBEY. I won't make you.

Mr. WILEY. You said someone was afraid of Siegel.

The CHAIRMAN. Would you say that, while Siegel lived, you didn't have any trouble, but after Siegel got killed then they started to try to edge you out of the Golden Nugget, and the reason you didn't have any trouble before that was that they were afraid of Siegel?

Mr. SEDWAY. I would presume that, being that we never had any difficulty before that, and certainly they don't have to worry about me. I am not going to do anything—which we have been out there, and I walked away from it, and that was the end.

The CHAIRMAN. They were afraid of Siegel, so they didn't bother him, but they weren't so afraid of you; is that the thing?

Mr. SEDWAY. I don't—

The CHAIRMAN. Let's get on.

[*Section edited.*]

Senator TOBEY. Would you mind telling us what your net worth is now? What do you consider your net worth to be today?

Mr. SEDWAY. I wouldn't know offhand.

Senator TOBEY. A million dollars or more?

Mr. SEDWAY. No; I wouldn't know offhand. It is not a million dollars; no, sir.

Senator WILEY. What income have you been drawing out of the place?

Mr. SEDWAY. We draw no income at all.

The CHAIRMAN. What is your income per year? What was your income last year?

Mr. SEDWAY. I invested in properties around here, and I have been successful. I just sold a piece of property for $70,000, which I had a partner. I sold another piece of property for $6,500 which cost me $2,000. This piece that I sold for $70,000 originally cost me $14,000, and I still have three quarters of it left, more than that, maybe four-fifths of it left.

I bought a long time ago. I am talking about highway property on the Strip.

The property adjoining the Flamingo I have with associates. I have 50 percent, and they have 50 percent. We sold 700-foot frontage for $70,000. We still have the difference to a half mile frontage.

Mr. HALLEY. When did you acquire that?

Mr. SEDWAY. Acquired it in 1944, and I bought it, I bought the whole thing for $14,000.

Mr. HALLEY. You mean your 50 percent?

Mr. SEDWAY. No I bought the whole thing and then sold 50 percent of it to these two fellows for $25,000 2 years ago, or a little more. I sold it to them for $25,000, and since then it went up so that we sold just 700 feet for $70,000.

The CHAIRMAN. What was your net income last year?

Senator WILEY. What did you return?

Mr. SEDWAY. I don't know offhand.

The CHAIRMAN. Approximately how much?

Mr. SEDWAY. About $30,000, $35,000.

Senator WILEY. You don't get anything out of the Flamingo?

Mr. SEDWAY. I get my room; I get my board.

Senator TOBEY. This question isn't meant to be impertinent. We try to learn something in all these things. We are sitting down here talking with other men who have been in the gambling business, and the point I make is a little deeper than that. You have been in this business all your life, and they are all playing the same games and they are all peeling off from it. You are growing rich, so to speak. The worst of it is that those of us who—I will speak it pretty clear: You don't contribute a thing in the way of production that makes real wealth. What you do is peel off in these games of chance. If you had your life to live over again, would you play the same kind of game again?

Mr. SEDWAY. No, sir.

Senator TOBEY. We have a country we love, all of us, and you and I are part of it; we are citizens. You simply wonder, after all, after the 60 or 70 years we live here, what it all amounts to after it is all said and done. You are in cahoots with a lot of people like Bugsy Siegel, and you wonder whether it all pays or not or what it amounts to, and why men do these things. I look upon these people in my State of New Hampshire that till the soil and make $2,000 a year as a lot richer than these people down here. They have got peace of mind and can look everybody in the eye.

Mr. SEDWAY. Senator, you see what it got for me, three coronaries and ulcers.

Senator TOBEY. What I am asking is this: What does it all amount to? Why do men play the game this way? What makes it attractive to them? What is the matter with men?

Mr. SEDWAY. Just go into that type of business and you get into it and you stay in it.

Senator TOBEY. You say you knew Lucky Luciano? He is a moral pervert and the scum of the earth, Lucky Luciano, and he is playing the game over there still in Italy.

When decent men want to make a living, these men peel it off. They are rich; they are poor. They may have money but that is all they have got.

Mr. SEDWAY. We don't get as rich as you think we do. This is hard work. I work pretty hard in this business.

Senator TOBEY. But you got the rich end all the time. If you put the same talent you have got toward constructive things in life, producing something that makes real wealth and human happiness, men would arise and call you blessed.

We find these men all over the country. What has come over the world? What are the dangers: Love of money and power. There are some finer things in the world.

Mr. SEDWAY. You asked me if I would want to do it over again. I would not do it over again. I would not want my children to do it again.

Senator TOBEY. I feel very earnest about it. It is a cancer spot in the body politic.

[*Section edited.*]

Mr. ROBINSON. When you were in Los Angeles, were you acquainted with Big Greenie Greenberg?

Mr. SEDWAY. No, I never knew him.

Mr. ROBINSON. Did you hear of Big Greenie Greenberg in Los Angeles?

Mr. SEDWAY. I heard of him after he was killed.

Mr. ROBINSON. Was Mr. Siegel indicted for that murder?

Mr. SEDWAY. Yes, sir.

Mr. ROBINSON. Did he ever discuss it with you?

Mr. SEDWAY. No, sir.

Mr. ROBINSON. Was he ever brought to trial on it?

Mr. SEDWAY. Yes, sir.

Mr. ROBINSON. He was brought to trial?

Mr. SEDWAY. Yes, sir.

Mr. ROBINSON. In Los Angeles?

Mr. SEDWAY. Yes, sir.

Mr. ROBINSON. Or Brooklyn?

Mr. SEDWAY. What?

Mr. ROBINSON. In Los Angeles or Brooklyn?

Mr. SEDWAY. In Los Angeles, wasn't it?

Mr. ROBINSON. Because of the death of Abe Reles he was not convicted—the principal witness in the case.

Mr. SEDWAY. I think the case was after the defense rested. I think they asked for a directed verdict and it was given.

Mr. ROBINSON. In the meantime the principal witness, Mr. Abe Reles, fell out of a hotel in Coney Island, is that correct?

Mr. SEDWAY. I read that in the paper.

Senator TOBEY. Did he fall, or was he pushed?

Mr. SEDWAY. Police were with him in the room, so he must have fallen.

Senator TOBEY. What about this man McAfee? Do you know him pretty well?

Mr. SEDWAY. Yes.

Senator TOBEY. What kind of a fellow is he?

Mr. SEDWAY. A very nice fellow.

The CHAIRMAN. What did the Flamingo make last year?

Mr. SEDWAY. Offhand I wouldn't know.

The CHAIRMAN. Well, about, your best judgment.

Mr. SEDWAY. I would say, net after taxes, around $400,000—between $300,000 and $400,000. As we make it we throw it back in.

The CHAIRMAN. We appreciate the testimony you have given here. (Witness excused.)

The Atomic Energy Commission Explains Atomic Testing in Nevada

The development of the atomic bomb at Los Alamos, New Mexico, during the early 1940s is one of the most dramatic stories of the twentieth century, involving many of the great minds of the Western world. The subsequent detonations of atomic weapons over Hiroshima, then Nagasaki, ended World War II and ushered in a historical era that will forever be perceived as a watershed.

Nevada's role in this era cannot be overestimated. In 1950 a vast, barren stretch of land situated ninety miles northwest of Las Vegas was designated as the official continental atomic proving grounds for the United States. Between January 1951 and 1963, one hundred bombs were tested atmospherically at the Nevada Test Site, producing blinding bursts of light and the famous mushroom clouds.

In Nevada homes, many families set their alarm clocks on the evening of an announced test, rising at four or so in the morning to darkness and predawn quiet. They would assume customary positions for bomb watching: seated behind a picture window or standing on the front porch. Some took to the family car, still in their pajamas, and parked out of the line of trees and buildings, eyes turned in the direction of the test site until there appeared a singular moment of blinding light, one that left no doubt about the strangeness and power of an atomic explosion.

At first, enthusiasm for atomic testing gave rise to a new "pop" genre. Hairdressers in Las Vegas created mushroom coiffures; businessmen announced atomic "blowout" sales; and bartenders mixed atomic cocktails (equal parts champagne, vodka, brandy, finish with a splash of sherry). Stage sets of small American towns were constructed on the test site, and Las Vegas merchants rushed to donate mannequins, clothes for mannequins, china, silver, furniture, even food to make these "doomtowns" realistic.

However, by 1956 the mood in Nevada had shifted. Several tests undertaken in 1953 and 1954 sent cloud after cloud containing radioactive fallout to parts of Nevada and Utah and as far east as Albany, New York. In 1956 a young child named Butch Bardoli, whose family ranch lay less than one hundred miles north of the test site, was diagnosed with leukemia. After his death, his parents and neighbors pointed to fallout as the probable cause of his illness.

It was against a backdrop of mounting concern over fallout that the Atomic Energy Commission (AEC) in late 1956 produced a public relations booklet entitled *Atomic Tests in Nevada*, excerpts from which appear below. It was sent to every school in Nevada and Utah. The booklet is small, three inches by five inches, with a green cover, and hence it is sometimes called "The Little Green Book." It includes cartoonlike drawings of rural Nevadans and a careful rationale for atomic testing in the state.

In 1963 atomic testing was moved underground. In 1993 the United States imposed a moratorium on all nuclear testing. Now "atomic tourists" can book air-conditioned bus tours through the once active region to peer at the abandoned relics of "doomtowns" and view charred and twisted remains of railroad bridges, tanks, telephone poles, and bank safes placed on the site to test their durability against the heat, blast, and radiation of an atomic bomb.

—Michon Mackedon

PROTECTION OF THE PUBLIC

You people who live near Nevada Test Site are in a very real sense active participants in the Nation's atomic test program. You have been close observers of tests which have contributed greatly to building the defenses of our country and of the free world. Nevada tests have helped us make great progress in a few years, and have been a vital factor in maintaining the peace of the world.

Some of you have been inconvenienced by our test operations. Nevertheless, you have accepted them without fuss and without alarm. Your cooperation has helped achieve an unusual record of safety.

To our knowledge no one outside the test site has been hurt in six years of testing. Only one person, a test participant, has been injured seriously as a result of the 4.5 detonations. His was an eye injury from the flash of light received at a point relatively near ground zero inside the test site. Experience has proved the adequacy of the safeguards which govern Nevada test operations.

[*Section edited.*]

EFFECTS OF NUCLEAR DETONATIONS

A nuclear explosion releases tremendous energy, equivalent in a so-called "nominal" burst to about 20,000 tons of TNT. This energy is released as heat, light, blast, and nuclear radiation.

The heat energy, released instantaneously, produces very hot gases at a high pressure, and the outward movement of these gases creates a shock wave, which is capable of severe destructive effects in the immediate area.

The instantaneous release of light is so great that devices detonated in Nevada, when fired before dawn, have produced a flash visible 400–600 miles away. At a distance of about 6 miles, the brilliant flash from a 20-kiloton burst—used as an example throughout this section—is 100 times brighter than the sun. . . .

[*Section edited.*]

THE ATOMIC CLOUD

As the fireball rises, the atomic cloud forms. If dirt and debris have been drawn up into it, they become coated with radioactive materials and immediately start falling to earth. As the cloud rises, it expands, begins losing its radioactivity by decay, and floats away.

The radioactive particles within the cloud are initially of a wide range of sizes. Extremely small particles are apt to be fission products; larger particles are more likely to consist of fission products condensed on dust and debris of the air or sucked up from the ground.

As the radioactive particles begin to descend to earth, they are carried transversely by the winds. The larger particles tend to settle first. Fallout—the descent of the particles back to earth—may occur in the immediate vicinity of the burst or thousands of miles away.

[*Section edited.*]

THE FLASH OF LIGHT

The effects of the flash of light are essentially no different from those of sunlight. If you look directly into the sun (or at a photographer's flash bulb), you get black spots in front of your eyes for a few seconds or a few minutes. If you were much closer to the sun or if you used binoculars, eye damage might result.

On-site the thermal (heat) waves can injure eye tissues and cause permanent eye damage if one looks directly at the fireball. This is also true in the air above the test site. At shot time all personnel on or above the test site wear extremely dark glasses or turn away; binoculars are prohibited; and road traffic may be halted.

Off-site the same precautions should be followed by anyone in line of sight with the expected burst. The flash can cause "black spots" so that momentarily you can't see, or the flash can startle you if it is unexpected. This effect can be experienced at night many miles away. The greatest caution needs to be used by drivers of vehicles or the pilots of aircraft who might have an accident if momentarily unable to see, or if startled.

The brightness of the light striking your eyes depends of course on whether it is night or day (at night, more light enters the dilated pupils), whether there is direct line of sight to the fireball, on distance, on atmospheric conditions, and to some extent on the yield of the device.

A majority of Nevada shots must be in the predawn hours of darkness and will require precautions against flash.

POST EXPERIENCE WITH FLASH

There have been no known cases of serious eye damage from light effects to people off-site. Some observers on nearby mountains, who did not wear dark glasses nor turn away, have reported temporary blind spots.

[*Section edited.*]

THE SOUND, OR BLAST

Shock waves go out in all directions from the detonation. Some strike the earth and are dissipated. Some are reflected back to earth from various atmospheric layers. If they reach earth at an inhabited point they may be felt or heard.

Waves propagated through the troposphere (up to 6 miles high) cause sharp cracking and banging noises in the nearby site region. The strength of waves hitting in the nearby region depends on temperature, and wind structure of the atmosphere, on altitude of the detonation, and on its yield. The point at which the wave will strike the earth is dictated by the altitude of the detonation and the meteorological structure of the atmosphere at that moment. Wind direction causes directional variation in blast. If the weather creates a lens effect in the atmosphere, blast intensity may be focused at a particular point and may be strong enough to break windows.

. . . Persons driving or sitting in automobiles should open the car windows. Another simple precaution is to stay away from large glass windows at shot time (windows usually break outward).

Thomas H. Saffer Witnesses an Atomic Test at the Nevada Test Site

"The loudspeaker started the countdown. 'Ten . . . five, four three, two, one.'" With these words, military personnel in the Nevada desert prepared themselves for a remarkable experiment—an experiment designed to determine the effects of atomic bomb radiation on human beings. Soon after the detonation of the first atomic bomb in New Mexico in July 1945, the U.S. government began seventeen years of these experiments. Two outdoor laboratories were created—one in the Marshall Islands and the other in southern Nevada, just ninety miles northwest of Las Vegas. Through 1979, the United States conducted 626 nuclear detonations in the United States alone, and approximately 200,000 military personnel took part in some way. Thomas H. Saffer was one of these men. A newly commissioned marine lieutenant in 1957, he was sent to witness three atomic detonations in the Nevada desert. Years later, Saffer

These cartoons appeared in the Atomic Energy Commission's 1957 pamphlet on atomic testing in Nevada. Although they were certainly well-meaning attempts to entertain the reader, today they seem condescending and dismissive toward Nevadans. A similar attitude can be found in the pamphlet's text, where Nevadans are assured that atomic testing is completely safe. Atomic Tests in Nevada, *United States Energy Commission, March 1957*

recorded his experiences in a book, *Countdown Zero;* an excerpt detailing one of these experiences follows.

After leaving the military, Saffer became an advocate for the veterans of these tests, as it became apparent that many suffered high rates of cancers. For example, a Centers for Disease Control study showed that atomic-blast witnesses developed leukemia at more than three times the normal rate. Eventually, the U.S. government accepted responsibility and established compensation for atomic veterans. The Radiation-Exposed Veterans Compensation Act of 1988 established compensation for veterans who participated in "radiation-risk activities" such as atmospheric nuclear testing and subsequently developed any of fifteen specified cancers.

—John B. Reid

At 6:15 the disembodied voice we had heard earlier over an unseen loudspeaker boomed again. "Gentlemen, proceed to the trenches." In the soft light of the desert dawn, we filed silently toward the narrow enclosure that would hold us captive for what would seem an interminable period. Entering through a cut in the trench wall nearest us, we walked down a slight dirt incline to the powdery bottom. The trench resembled those used during World War I, except that there were no ledges for footing or seating. They were two and one-half feet wide with vertical walls five and one-half feet high.

After moving down the dusty incline, I turned right, walked a few yards, and stopped. I stood there, awaiting further instructions.

The loudspeaker barked an order, "Face left, put your gas masks on, and replace your helmets. Kneel on your left knee and remain in this position. Do not stand. I repeat, do not stand." I obediently followed the command and placed my left knee on the powdery desert dust that lined the bottom of the trench. The coolness of the earth penetrated the thin layer of cloth between my knee and the desert floor.

"Place your left forearm over your eyes. Close your eyes lightly and do not open them. It is now H minus five." I felt my eyelashes brushing the plexiglass lens of the gas mask as I followed the brusque order of the voice.

In the control tower, Johnson and the young designer of the weapon scanned the lighted panel and watched carefully as the color of each individual light changed from red to green. Everything was proceeding as scheduled. Priscilla would soon fill the sky above Frenchman Flat with a kaleidoscope of nuclear colors.

We remained kneeling in the trench, bent low to the ground, filled with anxiety and anticipation, not knowing exactly what to expect.

"It is now H minus thirty seconds and counting."

The only sound was my own breathing and the humming of the loud-speaker. I began to perspire and felt the moisture collecting on my cheeks inside my gas mask. I nervously stroked the stubble on my chin with my right hand and then felt beneath my field jacket to assure myself that the film badge was still there. It was clipped to the flap on my left breast pocket on my utility jacket. I strained to keep my eyes closed tightly.

The loudspeaker started the countdown. "Ten . . . five, four three, two, one."

At zero, I heard a loud click. Immediately, I felt an intense beat on the back of my neck. A brilliant flash accompanied the heat, and I was shocked when, with my eyes tightly closed, I could see the bones in my forearm as though I were examining a red x-ray. I learned many years later that I had been x-rayed by a force many times greater than a normal medical x-ray.

Within seconds, a thunderous rumble like the sound of thousands of stampeding cattle passed directly overhead, pounding the trench line. Accompanying the roar was an intense pressure that pushed me downward. The shock wave was traveling at nearly four hundred miles per hour, pushed towards us by the immense energy of the explosion. The sound and the pressure were both frightening and deafening. The earth began to gyrate violently, and I could not control my body. I was thrown repeatedly from side to side and bounced helplessly off one trench wall and then off the other. Overcome by fear, I opened my eyes. I saw that I was being showered by dust, dirt, rocks and debris so thick that I could not see four feet in front of me. I could not locate the person who had been nearest to me in the trench. A light many times brighter than the sun penetrated the thick dust, and I imagined that some evil force was attempting to swallow my body and soul. I thought the world was coming to an end. I was certain that, with the raging, angry shaking of the earth, the very ground beneath me would be rent asunder. If what I was experiencing was an example of nuclear war, I wanted no part of it. I saw no way that friend or foe, marine or foreign adversary could survive such an experience.

As the initial sound wave bounced off the surrounding mountains and returned, we were struck by a second shock wave. A loud noise comparable to a tremendous clap of thunder made me cringe. The trembling of the earth mercifully ended at last.

I had been bounced helplessly around in the trench for ten to twelve seconds that seemed like an eternity. I felt as though I had been attacked and savagely beaten by a gang of toughs who hammered on my helmet and tore at my clothing from all sides. I was alive but dazed. No one had prepared me for what I had experienced. Had something gone wrong or was my encounter typical of a nuclear explosion?

Priscilla had not been the 14-kiloton lady we had been promised. She had erupted with the overwhelming force of a 38-kiloton monster. Whose decision was it to place us only two miles from such a vengeful creature?

Arthur Miller on Nevada and *The Misfits*

When playwright Arthur Miller first visited Nevada in 1956, the state's empty landscape and colorful individuals captured his imagination. His earlier plays, such as *Death of a Salesman*, explored the relationship of the individual to society and the moral consequences of adapting to a life that society sanctioned but the heart rejected. Nevada provided a perfect backdrop for this exploration as an empty stage that could be manipulated to create a world for his ideas.

The following excerpts from Miller's autobiography discuss his initial impressions of Nevada when he came from New York to get a divorce. This visit resulted in a personal epiphany for him. Fueled by his ardor for Marilyn Monroe, with whom he was in constant communication, Miller decided that Nevada's emptiness and freedom allowed for a "creative life with undivided soul," one in which individuals could have choice and dignity. He envisioned Monroe as his ideal, a symbol of liberation and joy, her life illustrating the "strength of one who has abandoned the illusions of a properly ordered life" for her own self-determined life. These images and ideas inspired his screenplay for *The Misfits*, which explores the choices of characters who would not accept the compromises of a mainstream world, people who chafed against concessions and control until they could no longer fit into the society that they had once rejected.

Unfortunately, Miller's ideas were just more projections of his own imagination. By the time he arrived to film the movie, his relationship with Monroe had deteriorated; by the end of filming, they lived in separate hotels. The filming itself was grueling and tension filled for the actors and crew. Miller constantly rewrote the script, forcing the cast to memorize lengthy changes every night. Several cast members, particularly Clark Gable, suffered from fragile health, exacerbated by filming in the heat and desolation of the desert near Pyramid Lake. The pressure of constant observation by a team of photographers, including Henri Cartier-Bresson, further increased the tension on the set. In the end, the desert did not provide Miller's catharsis. His epiphany faded, and he learned that even Nevada extracts a price for individual freedom: "Nevada thus became a mirror to me, but one in which nothing was reflected but a vast sky."

—Tanya Reid

Pyramid Lake, Nevada, was a piece of the moon in 1956, long before the marina, the hotdog stands, and the roar of outboards blasted away its uninhabited, enigmatic enchantment. It was a gray, salty lake miles long, surrounded by a Paiute Indian reservation, a forbidding but beautiful place occasionally favored by movie companies shooting scenes of weird monsters in outer space. I had come here to live out the six-week residency required for the otherwise easy Nevada divorce, the New York State law still requiring a finding of adultery. Saul Bellow, with whom I shared an editor, Pascal Covici of Viking Press, was in Nevada for the same reason, and Covici had asked his help in finding me a place to stay. Bellow had taken one of the two cottages facing the lake. I took the other. He was then working on his novel *Henderson the Rain King*. I was trying to make some personal contact with the terrain where I had landed after exploding my life.

Fittingly, this being Nevada, home of the rootless, the wanderers, and the misfits, the only phone between our cottages and Reno, some forty miles away, was in a lone booth standing beside the highway, a road traveled by perhaps three vehicles a day and none at night. Nearby were the empty cottages of an abandoned motel for people waiting out their divorces. Only its owners lived there now, a troubled couple, the man a fairly scrupulous horse breeder whose half-dozen thoroughbreds grazed untied along the lakeshore. He, his wife, or their hired man would drive over to summon one or the other of us to the phone booth for one of our rare calls from what had come to seem an increasingly remote United States. Surrounding us was a range of low, iron-stained mountains perpetually changing their magenta colors through the unbroken silence of the days. Saul would sometimes spend half an hour up behind a hill a half-mile from the cottages emptying his lungs roaring at the stillness, an exercise in self-contact, I supposed, and the day's biggest event. He had already accumulated a library here large enough for a small college.

A mile across the lake an island—full of rattlers, we were told—could be seen as though it were a hundred yards away, so clear was the air. The Indians kept removing the federal warning signs from an area of quicksand at the shoreline, hoping to do in any Reno fishermen who might venture out too far in their hip boots, but visitors were rare and only a few were said to have been sucked under, their bodies sinking for miles into the gorge that the lake had filled, to rise periodically over months or years and sink again, borne by a clockwise current. Strange broad-mouthed fish lived in the lake, whiskery and forbidding, of an unevolved kind found only here, it was said, and in a lake in India. I had a vision of an Indian eagle flying the ocean and dropping one of its unique eggs here. Once a week we would drive to Reno in Saul's Chevrolet to buy groceries and get our laundry done. No car ever passed us during the forty-mile trip, and we overtook none. It was a fine place to think, if you dared, plenty of space in which to hope and privacy to despair. I had moved into the unknown, physically as well as spiritually, and the color of the unknown is darkness until it opens into the light.

But there were only glimmers so far. Divorce, I suppose, is to some degree an optimistic reaching for authenticity, a rebellion against waste. But we are mostly what we were, and the turtle stretching toward delicious buds on high does not lighten his carapace by his resolve. I had to wonder sometimes if I had managed to evade rather than to declare the reality of myself. Marilyn [Monroe] was shooting *Bus Stop*, directed by Joshua Logan, and in her scrawled notes to me she sounded harried too. The play had been a great hit, and the role seemed made for her. Despite her usual trepidation, she had looked forward to working with Logan, the respected director of a great many Broadway hits, among them *South Pacific* and *Mister Roberts*. That nothing I could say seemed to cheer her up was bewildering, although the promise of our coming new life, she said, made her look ahead with a kind of hope for herself that she had never felt before.

The motel owner woke me one night to tell me I was wanted on the phone. It was after eleven, well past Marilyn's bedtime while filming. The truck bumped along the sandy path to the phone booth, lit inside only by the greenish glow of the moon. Every star seemed to crowd the sky across the great Western vault. The air seeping in under the door of the booth was cold on my bare ankles.

Her voice, always light and breathy, was barely audible. "I can't do it, I can't work this way. Oh, Papa, I can't do it . . ." Jokingly at first, then as a habit, she had been calling me this, but there was no joking here; she was desperate and near weeping. She sounded strangely private, almost as though she were talking to herself, not even bothering with pronouns. "Says I did the scene with vulgarity. What is it, a registered nurse? Can't stand women, none of them can, they're afraid of women, the whole gang of them. Vulgar! Supposed to rip off my tail, this thing I have sticking out of my costume in the back, but angrily so it makes a mockery of me so I can react, instead of like just lifting it away I didn't even know he'd done it. So I said rip it off, be angry with me so I can make it real when I react, but they're afraid to act nasty because the audience might not approve, you see what I mean? I'm no trained actor, I can't pretend I'm doing something if I'm not. All I know is real! I can't do it if it's not real! And calls me vulgar because I said that! Hates me! Hates me!

"Supposed to run out into the rodeo and my shoe came off and I could see him start to call cut, but then he saw the crowd laughing and so happy so he let me run back and get my shoe and go on with the scene, but he was ready to cut if I hadn't of gone on! Because I knew the minute it happened it would be good, and it was, but he doesn't know!"

But all this was overlay, a swollen sea of grief heaved under it, and now she began to sound high and inspired. "I don't want this, I want to live quietly, I hate it, I don't want it anymore, I want to live quietly in the country and just be there when you need me. I can't fight for myself anymore. . . ."

I asked if her partner, Milton Greene, couldn't help, and her voice went deeper into secrecy; he was there in the room with some other people. But he was afraid to stand up to Logan for her.

As such, her complaints about Logan—which smacked a bit of frantic actor talk—mattered less to me than a new terror I was hearing, an abandoned voice crying out to a deaf sky, and the dead miles between us choked me with frustration; whatever the truth about Logan, her sincerity was unquestionable, for she was dancing on the edge and the drop down was forever. This was the first time she had sounded so unguardedly terrified, and I felt the rush of her trust in me. She had concealed her dependency before, and I saw suddenly that I was all she had. I recalled her telling me months ago that she was putting off signing a contract that Greene and his lawyer had been pressing on her to set up her new company; it gave Greene fifty-one-percent control against her forty-nine. In return for his share he would bring in new recording and film projects that would not require her participation, but so far the new company's assets consisted only of her and her salary. She had not wanted to dwell on this, had tried to turn from the implicit betrayal, and even now as she reported her disappointment in Greene's failure to protect her from Logan, she seemed to shy from any open anger with him. For myself, I wished she could trust him; I had had only the minimum necessary interest even in my own business affairs, leaving most of the decisions to lawyers and accountants to keep myself free to work. I hardly knew Greene; it was faith itself I instinctively did not want to see her lose.

I kept trying to reassure her, but she seemed to be sinking where I could not reach, her voice growing fainter. I was losing her, she was slipping away out there, and with partner and friends so close by. "Oh, Papa, I can't make it, I can't make it!" Her suicide leaped up before me, an act I had never connected with her before. I tried to think of someone I knew in Hollywood who could go and see her, but there was no one, and suddenly I realized I was out of breath, a dizziness screwing into my head, my knees unlocking, and I felt myself sliding to the floor of the booth, the receiver slipping out of my hands. I came to in what was probably a few seconds, her voice still whispering out of the receiver over my head. After a moment I got up and talked her down to earth, and it was over; she would try not to let it get to her tomorrow, just do the job and get on with it. Lights were still revolving behind my eyes. We would marry and start a new and real life once this picture was done. "I don't want this anymore, Papa, I can't fight them alone, I want to live with you in the country and be a good wife, and if somebody wants me for a wonderful picture . . ." Yes and yes and yes and it was over, and the healing silence of the desert swept back and covered it all.

I left the highway behind me and walked toward the two cottages and the low moon. I had never fainted before. A weight had fallen and my lungs felt scored, as if I had been weeping for a long time. I felt healed, as though I had crossed over a division within me and onto a plane of peace where the parts of myself had joined. I loved her as though I had loved her all my life; her pain was mine. My blood seemed to have spoken. The low lunar mountains outside my window, the overarching silence of this terrain of waste and immanence, the gloomy lake and its unchanging prehistoric fish swimming longingly toward India forever—I felt my happiness like a live glow in all this dead, unmoving space. I tried to recall a play about people who suffer but do not fail and saw suddenly the inexpressible happiness that tragedy reveals. Suddenly the hidden order, life's grin of continuity; as I had felt it tonight, as though her being had been maturing in me since my own birth. The anguish of this past year, the guilty parting with children and the wrenching up of roots, seemed now the necessary price for what might truly be waiting just ahead, a creative life with undivided soul. For the first time in months or maybe years, a fierce condensing power of mind moved in me, the signal to write, but only something as simple and as true as tonight. To be one thing, sexuality and mind, appetite and justice, one. All our theatre—my own of course included, but that of the masters too—seemed so paltry now beside the immensity of human possibilities. It had all been written by unhappy men—Ibsen a paranoid with a lust for young women he could not dare acknowledge; Chekhov, fatally ill and all but abandoned by an unfaithful wife; Strindberg, in terror of castration. Where was the broad marble brow of the Greek vision, the sunlit wholeness of a healthy and generous confrontation with catastrophe? She, in her fogged, blundering search, was an unaware exemplar. She had accepted the role of outcast years ago, even flaunted it, first as a casualty of puritanical rejection but then with victorious disorder; from her refusal to wear bras to her laughing acknowledgment of the calendar photos, her bracing candor—so un-American especially now in the new empire preparing to lead the war-crippled West—was health, the strength of one who has abandoned the illusions of a properly ordered life for herself. With all her concealed pain, she was becoming enviable, the astonishing signal of liberation and its joys. Out of the muck, the flower. And soon, an amazing life . . .

Nevada was easy to define, hard to grasp. On the left of the highway to Reno a black tar-paper box about twenty feet square stood on stilts with a roughly made ladder descending from the middle of the floor and disappearing into a hole in the ground. A Cadillac, dusty but new, was parked nearby. The owner was a small man dressed in boots and jeans and a sweaty broad-brimmed hat, cheerful and friendly. When he needed a little cash he would descend the ladder from his living room and go down the hole into his silver mine. It was simple but hard to absorb, somehow. Especially when I learned that he kept a grand piano in his stilt house and played only chopsticks on it. None of this thought particularly noteworthy among Nevadans.

After a week or so out on the desert with two rodeo men whom I had met in Reno, hunters of wild mustangs in their off times, we came on an abandoned shack in the middle of nowhere, a shelter put up by some long-gone rancher and used now for a lie-down by anybody who happened by. The lone window had lost its panes, the door hung open on one hinge. Several hundred magazines lay strewn about. They were of two types, *Playboy* and its clones, and Western stories. In the corners the piles were a foot thick, indicating that hundreds of cowboys must have come by with their magazines over many years, to rest and read and dream. My two friends couldn't understand why I thought it strange that men who had lived on horseback for years looked to the movies for their models and could imagine no finer fate than to be picked up for a film role. The movie cowboy was the real one, they the imitations. The final triumph of art, at least this kind of art, was to make a man feel less reality in himself than in an image.

Four years later, one of these men showed up on location when we were shooting *The Misfits,* and after a good reminiscing talk, he watched from beside the camera as Clark Gable happened to be telling Marilyn some details of his character's past, which I had drawn from this cowboy's life. When the scene was finished he turned to me shaking his head, excited and pleased: "Sounds real as hell." But he clearly showed no sign of recognizing his own biography as the source, or even the possibility of such a metamorphosis. Nevada thus became a mirror to me, but one in which nothing was reflected but a vast sky.

Out on the desert, far from any vehicle track, there were sometimes signs of life underground: in the midst of sage and sand a pair of shorts hung on a stick to dry in the sun, or a T-shirt. My friends never ventured close, although they claimed to know some of these residents of holes in the ground. They were men wanted by the law, for murder more often than not. The state police knew they were out there, and nobody inquired why they were never picked up, but payoffs were inevitably suspected.

In Reno on our weekly shopping and laundry expeditions we saw the town differently than tourists do looking for fun; after a few weeks the tawdriness of the gambling enterprise grew depressing. Next to the supermarket checkout counter, women carrying babies would drop their change into waiting slot machines, but from the indifferent blankness of their faces they had no anticipation of winning. It was as joyless a routine gesture as discarding a Kleenex out a window, tired and blind and thoughtless. Just a lot of women in jeans and worn sneakers giving away money.

Toward dusk one night in a tiny town of some eight or ten houses on a single dogleg street, the two cowboys and I bought stringy steaks from a little grocery store at the edge of the desert. The grocer simply reached up to a side of beef hanging over his cash register and started cutting. We also bought a long spongy white bread and some salt, and went outside and built a fire of dried sagebrush and roasted the meat on sticks. The juices, spiked with sage, drenched the bread. Each of us must have eaten several pounds of beef, and it was one of the best meals I have ever had. The moon rose while we were digesting beside the fire, and the two men admired its appearance as though it were a woman, with those faint smiles that show a man is imagining something.

There was an occasional week when they did the rounds, servicing two or three women waiting in various beds in the area, but they almost always referred to them with respect. There was always a nice trickle of would-be divorcees flowing in from all the states, and the variety of their personalities fascinated my friends. Being divorced themselves, they sympathized with the difficulties of staying married. Under all that sky and amid those eternal mountains they understood weather and animals and each other, but the women were forever the mystery. The older of the two, Will Bingham, a rodeo roper in his early forties, had left a wife and a six-year-old daughter whom he occasionally stopped by to visit in a small town in the north of the state. He led a lone, self-sufficient life that he seemed to think inevitable if not ideal, but the guilt of having left his child was always with him. The sensitivity of some of these brawny Western men was somehow reassuring, something I did not recall reading about, except for hints of it in Frank Norris's forgotten masterpiece, *McTeague*.

[*Miller returned to Nevada for the filming of* The Misfits *from his screenplay and starring his wife, Marilyn Monroe.*]

I had written the rodeo scene to take place in a certain town, its name faded from memory now, far out in the desert. I had come across it one day with the two cowboy horse-hunters: a string of slatternly houses made of unpainted gray pine boards, and another string of bars, about eight or ten in all, facing an impromptu rodeo ring in front of a rough bleachers. Beyond the ring was a church atop whose steeple a wooden cross tilted over, ready to fall into the street, a reasonable symbol of what I was after in the film. The line of bars had one long dent in front where drunks had banged cars and trucks into them, men from the nearby wallboard plant who worked in clouds of white gypsum dust all day. Inside bullet holes showed in the ceilings and walls, with whole pockets dug out of some wooden bars by quick fire. It was the only town in Nevada where a man could legally carry sidearms, and a great many did, big forty-fives strapped to their thighs. During my Nevada time I had been there one Saturday night when the sheer fury of the customers was like a fever in the air, and I had to wonder if the grinding emptiness of their lives had driven them to want to kill or threaten to kill or be killed. It was never a question of robbery, just of two men starting a brainless argument that ended in shooting, a kind of mass sex, it seemed, with bloodshed as the climax of the rodeo itself.

As it turned out, we could not work in that town because there was insufficient water to supply cast and crew, and because of its distance from Reno and our hotels. We found another town, with better facilities and plenty of room for us: it had been deserted decades before by its entire population when some nearby mine gave out. Weathered signs were applied on the store windows or hung askew over the street. It was all very strange to think we were shooting where a real population had once lived, people who had doubtless had great hopes for a good life and now had vanished.

But another place where I had spent some time with my cowboy friends—a house owned by a Mrs. Styx—was used as Roslyn's temporary Nevada residence. It overlooked one of the rare green valleys in that desiccated area, with some trees and enough good grass for a few cattle. Anticipating a need for more space in which to move the camera around, production people had sawed through the corners of the house to make them removable at a moment's notice by turning a few bolts. In a morning a vegetable garden was set in place out front, as the story required, and shrubs planted. One quickly forgot these were all new. The oddness about it was that like demented gods, we had taken a reality and created a fake.

I was finding it hard to remember that in reality Clark Gable was not the cowboy who had inspired the Gay Langland character. It was during this part of the shooting that the original cowboy suddenly showed up to look on for a few hours, and I could not help feeling disappointed by a certain thinness about him as compared to Gable's more satisfying roundness and density. Of course I was part of Gable's character, as I was not of the cowboy's.

Grant Sawyer on Getting Tough on Gaming Control

Grant Sawyer (1918–96) may have been Nevada's most influential governor. Raised in Idaho by his divorced mother, he spent summers in Nevada with his father, a doctor and Democratic politician, and his second wife, historian and educator Byrd Wall Sawyer. Sawyer graduated from the university in Reno and received his political education going to law school in Washington, D.C., while working in the office of Senator Pat McCarran. One of many "McCarran Boys" whom the senator put through law school, he returned to Nevada, won election as district attorney of Elko County, received an appointment to the Board of Regents, and was active in state Democratic politics.

When Sawyer ran for governor in 1958, he was the underdog. He took advantage of that, criticizing the political machine that ran the state after McCarran's death and proclaiming, "Nevada's not for sale." He sought to project an image of progress, and Nevada needed it. The state was reeling from charges that organized crime controlled gaming and that it was a racist state, known as the "Mississippi of the West." Many of Sawyer's efforts on behalf of civil rights were stymied, thanks to legislative inaction, although he was able to push through the passage of the Nevada Equal Rights Commission. Sawyer called himself "fiscally conservative, and liberal on civil rights," at a time that the vast majority of Nevadans remained conservative on both issues.

His quest for stricter gaming control proved much more successful. Sawyer was largely responsible for creating the Gaming Commission and the Black Book, or List of Excluded Persons, yet as governor he opposed corporate gaming, reasoning that it would serve as a front for organized crime. The law allowing corporate gaming passed once he left office, and he was right: at first, organized crime took advantage of the law. Later, this law combined with state enforcement, federal prosecutions, and the advancing age of the casino owners to drive out organized-crime interests. Sawyer contributed even after leaving office. For twenty years as Democratic national committeeman and then afterward, he was a gray (or, more accurately, salt-and-pepper) eminence, taking public stands and advising younger politicians. With Las Vegas attorney Sam Lionel, he cofounded a law firm that became the leading corporate gaming firm in Nevada, and he remained an important power in state politics. The state building in Las Vegas, a Las Vegas middle school, and a center at the University of Nevada, Reno, are named for Sawyer. He is also remembered as the governor who changed his state.

—Michael Green

When I took office I wanted gaming control to be strengthened; and with the support of some legislators (from both parties, as I remember), I proposed that the Tax Commission should henceforth be dedicated exclusively to tax matters, and replaced as gaming regulator by a state gaming commission, with the Gaming Control Board given the responsibility for enforcing the gaming laws. . . . Although there was some opposition, no partisan dispute developed, and the proposal was enacted into law. . . .

For my appointees to both the commission and the board I went with people who had a high profile in law enforcement . . . and people who were familiar with gaming and shared my belief that its control was dismally inadequate in Nevada. It made no difference to me whether they were Republican or Democrat, but they had to be people who could command respect on the national level as well as the state, because our relations with federal authorities were not good. In appointing members to the board or commission, I looked for integrity. Can this person be trusted? There are so many ways that members can be gotten to, and not just with money. You had to be sure that your appointees were incorruptible: that they would not take advantage of their positions financially or otherwise; that they wouldn't even take free tickets to a ball game. I wouldn't put any of my friends on the commission or the board, either . . . they didn't have the qualifications, and in addition to that, I know my friends, and that is the last place I would want some of them! [laughter] And I didn't appoint anybody to the commission from the gaming industry, which was a matter of some concern to them. But at that time there was a lot of rumor and gossip about crime and corruption in Nevada gaming—it was a national issue (there had even been congressional hearings on it), and I felt that members had to be above any possible reproach.

I was in a vulnerable position. If I made a mistake in my appointments my whole career would be on the line, because appointments are made by the governor alone. The senate has always wanted an advice and consent role regarding gaming control, but they've never gotten it; and I wouldn't favor it even now, because to be an effective executive you have to decide who is going to be on the boat and who is going to be running it. A bunch of people who meet every two years, coming up with their buddies and their favorites . . . that can't make for a very good operation. . . .

Back when I was governor we were dealing with a different breed in gaming than we have today. Many in the industry were alleged to have come from unsavory backgrounds, from the mob as it were, and they were experts at applying leverage and exerting undue influence—if not with money, then by other means, such as catching you in a compromising position. As governor I had to be constantly aware of this, to the point that I almost had to have a protector around me all the time. I couldn't even stay in a hotel room by myself! I had to have people around me who could not be gotten to, and I selected only men whom I knew well or who came to me with very strong recommendations. . . .

In my inaugural address to the legislature I said that it was the policy of my administration that we would not tolerate any organized crime influence in Nevada, and I invited the FBI to tell us if they knew of any mob presence in the state. Although I questioned the alleged extent of mob influence, I wasn't so dumb that I didn't realize that some of the licensees came out of organized criminal backgrounds. There wasn't really anything I could do about those who were already here and licensed before I was elected except watch them carefully; but when a new applicant for a gaming license came along, one of the first inquiries would be to the FBI to see if they had a rap sheet on that person (they would always provide us with a copy if they did), and during my eight years as governor I don't believe we licensed anybody who later turned out to have ties with organized crime. . . .

In the summer of 1961 [Nevada Attorney General] Roger Foley learned of a federal strike force that was being put together to invade every major casino in Reno and Las Vegas—the Department of Justice asked him to deputize sixty-five federal agents to carry out this big raid on Nevada gambling. I was stunned. The day after Roger told me, we got on a plane and went to Washington and I made an appointment to see the attorney general. To my recollection it was on a weekend, because when I was shown in to see Bobby Kennedy I found him dressed for a game of tennis or something. I asked if he was planning to raid Nevada; and if so, why? We had a heated discussion, to say the least, and there was no give or compromise on his part at all. He looked at Nevada, as many people then did, as a den of iniquity . . . everybody who lived in or came to Nevada was corrupt, including me, and to clean the state up he was ready to assign a substantial force of agents to raid it. I took great exception to that, because we had a pretty effective enforcement policy in Nevada by that time. And apart from everything else, Bobby's plan made no political sense; the last time I had seen him before this was in Los Angeles at the 1960 Democratic convention, when he came to my room pleading for the Nevada votes for his brother.

We had tried desperately to cooperate with the FBI in an exchange of information, and we had offered numerous times to clean up anything that the attorney general, his staff, or the FBI felt was going on—if they would simply tell us, we would take care of it. But here in the middle of what we thought was a cooperative effort to deal jointly with our problems, I discovered this secret plan. The media sensationalizing that would attend such a federal raid could do our state great damage, and I was shocked that neither the Nevada attorney general nor myself had been extended the courtesy of being informed. There were already more federal agents per capita in Nevada than any place in the world [laughter], and I suspected that the planned invasion in force was a publicity stunt as much as anything else. Bobby Kennedy wanted to show the people of the United States that he was the guy to clean up all sin and corruption, and Nevada was a great place to start.

You had to experience the attitude of Easterners concerning Nevada. . . . It was then almost endemic in the bureaucracy and the Washington establishment, and we are seeing it now with the nuclear dump issue when senators and congressmen refer to Nevada as a wasteland. It was that attitude that Bobby Kennedy projected: "You are a bunch of peasants out there; you're all sort of sleazy. We here in the East, who know all, are going to come out there and set you right, whether you like it or not." As a personal matter I was particularly offended, because I got the impression that Bobby looked upon me as someone who had just stepped out from behind a crap table; and he seemed to imply that I was connected with the mob, which really burned me up. I remember pounding the table and just feeling that I was making no progress with him at all.

The day after my confrontation with Bobby I went up to the White House. I had not gone to Washington intending to see the president, but after receiving no satisfaction from Bobby I felt it was necessary, and Jack Kennedy and I met alone in the Oval Office. As I told him the story and described the devastating effect I thought this raid would have on Nevada, I got the impression that he knew nothing about his brother's plan. I explained the progress we were making in the state with respect to enforcement and control, and said that I thought the planned action was a precipitous move on the part of his attorney general. Not only would it be terribly damaging to Nevada, it would accomplish little in the national context. The president was very cordial, very nice. He made no commitments, but the raid never occurred. . . .

Even after my meeting with President Kennedy, although the raid was canceled, the general situation in Nevada improved very little. In 1963, Carl Cohen, a 10 percent shareholder in the Sands, found microphones in his office, and I believe in his house, and other top-ranking casino executives in this state were wire-tapped. This was disgraceful. If you have a federal law, you should abide by it everywhere, not just everywhere but Nevada! We also had state laws that prohibited this kind of eavesdropping without court sanction.

In November that year I wrote to Attorney General Kennedy and enclosed some of the news clippings of the wiretapping . . . in essence I was asking what was going on. My impression was that none of these wiretaps had been sanctioned under federal law; I doubt that any court had ordered them or endorsed them, and I took the position publicly that Bobby Kennedy and J. Edgar Hoover were violating federal and state law. I'm sure I was right, but *nobody* dared move against J. Edgar Hoover in those days; and although he and Bobby Kennedy were not friends, Kennedy would do nothing to restrain Hoover and the FBI. Between the two of them, they were trampling on the constitutional right to privacy of the citizens of this country. . . .

Sam Giancana, subpoenaed, by a Chicago federal grand jury investigating organized crime, disappeared in the summer of 1963. It was later discovered that he was staying at Frank Sinatra's Cal-Neva Lodge at Lake Tahoe. Giancana was a hoodlum of national repute who was listed in the black book, and there was no question that the Cal-Neva was violating Nevada gaming regulations, but when officials of the Gaming Control Board launched an investigation, Sinatra bullied, badgered and harassed them. He was so rude to the Gaming Control agents that it was almost unbelievable. I read a telephone transcript in which he used every filthy word in the book . . . arrogant, threatening language! He dished out astonishing abuse—who were we in Nevada to question *him*? . . .

Because he was Sinatra, it was obvious that we would have a problem enforcing regulations; but when the board came to me, I said, "Go for it!" I told [Gaming Control Board chairman] Ed Olsen, "He's no better than anybody else, and you do with him exactly as you would with anyone in that situation. Give no through to who he is, or who he thinks he is. Do the right thing, and do not be intimidated by him." Sinatra hired an attorney who wrote a couple of threatening letters to me, but the Control Board proceeded against him and he finally gave up his gaming licenses, both at the Cal-Neva and at the Sands. He gave the Sands license up voluntarily when it was made very clear that if he did not, it would be taken from him. Sinatra has spent a lot of years trying to get even.

I later had a brief discussion with President Kennedy about this episode during a short visit he made to Las Vegas. He landed at the airport, and [Senator Alan] Bible, [Senator Howard] Cannon, [Representative Walter] Baring and I all rode with him in an open car to the Convention Center, where he made a speech. He said to me, "What are you guys doing to my friend, Frank Sinatra?"

I said, "Well, Mr. President, I'll try to take care of things here in Nevada, and I wish you luck on the national level." [laughter] That was about the end of that.

James B. McMillan on the Civil Rights Movement in Las Vegas

Young dentist James B. McMillan (1917–) moved from Detroit to Las Vegas in 1955 for a fresh start in a place with warm, sunny days. Within a year he was leading the city's civil rights movement, and he successfully negotiated the integration of Las Vegas's public places without arrests or bloodshed. Like many of his contemporaries, though, McMillan came to realize that integration alone did not resolve all the problems of racial discrimination.

From the early years of Las Vegas until the migrations of African Americans to the city increased in the 1930s, relatively fluid interactions characterized race relations in Las Vegas, where African Americans numbered only about 50 in 1925. Members of the minority group faced no housing restrictions, and Fremont Street gaming establishments did not exclude African American customers. Similar patterns existed in northern cities such as Detroit and Cleveland in the nineteenth century. In these cities as in Las Vegas, migrations of significant numbers of African Americans into the cities led to increased racial restrictions. As the Las Vegas African American community grew in the 1940s (from 178 in 1940 to 2,725 in 1950), racial restrictions began to appear with more frequency. Restrictive covenants and informal zoning measures gradually restricted black individuals and businesses to the neighborhood known as the Westside. Gaming businesses changed their policies as well. Because many of Las Vegas's tourists came from areas where racial segregation was expected, the city's bars and gaming establishments excluded African Americans by the mid-1940s.

McMillan arrived in Las Vegas at a propitious time. Two events had ignited the national civil-rights movement: the 1954 *Brown v. Board of Education* decision that challenged the constitutionality of segregated schools, and the successful Montgomery bus boycott of 1955–56. McMillan seemed to possess charisma and leadership ability, and he was elected president of the local NAACP branch after attending only a few meetings. Under McMillan's leadership, the Las Vegas NAACP adopted an assertive direct-action plan to complement its traditional political lobbying activities. McMillan's first project was the successful boycott of a dairy that delivered to the Westside but refused to hire African American employees.

McMillan's most important work, his challenge to racial segregation in downtown Las Vegas in 1960, is the subject of most of the interview excerpt printed below. Encouraged by the Greensboro sit-in that February, McMillan wrote a letter to Mayor Oran Gragson that threatened disruptive protests unless the city took significant steps to end segregation. Remarkably, the city responded to this threat with an order to integrate all public places within the city's borders and a voluntary agreement for resorts on the Strip to do so as well. In this excerpt from an oral interview, McMillan repeats a controversial version of the tale. According to McMillan, he had a private meeting with Gragson and city commissioner Reed Whipple in which they asked him to drop his demands in exchange for some minor concessions. Both Gragson and Whipple have denied that this meeting ever took place.

Mirroring the national civil-rights movement, McMillan's happiness at this initial success gradually turned to frustration upon his realizing that racial integration did not solve all the problems of racial discrimination. African Americans continued to be restricted to the Westside neighborhood and its often substandard housing, medical facilities, and schools (as late as 1970, 22,000 of the 24,760 African Americans in Las Vegas lived in the Westside). In addition, job discrimination continued, as most Las Vegas businesses hired African Americans for only the most menial jobs. The Las Vegas NAACP made some progress in these areas. In 1965 the Nevada legislature passed a strong civil-rights bill that prohibited discrimination in public places and in employment. A busing order integrated the schools to some extent in the 1970s. And in 1971, the Nevada legislature passed a strong open-housing law that ended legal residential segregation in Nevada.

—John B. Reid

It was 1960. Oran Gragson was mayor and I was president of the NAACP. We had the Voter's League. Throughout the country there were sit-ins, and in the South people were fighting to eliminate discrimination. The national NAACP office sent out correspondence to the presidents of all the branches saying that each branch should do everything possible to eliminate all vestiges of discrimination in its region. As I read it I asked myself, "What can we do to really start a movement here to eliminate segregation?"

Dave Hoggard and I got together that night and talked about it. I said, "Dave, we're going to write a letter to the mayor, tell him we've received instructions from national headquarters to take action against segregation in this community. I'm going to give him thirty days to respond, thirty days to tell us what he can do to help eliminate discrimination in the city of Las Vegas." We wrote the letter and I sent it to the mayor's office. I didn't expect an immediate response, but I thought that the tone of the letter might shake up white people, get them to think that we were stirred up and that we might actually do something this time. Three or four days later Alan Jarlson, a reporter for the *Sun* who worked city hall, was in the mayor's office. He saw the letter and called me and said he wanted to use it as the basis for a story, to get the news out. I said, "Well, good. Be my guest."

At that time most of the newspaper people and the television and radio people were tight with the establishment in this town. Nothing got out that would rock the boat. Hank Greenspun, the editor and publisher of the *Sun*, was the exception, and he was our early salvation. Greenspun loaded his "Where I Stand" columns with civil rights issues. In contrast the *Review-Journal*, which John Cahlan and his brother Al ran, never had anything good to say about blacks or eliminating segregation; in fact some people believe that the R-J went so far as to deliberately cover news about blacks in a negative way. We were lucky that there were two papers. If it hadn't been for Hank Greenspun and his son we wouldn't have had a chance to get anything in front of the public. Greenspun ran Jarlson's story the next day, and all of Las Vegas knew that the NAACP was threatening a boycott if something wasn't done immediately to end discrimination.

There was a national radio program broadcast from the Fremont Hotel, and this guy took the newspaper story and put it out that night on the radio: "The NAACP threatens a boycott on the Las Vegas Strip in thirty days if there is no response to their request to negotiate a desegregation agreement." When that went out on radio throughout the United States, all hell broke loose. Radio and television stations and newspapers everywhere picked it up. This was a tremendous story, to have this type of thing happen in Las Vegas, the convention city of the United States. Our local politicians *had* to start doing something.

I was dumbfounded by what had happened. Who would ever have thought that our letter could cause this much trouble? I was just as happy as I could be, and most of the black community was happy, walking around talking about it on their jobs and what have you. But some people were frightened and some of the ministers were frightened, saying that if we went and started a disturbance on the Strip, our side of town could wind up being burned down. But I stayed forceful, and the common people didn't want to hear that crap even if their ministers were speaking it. The ministers were saying, "Go easy, Mac. Go slow," but they did work with us from the very beginning. We even had meetings in the churches to plan our tactics, and this went on for several weeks.

Shortly after the news broke I had a meeting with Oran Gragson and Reed Whipple in my office. They tried to convince me to call off the demonstration, saying that it wouldn't be good for the city and the county, and they promised to be much more responsive to the black community in the future with city jobs and so forth. Reed Whipple, who was with the First National Bank at that time, said he would see to it that blacks could get loans to buy houses and start businesses and this and that. But they claimed they didn't have the power to do anything about segregation in the hotels and casinos and elsewhere. I turned them down. The demonstration was still on.

After the mayor and Whipple met with me there was no other movement to solve this thing. I'm wondering what in the hell I'm going to do now. I was getting death threats, telephone calls, letters, Ku Klux Klan people . . . my kids would answer the phone and they would wake up screaming at night because people threatened to throw bombs in the house. Bob Bailey and a group of men in the black community walked and stood guard around my house for ten days to make sure that we didn't have any fire bombing or shooting or anything like that.

After I turned down Gragson and Whipple, I had just ten days left to organize the demonstration. I'm threatening to have people picket with signs, people walking on the strip, blocking traffic, going into hotels, being arrested precisely thirty days from the date I had sent the letter. It didn't look like we could pull it off. We were having pep rallies in the churches, and the press and television people would cover these—we would make inflammatory statements about what we were going to do and how bad it was going to be. But that was all I had going for me. I didn't have any plans made for the march; I didn't have any groups volunteering to go into the hotels and get arrested and maybe get hit over the head. . . . I'm hanging. I'm about to be out there with nothing covering my naked ass. I'm thinking I might have to leave town, because I'm going to fall on my face: "This isn't going to happen. These people are not going to march, and we're going to be ruined forever in this town." The only thing that I had going for me was that the Caucasians had not faced this type of thing before and they really didn't know what was going to happen. They were afraid.

Then we got a break. Oscar Crozier called me up. He'd been in touch with some of the underworld people that was involved in running the Strip hotels. He said, "I want to talk to you, man."

I said, OK, come on by the house."

Oscar told me that the people who owned some of these hotels had flown in to Las Vegas and had a meeting: "They said they want to know what you're about—this boycott, this marching and all of this. They told me to tell you to cool it or you might be found floating face down in Lake Mead."

I said, "Oscar, they can't get off that easy. Tell these people that I'm not a gambler. I don't have any money. I'm not trying to cut into their business. All I'm trying to do is make this a cosmopolitan city, and that will make more money for them. You tell them that and let me know what they say." I was almost ready to throw in the towel. If he had come back to me and said, "Man, they said no. You better cut this crap out," I would have peeked at my hole card.

A couple of days later Oscar called again. "Mac," he said, "it's OK. They're going to make their people let blacks stay in the hotels. They're going to integrate this town. You can make the announcement that this thing has been settled and that there will be no more discrimination in public accommodations. Black people can go into restaurants and stay at hotels and gamble and eat and everything else." He told me that what I had to do was call the Desert Inn and ask for Mr. Taylor, who was running the place for Moe Dalitz at that time. "He will tell you that they have given you the final OK."

I said, "I'm not going to make any announcement until a couple of days before the deadline we gave the city."

Oscar said, "That's OK."

After I got the information from Crozier, three ministers came into the office and said, "Mac, we just can't support you any longer. You're going to get our town burned down. You have to call off this march."

I said, "You mean to tell me you're going to leave me hanging out here like that?"

They said, "We don't care, we don't want you to march. We can't support you."

These were prominent men in the community, but I had lost all respect for them. I told them, "Well, I want you guys to know that you don't have to worry about your town being burned down. It's all settled. Don't say anything about it until I tell you to."

Everything Oscar Crozier told me came true. I phoned Taylor and said, "I'm supposed to call you in regard to this march and demonstration that we're going to have. And you're supposed to tell me that I don't have to have the march, and that you have accepted all the terms that we have talked about."

Slowly he said, "Yes, that's correct. It's been settled. We have accepted your terms."

Hank Greenspun had been working behind the scenes with some hotel owners, and he and I called a meeting at the Moulin Rouge to announce the settlement. There were churches in West Las Vegas where we probably could have met, but I suggested that we should meet at a neutral site. The place wasn't fixed up or anything for it—chairs were all stacked up in the hall, and we just moved them around and pulled the table out and had the meeting. David Hoggard, Woodrow Wilson, Bob Bailey, Donald Clark and I were there for the NAACP. We had the justice of the peace, the sheriff, Governor Grant Sawyer, Oran Gragson . . . all of these people came, and the press was there. We announced that there would not be any demonstrations, because discrimination in hotels and public accommodations on the Strip had ended. The following day we formed teams of NAACP men and women to go out to the hotels to test them. And all the hotels accepted them. They could go to the tables to gamble; they could go to the restaurants and eat; they could make reservations for rooms.

Years later the Moulin Rouge was named a historic site because that's where we supposedly met to sign the agreement that segregation would be ended in the city of Las Vegas. But there was nothing signed, and politicians had nothing to do with it. Governor Grant Sawyer was in Washington talking with the Kennedys or whatever when this damn thing busted in the papers. He got on a plane and flew back here quick, and I met with him and told him it had all been settled. Other politicians were at our meeting to announce the agreement, but they had done nothing. All of their hand wringing and all of their rhetoric didn't mean anything: they didn't own the hotels; they didn't own the gaming joints; they didn't own the restaurants. This thing was settled by Oscar Crozier and a handful of powerful hotel owners, and politicians played almost no role in it.

The hotels had settled because it was good business to settle. They knew that some southerners wouldn't want to gamble at an integrated casino, but they also knew that they needed to make sure that the convention business stayed, and that white people would not boycott Las Vegas. Money moves the world. When these fellows realized that they weren't going to lose any money, that they might even make more, they were suddenly colorblind.

[*Section edited.*]

I've long wondered whether I did the right thing by turning down the offer Mayor Gragson and Reed Whipple made when we were threatening to demonstrate on the Strip in 1960. We had momentum, but the mood of the country at that time would have given us integration anyway in three or four years. By insisting that it happen now, I lost a great opportunity to get red lining stopped, and to be given loans and mortgages and jobs to placate us. That could have been the right way to go . . . opening up the city, eliminating segregation, didn't do anything but help the white establishment make more money. No economic benefit, nothing for black people. I thought that with a desegregated city, blacks would still go to black businesses and spend their money; but I soon saw how mistaken I was.

You can have all the civil rights you want, you know. You can get a job sweeping the floor downtown in a hotel or be a cocktail waitress, but if you don't have capital in your community . . . I hate to say this, but in Las Vegas, through the success of the civil rights movement and our NAACP actions, we actually hurt the black population. When blacks were confined to the Westside, that's where their money stayed: we had five black gaming joints and two Chinese joints in our community that would hire black people, put them to work. All the money was going into black hands where we could develop the community—restaurants, stores, gaming, and things. Then when we got civil rights, and we could eat, shop and gamble anywhere, all this business moved to the white man. Before desegregation Jerry's Nugget was just a slot joint on the fringe of the black community, and now it's . . . Jerry's Nugget didn't give us a damn thing. They got a lot of black business, but they only hired two or three black dealers for the whole operation. Here's how we lost all our money, all our capital: we were OK (sad to say this) as long as white people forced us to stay in our community, but when we solved that problem and tore the barrier down and could take our money and go, that's what we did. I'm saying that black businesses went under when we got our civil rights.

When desegregation finally came, and blacks began taking their money elsewhere, white businesses on the Westside were hurt too. The Westside had two clubs that were owned by Orientals, and it really didn't hurt my conscience at all that they lost all of their black business. In fact, I was happy. They hadn't been doing anything to help blacks anyway except hiring a few, and they were taking the money and sending it to San Francisco or wherever it was. They weren't putting anything back in the black community. The black clubs were the ones that I felt sorry for, and the grocery stores and little shops. I thought that desegregation would make the town different, and the atmosphere would be better if we could go anywhere we pleased. But for thirty years after we won our battle I didn't see any construction going on in west Las Vegas. So there's a downside to integration.

Sammy Davis Jr. on the Segregation of African American Entertainers in Las Vegas

Sammy Davis Jr. (1925–90) was an African American entertainment legend with numerous stage, screen, and recording triumphs. Born before the civil-rights legislation of the 1950s and 1960s, Davis began his show-business career in a racially segregated United States. He began entertaining at the age of three in his father's vaudeville act. This group eventually became the Will Maston Trio, with Davis Jr. and Davis Sr. joined by Will Maston. This group's act, in particular the energetic and multifaceted style of Davis Jr., attracted a wide and diverse audience as they toured the country with their nightclub act. The trio, and then eventually Davis Jr. as a solo act, became more popular with white audiences as racial barriers gradually receded.

Davis's excerpt below describes his experiences of the racial barriers in Las Vegas. These barriers were considerable; in fact, Las Vegas became known as the "Mississippi of the West" for its strict racial barriers. Before 1960 African American entertainers were allowed to perform for white audiences, but they were not allowed to stay in the hotels that employed them. Instead, they stayed in rooming houses in the Westside, Las Vegas's African American neighborhood. As seen in the excerpt below, Las Vegas gradually allowed its African American stars access to its wonders as long as they stayed within prescribed boundaries. In 1960 hotels on the Las Vegas Strip voluntarily accepted racial integration of their public spaces. Davis continued to work there through the 1970s and 1980s.

—John B. Reid

In Seattle, after our fourth show, the musicians would sit in with a college band run by a kid named Quincy Jones. I went along with them and we played, sang, and experimented with new things until dawn.

There was a note under my door when I got home one morning. "Wake me whenever you come in. Don't worry. Everything's fine. Will."

I heard the springs of his bed creak, then his slippers swooshing across the floor. He opened the door, rubbing his eyes, smiling. "Go get Big Sam."

I looked from one to the other. "Okay, now we have a pajama party. What's it all about?"

Will said, "We're booked as the opening act at El Rancho Vegas in Las Vegas, Nevada. For five hundred dollars a week." He smiled, pleased. "Mose Gastin, now let me hear you say we're going to be buried."

The trade papers were bursting with news about Las Vegas. It was starting to become a show town. El Rancho and the Last Frontier were the first luxury hotels and there was talk about new hotels being planned to go up near them.

My father was heating coffee on the hot plate. "The word is they're payin' acts twice as much as anywheres else. Free suites and food tabs." Will said, "They're out to make it the number one show town." I listened to them like I was watching a ping-pong game. . . . "The whole business is watching what's happening in Vegas."

I walked over to Will. "Massey, I'm going to do those impressions."

He got out of bed and stared out the window. I knew by his long silence that he wasn't going to fight me. Finally, "Sammy, I don't think you can get away with it. Still, you're a third of the trio and you've seen a lot of show business so I won't stop you. I'm just going to hope you're right."

I looked around backstage while we waited to rehearse. The band was the biggest we'd ever worked with, the floor of the stage was springy and slick, the lighting was the most modern I'd ever seen. I was standing next to the stage manager. I asked, "Do I have it right about our rooms, that they're a part of our deal here?"

The manager came over to us as we finished rehearsing. "Sorry. We can't let you have rooms here. House rules. You'll have to find a place in the—uh, on the other side of town."

I picked up our suitcases. "Let's go, Dad, Will."

The hotels we'd passed in the town itself looked awful compared to El Rancho but even they were out of bounds to us. The cab driver said, "There's a woman name of Cartwright over in Westside takes in you people."

It was Tobacco Road. A three- or four-year-old baby, naked, was standing in front of a shack made of wooden crates and cardboard that was unfit for human life. None of us spoke.

The driver sounded almost embarrassed. "Guess y'can't say a lot for housing out here. Been hardly any call for labor 'round these parts. Just a handful of porters and dishwashers they use over on the Strip. Not much cause for you people t'come to Vegas."

The cab stopped in front of one of the few decent houses. A woman was standing in the doorway. "Come right in, folks. You boys with one of the shows? Well, I got three nice rooms for you."

When she told us the price Will almost choked. "But that's probably twice what it would cost at El Rancho Vegas."

"Then why don't you go live at El Rancho Vegas?"

"Pay her the money, Massey. It's not important."

Will counted out the first week's rent. My father smiled sardonically at her. "Looks like if the ofays don't get us, then our own will."

"Business is business. I've got my own troubles."

My father followed me into my room. "Not half bad." I nodded and started unpacking. He sat down and I could feel him watching me. I threw a shirt into a drawer and slammed it closed. "All right, Dad, for God's sake what is it?"

"*That's* what it is. Exactly what you're doin,' eatin' yourself up, grindin' your teeth. Y'can't let it get t'you, Poppa [a nickname for Davis Jr.]. I know how you feels. But the fact is, when it comes time to lay your head down at night what's the difference if it's here or in a room at El Rancho?"

"Dad, I don't give a damn about their lousy rooms, I really don't. Right now, the only thing in this world that I want is their stage!"

As I danced, I did Satchmo. I shuffled across the stage like Step'n Fetchit. Then I spun around and came back doing the Jimmy Cagney walk to the center of the stage and stood there, facing my father and Will, doing Cagney's legs-apart stance, the face, and then "All right you dirty rats!" For a moment there was no sound from out front—then they roared.

In the wings Will smiled warmly. "I'm glad I was wrong, Sammy." My father laughed and hugged me. "Poppa, you was *great!*" He put me down. "Whattya say we get dressed after the next show and go look around the casino. I got fifty dollars that's bustin' t'grow into a hundred."

We went out the stage door and around the building. The desert all around us was as dark as night can be but the casino was blazing with light. The door opened and as some people came out there was an outpour of sounds such as I'd never before heard: slot machines clanging, dealers droning, a woman shrieking with joy—and behind it all, a background of the liveliest, gayest music I'd ever heard. As I held the door open for my father, my head went in all directions to slot machines, dice tables, waiters rushing around with drinks, a man carrying a tray full of silver dollars.

I saw a hand on my father's shoulder. A deputy sheriff was holding him, shaking his head.

We rode to Mrs. Cartwright's in silence. They got out of the cab and I continued on downtown where there was a movie theater, where for a few hours I could lose myself in other people's lives.

A hand gripped my arm like a circle of steel, yanking me out of my seat, half-dragging me out to the lobby. "What're you, boy? A wise guy?" He was a sheriff, wearing a star badge and the big Western hat. His hand came up from nowhere and slapped across my face. He'd done it effortlessly but my jaw felt like it had been torn loose from my head. "Speak up when I talk to you!"

"What'd I do?"

"Don't bull me, boy. You know the law."

When I explained I'd just gotten to town and had never been there before, he pointed to a sign. "Coloreds sit in the last three rows. You're in Nevada now, not New York. Mind our rules and you'll be treated square. Go on back and enjoy the movie, boy."

I had no choice but to go in. A Mickey Rooney picture was on. After a while I glanced up to catch a song he was doing and I looked away, still steaming. Then I looked up again and I forgot the cop and the theater and the rules and I was dancing across the campus in a college musical. An hour later I was Danny Kaye git-gat-gattling my way through the army. Then the lights went on and I was sitting in the last row of an almost empty movie theater, and again I was a Negro in a Jim Crow town.

I went back to Mrs. Cartwright's and slammed her dirty, gouging door and swore to myself that someday it would be different. I tried reading but I couldn't keep my mind on the book. I felt closed in so I went out for a walk but the sight of all the poorness drove me back to my room. I stared out the window at the glow of the lights from the Strip in the distance until it faded into the morning sun.

I should have been tired the next night but as eight o'clock drew near I was vibrating with energy and I couldn't wait to get on the stage. I worked with the strength of ten men.

We did our shows and went out to get a cab to Mrs. Cartwright's. I looked away from the lights of the casino but I couldn't avoid hearing the sounds. Night after night I had to pass that door to get a cab. Once, between shows, I stood around the corner where nobody would see me, and waited for the door to open so I could catch the short bursts of gaiety that escaped as people went in and came out. I sat on the ground for an hour, listening and wondering what it must be like to be able to just walk in anywhere.

[*Section edited.*]

In Vegas, for twenty minutes, twice a night, our skin had no color. Then, the second we stepped off the stage, we were colored again.

I went on every night, turning myself inside out for the audience. They were paying more attention and giving us more respect than ever before, and after every performance I was so exhilarated by our acceptance onstage that I really expected one of the owners to come rushing back saying, "You were great. To hell with the rules. Come on in and have a drink with us." But it never happened. The other acts could move around the hotel, go out and gamble or sit in the lounge and have a drink, but we had to leave through the kitchen, with the garbage, like thieves in the night. I was dying to grab a look into the casino, just to see what it was like, but I was damned if I'd let anyone see me like a kid with his nose against the candy store window. I wanted to believe "If they don't want me then I don't want them either," but I couldn't help imagining what it must be like to be wanted, to be able to walk into any casino in town. I kept seeing the warmth in the faces of the people we'd played to that night. How could they like me onstage—and then this?

My father spent his time around the Westside bars and casino but I went to my room trying to ignore the taunting glow of light coming from the Strip, bigger and brighter than ever, until finally the irresistible blaze of it drew me to the window and I gazed across at it knowing it was only three in the morning, which is like noon in Las Vegas, feeling as wide awake as the rest of the town which was rocking with excitement. I pictured myself in the midst of it all, the music, the gaiety, the money piled high on tables, the women in beautiful dresses and diamonds, gambling away fortunes and laughing.

It took a physical effort to tear myself away from the window. I forced it all out of my mind and kept telling myself: Someday . . . , listening to records and reading until I was tired enough to fall asleep, always wondering when "someday" would be.

[*Section edited.*]
[*Later Las Vegas loosened its racial segregation, and Davis experienced the change firsthand.*]

The phone rang. "Sammy, I'm at the Morris office and something just came up. How fast can you get down here?"

"I'm in the middle of packing, Massey, I'm not dressed."

"Then get dressed. You'll be glad you did."

The receptionist led me to the room where Will and my father were waiting with one of the agents from the nightclub department.

Will said, "We're playing Vegas. We'll be working the Old Frontier and we'll be *living* at the Old Frontier! In the best suites they got!"

"You mean right in the hotel?"

"And free of charge besides, and that includes food and drink *and* $7500 a week."

I resented the excitement I felt over it. "I don't know, Massey, I just don't know if anything's worth crawling in there like 'Gee, sir, y'mean you'll really let us live at your goddamned hotel?'"

"Sammy, we're not crawling to nobody."

The Morris guy smiled. "*Crawling.* It's not good business to pass up an attraction that'll bring people to the tables. To get you now, they'll break their necks, let alone a ridiculous custom."

"When do they want us?"

"They're asking for November." He looked at a sheet of paper on his desk. "That means you play Detroit, Chicago, Atlantic City, Buffalo, Syracuse, Bos-

ton, and then into Vegas. That's twelve straight weeks with no day off except
for traveling. . . .

I wasn't looking for days off. If Vegas could open up to us like that then it was
just a matter of time until the whole country would open up, and I couldn't
wait to hit the road and sing and dance my head off toward that moment.

It was a gorgeous crisp November morning as I stepped off the train in Las
Vegas. My father and Will were waiting for me on the platform. I searched
their faces. "Well?"

My father made a circle with his thumb and forefinger. "The best."

"No problems?"

Will shook his head. "They're bending over backwards." I put my arms
around both their shoulders and we walked through the station.

They stopped in front of a beautiful, brand new Cadillac convertible. I
looked at my father. "Damn! You musta hit a eight-horse parlay to get your
hands on this baby!"

He tossed me the key. "Well, seein' as you like her, she's yours. Will and me
bought it for you as a sorta advance birthday present." I took a slow walk
around the car and stopped in front of the "S.D. Jr." they'd had painted on the
door. "Well, climb in, Poppa, and let's see if she drives."

They slid in alongside me and I put the top down. "Might as well let 'em see
who owns this boat." I put it in gear and we rolled away from the station. I ran
my fingers over a clear plastic cone which jutted out from the center of the
steering wheel, enclosing the Cadillac emblem. "I don't know how to thank
you."

Will said, "Don't thank us, Sammy. Thank show business. That's where it all
come from."

I couldn't get serious if my life depended on it. We stopped for a light and I
pulled out the ash tray. "Hey, fellas, whatta we do when this gets filled up?"

My father came right in on cue. "We throws this car away and gets us a *new*
one."

Will smiled. "You boys keep doing old jokes like that and we'll be back riding buses."

As we got onto The Strip, I slowed down. "We just drive straight up to the
front entrance, right?"

My father laughed. "Like we own the place." He was as giddy as I had been a minute before. "We don't even have t'bother parking the car. They got a man standin' there just to do that and all you do is slip him a silver dollar and he tips his hat and says, 'Thank you, sir.'"

As we approached the hotel I saw the big sign out front, "THE WILL MASTIN TRIO FEATURING SAMMY DAVIS, JR." I turned into the driveway and pulled up in front of the entrance. A doorman hurried over and opened my door. "I'll take care of it for you, Mr. Davis." I gave him a five and he tipped his hat. "Thanks, Mr. Davis." A bellman came over. "Take your luggage, Mr. Davis?" I pointed to a cab just pulling up. "It's in that one, baby. My valet will give it to you."

The door closed and we were alone in a huge, beautiful suite. I collapsed onto the bed, kicking my legs in the air. "I don't *never* wanta leave this room! I'd sign a contract to stay here for the rest of my natural!" I got up and looked around. There was a large basket of flowers in the living room. The card read: "Welcome to the Old Frontier" and was signed by the manager.

My father was standing behind a bar in the corner of the room. "Glasses, ice, soda, cokes, scotch, bourbon hell, they didn't slip up on nothin.'"

"Well, I guess this is about as First Cabin as anyone can ever hope to go."

Charley Head, the man I'd hired in L.A., came in leading four bellmen carrying my luggage. I walked my father and Will to the door. "How about your rooms?"

"Almost the same layouts. Right down the hall."

I inspected the suite while Charley started unpacking. "Pretty nice, huh, baby?"

He didn't look around. "I'll let you know when I see where they put me."

Oh God, I hadn't thought about that. "Well, look, you let me know, and if it's not okay you'll stay in here with me." He just kept unpacking. I could imagine how he felt. "Let me help you, baby, and we'll get it done faster."

Morty was rehearsing the band. I sat in the back of the room listening, and checked John out on the lights.

When Morty gave the guys a break I called him aside. "Baby, I'll open with 'Birth of the Blues.'"

"You're joking! What'll you go off on?"

"We'll use 'Fascinating Rhythm.' Look, we throw away all the rules here. The plotting of a show for a Vegas audience is different than anywhere else. For openers, the hotels are all but giving away the best shows that money can buy, so the average cat who comes in to see us has been in town for a few days and he's already seen maybe six or eight of the biggest names in the business. This same guy may never see a live show from one end of the year to the next when he's home but after a few days here he's Charley-Make-Me-Laugh. Now, above and beyond that, plus the normal nightclub distractions, if I don't hook that guy right from the start and hang on to him I'm dead, because he'll be watching me but he'll start wondering if when he leaves maybe he should try ten the hard way. So, it's like when we make records: we do or die in the first eight bars." He whistled softly. "And on top of that, where in a normal club if I start off a little slow I can always stay on until eventually I get 'em and they leave saying, 'Hey, isn't it nice the way he does those long shows,' in Vegas the headliner has exactly fifty-two minutes, including bows. They're in the gambling business here and everything's timed down to the split second: there's no dancing after the shows and your check is collected before the show breaks. Those doors lead into the casino and they want the people to walk through them *on time!* There are just so many minutes in each day and the hotel anticipates a certain amount of gambling revenue for each one of them. I can't steal any of that time to make sure I come off smelling like a rose. They pay me to bring customers to the tables, not to keep them away. So, watch me extra carefully for the cues, baby, cause once I'm out there it's fight-for-your-life time."

[*Later, Davis was forced to confront that racial discrimination had not disappeared from the Las Vegas scene.*]

The living room was jammed and I went from group to group, saying hello, soaking up the flattery. I sat down next to Mama. "You have a good time tonight?"

"Just seeing what people think of you and how they're treating you is a good time for me, Sammy. I'd better be getting my sleep, though. And don't you stay up too late neither. You need your rest."

I walked her to the door. "Don't worry about me, Mama. I never felt better in my life."

There were still about a dozen people left. I sat down, Charley handed me a coke, and I lit a cigarette and relaxed into their conversation. Dave said, "Hey, whattya say we start at one end of the town and hit every place along the way?" His face, turned toward me, was still reflecting the excitement of the evening. "I hear there's a wild lounge act over at the Desert Inn. We could start there and then . . ."

"Baby, we're comfortable, it's late, we've got everything we want."

"It's only four o'clock. Come on, let's really celebrate."

"I don't know about those places, Dave." He looked at me, not understanding. "Baby, this is Vegas. It's one thing for me here where I'm working, but I'm not so sure about those other hotels. Now do you wanta see a lounge act, or a lynching?"

Somebody else said, "Are you doing modest bits or don't you know how big you are? They'll roll out a red carpet anywhere you go."

Dave said, "He's out of his mind and I'll prove it." He picked up the phone. "Maybe years ago it was one thing . . . hello, may I have the Desert Inn, please."

Conversation stopped. Dave lit a cigarette, crossed one leg over the other and blew smoke rings at the ceiling. "Connect me with the Lounge, please, darling. . . . Hello, I'd like to reserve a table for about twenty minutes from now for Sammy Davis, Jr. and a party of . . ." The burst of red across his cheeks was as though he'd been slapped. He lowered the phone back on the hook. "Sam . . . I did it again. I'm sorry."

I shrugged. "Let's not make a ninety-minute spectacular out of it." I could feel everybody looking at me, embarrassed for me. There were murmurs of "Well if that's how they are then who the hell needs 'em . . ." "They're a hundred years behind the times." The party was lying on the floor dead.

I stood up. "Charley, get hot on the phone with room service and have them bring over twenty steak sandwiches, and tell them we'll need a case of their best champagne, quick-style. Morty, do me a favor. Swing by the casino and find Sunny and the kids. Tell 'em it's a party. Invite everybody you see that we dig." I turned on the hi-fi set, loud. Within ten minutes the crowd of kids pouring in was drowning it out, and the room came alive like somebody'd plugged us in.

Dave came over to where I was standing. "You okay?"

"Thanks, baby. I'm fine."

I had the feeling of having waited all my life to own a raincoat and when finally I got one it wasn't working, the water was coming through. I had to get bigger, that's all. I just had to get bigger.

Lena Horne on Entertaining in Las Vegas

Lena Horne (1917–) was more ambiguous about Las Vegas than was Sammy Davis Jr. Like Davis, she is an African American entertainment legend with numerous successes on stage, in films, and as a recording artist. Like Davis, she was invited to bring her singing talents to the showrooms of Las Vegas in the 1950s. She had already become famous for her distinctive blues singing style and for becoming the first African American actress to sign a long-term contract with a Hollywood film studio. And like Davis, she experienced and overcame the racial discrimination endured by African American performers of this era. She refers to the discrimination she faced at the Copacabana club in New York in the excerpt below. In addition she describes her experience of the early days of Las Vegas entertainment (including an experience of Benjamin Siegel's power as boss at the Flamingo) and gives her candid observations of the downside to performing in Las Vegas showrooms.

—John B. Reid

By the early 1950s, of course, there were laws on the books in New York that were pretty effective in preventing the more obvious kinds of discrimination in public places.

Not all the incidents of these years were as serious, objectively or emotionally, as the one at the Copa. For instance, right after the war I made what amounted to a pioneering trek to Las Vegas—pioneering in the sense that I was the first Negro to star in a big club there and pioneering, also, in the sense that I went there right at the beginning of the expansion and glamorization of the big clubs on the strip.

I was playing the Flamingo, sharing the bill with a very famous Latin band. The leader was a real jerk—very snide when he introduced me, and not rehearsing and not disciplining the band at all. I took it for a couple of days and then called Lennie in California to ask him what to do. I was furious and ready to walk out on the whole thing.

He calmed me down a little and said he would call the manager of the club who was, of course, just the front man for the gents-up-top who really owned it. He made the call all right and told the guy what was happening. They discussed it back and forth for a while and the manager was sort of noncommittal. What did he care?—we were both under contract and business was good. Why should he stir around in the situation?

But then another voice came on the phone and said: "Don't think any more about it, Mr. Hayton. I didn't know that she was having any trouble, but she will not have any further trouble."

Lennie didn't recognize the voice, so he said, "Who's this?"

"This is Mr. Siegel."

Lennie thanked him and then called me back. "Darling, I just want to tell you not to worry. Mr. Siegel says he'll take care of everything."

"And who the hell is Mr. Siegel?" I said.

"You know, Bugsy Siegel."

Well, apparently Mr. Siegel sent a couple of his boys around to see the bandleader and give him a little lecture. At the next show he did not introduce me. One of the men in the band did, and it was a beautiful announcement. After that, the leader made very proper announcements. And I noticed that he and his band, who had been hanging around the club between and after the shows to gamble, were suddenly in a big hurry to pack up and get outside when they finished work. I thought it was pretty funny, watching them scurrying around, being nicer than nice. And I thought there was a kind of rude justice in it, too.

[*Section edited.*]

[*Later, Horne commented on the entertainment atmosphere in Las Vegas.*]

Las Vegas came to be a symbol of a great deal I hated in this business. It was and is where the big money is for a cabaret entertainer. I played the Sands for a decade. It was a beautifully run room, very classy. If you have to play Vegas, that is the room to play. But to me there was no gratification to performing there. You never know when you're working in Vegas quite what's happening to you. The audience is a captive one, but the thing that has captured them is the gambling. They really only come to see you in order to take a rest from the crap tables. And since they're still thinking about the crap tables, they aren't thinking about you particularly. There's no challenge in them, so you have no sense of discovery about your performance to gain through their reactions.

Besides that, there is usually, along the strip, no sense of competing with your peers. You're competing with what a headline of the moment has created, what a cliché of the moment has created, what a nakedness of the moment has created.

I might be working next to a place that has an attraction at the moment who is the world's best fire-eater. Well, that's fine; that's all show business, really and truly. But then, on the other hand, I think the world's best fire-eater is more show business than, for instance, the most divorced woman in the world, who is working at the place opposite us both, and who can't eat fire and who can't sing. It made me feel like a freak, that's all. The lure is only money and I'm not being a snob about it, but I have not always found that when you have money you have everything. And besides, it's still a prejudiced town.

Now, a lot of the good performers may think all this, and they still go back. One of them said to me, just recently, "What the hell—take your money and run." But the thing that galled me was that Vegas was the only big-money channel open to Negroes. TV was closed to us, movies were closed to us, Broadway was mostly closed to us. The only place we could get the big loot was Vegas!

That was hardly Las Vegas' fault, I know. But I had to resent it. And the resentment grew and grew until I stopped going there. In the end, it was just a personal thing. I welcomed the opportunity to go and work in physically bad, acoustically poor rooms, for less money, rather than go there. Maybe it was stupid. But in those rooms, if I made it, I could find me again. At least sometimes I could.

"The Seed" Poster: Rock, Art, and the History of Nevada

Among the people drawn to the mythology of Nevada were some of the earliest members of San Francisco's 1960s music scene. Seeking the freedom from social convention implied by the rural West, Chandler Laughlin and Mark Unobsky followed a friend to the Comstock in spring 1965. There they created the Red Dog Saloon in Virginia City, envisioning a community of like-minded individuals seeking to define their own identities and create their own lifestyles.

The proprietors of the Red Dog selected an early western theme, as homage to the freedom and simplicity of an earlier time. Their choice of wardrobe and decor was also an attempt to deflect public censure and make their alternative lifestyles appear less threatening to locals, by co-opting an appealing and respected traditional image. Laughlin and Unobsky remodeled the old Comstock House hotel into an early West ideal, with velvet drapes, crystal chandeliers, and an antique bar. Patrons and employees dressed in western costume, often carrying pistols. Laughlin and Unobsky found a kindred spirit when they met George Hunter. Interested in forging a uniquely American identity in opposition to the British invasion, George Hunter and his band, the Charlatans, had begun dressing in Edwardian clothes obtained from thrift stores in San Francisco. Although they had never performed for an audience, they were hired as the house band for the Red Dog, playing early Americana music such as "Wabash Cannonball" and some original songs.

As people traveled back and forth from Virginia City to San Francisco for supplies, word of the Red Dog began to spread. Most of the major figures of the San Francisco counterculture visited the saloon, including Neal Cassady, better known as Dean Moriarty from Jack Kerouac's *On the Road,* and Ken Kesey with the Merry Pranksters. Musical acts included Big Brother and the Holding Company, the Great Society, and Jefferson Airplane. Light-show pioneer Bill Ham brought his light boxes and produced kinetic light shows. The tolerant environment of the Red Dog even welcomed politicians from the state capital, including Governor Grant Sawyer, who danced with the cocktail waitresses.

The handbill for the Red Dog's opening night has become a valued artifact of music history as the first psychedelic art poster. Usually called "The Seed," the handbill uses a metaphor that implies a new graphic art style as well as the birth of a new alternative culture. The poster answered a need to produce and distribute information about forthcoming events simply and inexpensively, but it also functioned as an embodiment of the ethos of the Red Dog. Designed and hand drawn by band members George Hunter and Michael Ferguson, who also drew the Red Dog logo, the graphics evoke nineteenth-century posters, with their old-time craftsmanship and artisanry, in distinct opposition to the modern machine-made uniformity of sixties production. "The Seed" implied a new lifestyle aesthetic, one in which life was intimately connected to work, a lifestyle that could incorporate all aspects of a person's abilities, enthusiasm, and ambition—a lifestyle in which the life, itself, was art.

—Tanya Reid

Paul Laxalt's Reflections on His Relationship with Ronald Reagan

Paul Laxalt (1922–) came closer to presidential power than any Nevadan before or since. He became living proof of Pat McCarran's axiom about Nevada politicians—that no Nevada politician should aspire to the presidency, due to the moral reputation of

One of two posters used to advertise the opening of the Red Dog Saloon in Virginia City, "The Seed" is widely acknowledged as the first psychedelic poster. With their hand-drawn art and bold coloring, posters like this became symbols of the counterculture. Courtesy of John Wasserman private collection the state and the virtual necessity of having contacts among some of Nevada's prominent citizens with less-than-sterling reputations.

The son of Basque immigrants to Nevada, Laxalt climbed the ladder of Nevada politics immediately after graduating from law school in 1949. He served as Ormsby County district attorney (1951–54), Nevada lieutenant governor (1963–66), governor of Nevada (1967–70), and U.S. senator (1975–86). While governor, Laxalt befriended then California governor Ronald Reagan, as recounted in the excerpt below. Laxalt was an early supporter of Reagan for president—he even formed the first Citizens for Reagan Committee in the mid-1970s to advocate a Reagan challenge to Gerald Ford.

It was through this friendship that Laxalt's political fortunes rose. In 1980 Laxalt was a crucial link between Reagan—who viewed himself as and ran as a political outsider—and the Washington insiders with whom he had to work upon assuming the presidency. Due to their shared experiences and clear personal rapport, Laxalt was the most influential Republican in Congress throughout the Reagan presidency, and Reagan called upon him often for help and advice. In addition Laxalt's power helped several Nevadans receive high-profile jobs in Washington, D.C. For example, Nevadan Frank Fahrenkopf became chairman of the Republican National Committee, and Sig Rogich advised President Reagan and was appointed by President Bush to be assistant to the president for public events and initiatives.

Several reports suggest that Laxalt was Reagan's personal choice to succeed him in 1989. A Reagan speech delivered at a Laxalt fund-raiser in 1986 stopped just short of an endorsement: "Look to the son of the high mountains and peasant herders, to the son of the Sierra and the immigrant Basque family. Look to a man, to a friend, to an American who gave himself so that others may live in freedom." Laxalt was quoted as saying, "In Western parlance, this hired hand is ready to take over as foreman."

To the Republican Party, though, Laxalt did not seem to be the best choice to continue the Reagan program, and his 1988 campaign for president foundered early. His campaign contributions from alleged organized-crime figures Ruby Kolod and Moe Dalitz and loans from the Teamsters Union (with its suspected organized-crime ties) were too questionable to survive the intense scrutiny of a presidential campaign. With the end of Reagan's political career, Laxalt returned to private life as well. He lives and works in Washington, D.C., as a lawyer and lobbyist.

—John B. Reid

What turned out to be a unique personal and political friendship with Ronald Reagan started perfunctorily in 1964, during Barry Goldwater's ill-fated campaign for the presidency.

I was Nevada's Lieutenant Governor at the time and became the first state official in the West to announce my support for Barry. Ron was well-known because of his television and movie work, of course, and was stumping for Barry. Our paths crossed occasionally on the campaign trail in California and Nevada.

At that time, Ron was still thought of as little more than an entertainment figure, a movie star, although one active in his industry's internal politics and willing, as a concerned citizen, to use his name and connections to help candidates in whom he believed. Then, as now, the "household name" value of show business personalities was very valuable to any candidate, regardless of the office he or she was seeking.

It had been mentioned that Ron might run for public office, but in 1964 it was still in the early discussion stages.

My recollections of Ronald Reagan in those days are hazy, because we didn't really become well-acquainted until a few years later. I remember him as a stylish, charismatic individual, always smiling, with an instinctive ability to relate to an audience and to attract the interest of a crowd.

He was a natural campaigner, appearing totally at ease in any type of setting or situation. In observing him, I was impressed, but I had my doubts about whether he was "real." After all, any accomplished actor could deliver a ringing speech from notes.

NEIGHBOR GOVERNORS

In 1966, we were elected Governors of our respective states. Ron defeated Pat Brown, the father of future Governor Jerry Brown, and I defeated Grant Sawyer who, like Pat Brown, was seeking a third term.

This election marked the official start of our political association and personal friendship. We had frequent common problems as Chief Executives of neighboring states, and as we dealt with them, we became good friends.

Nevada and California have a relationship unlike that of virtually all other bordering states. On the surface, two more dissimilar states would be hard to find.

California, of course, is first among the separate but equal states of the Union, packed with people, loaded with natural resources, fat with things to do, places to go, people to see. It's the "land of milk and honey."

Nevada, on the other hand, is a land-locked state rich only in the barrenness of its high desert, poor in most natural resources and sparsely populated.

To many Californians, that which Nevada holds dear—the sagebrush wilderness of its interior—is nothing more than wasteland. To many Nevadans, the hustle, bustle and fervor of California is repugnant, representing a foreign way of life.

But Nevada has legalized gambling, which for more than six decades, has kept Nevada well-populated on a temporary basis with visiting Californians. It has drawn heavily on an influx of tourists from across the state line. Millions of Californians have left billions of dollars in Nevada casinos over the years.

During our Governorships, Ron and I would kid one another about this unique "love-hate" relationship between Nevada and California. Ron would jokingly threaten to close the borders and thus "bankrupt Nevada in 24 hours."

Paul Laxalt (*left*) and Ronald Reagan share the stage at a rally in Reno in 1982. Behind the scenes, Laxalt's friendship with Ronald and Nancy Reagan gave Nevada unprecedented access to the halls of federal power in the 1980s. Courtesy Special Collections, University of Nevada, Reno, Library

The Jarbidge Debates—*Elko County* v. *the Forest Service*

The South Canyon Road, located in Elko County's Jarbidge Wilderness, was the center of a dispute between the citizens and elected officials of Elko County, the U.S. Forest Service, and the conservation group Trout Unlimited in the late 1990s. In 1995 the Jarbidge River flooded, washing out the road. Later the U.S. Forest Service made plans to rebuild it. Trout Unlimited, however, challenged the preliminary environmental assessment on the grounds that further scientific evidence was needed to demonstrate that the road would not hurt the bull trout living in the Jarbidge River. After the challenge, the Forest Service proposed building a foot trail. This decision upset many Elko County residents. A citizens' revolt and legal brawl ensued. The struggle gained national attention, becoming a poster child for forces opposed to President Clinton's Roadless Areas Initiative.

In the state of Nevada, conflicts between the federal, state, and local governments and individual citizens over land ownership and usage are not unusual. This contentious atmosphere can be attributed to the fact that the federal government manages 87 percent of the land in Nevada. The South Canyon Road dispute also represents conflicts between the "New" and the "Old" West. As the western United States becomes increasingly urbanized and a service sector-based economy begins to supplant a rural and resource extraction-based economy, a preservationist ethos is gaining strength over its conservationist predecessor. This change has translated into less political, economic, and social power for the rural West. The conflict is, thus, as much about political voice as it is about the actual control of resources.

The two primary sources included in this section illustrate the underlying tensions that gave rise to the South Canyon Road controversy. The first item, *An Elko Proclamation*, was written by longtime Elko resident and doctor Hugh S. Collett. In this polemical section, Dr. Collett draws attention to the feeling of many Elko County citizens that federal agencies develop policies without local input. The second selection, the *Fact Finding Report*, speaks directly to the generally strained relations between the Forest Service and residents of northeastern Nevada. This report was the result of a task force created in December 1999 to examine former Humboldt–Toiyabe National Forest supervisor Gloria Flora's allegations of an unsafe working environment. In an open letter to Forest Service employees, she called attention to the contentious climate in this area of Nevada, citing it as the reason for her resignation as forest supervisor, a position she had held from July 1998 to November 1999.

—Rachel Harvey

AN ELKO Proclamation

Feb 11 2000 12:00AM By Hugh S. Collett, M.D.

By virtue of their arrogance which is deserved because of their superior intellect, the people of Elko County declare the District of Columbia to be a National Monument.

These people have looked at a map and some old books and thereby declare the District of Columbia to be a roadless area. Henceforth all roads in this roadless area will be barricaded and only foot traffic will be permitted. No wheeled vehicles will be allowed.

This monument area will be under the jurisdiction of the U.S. Forest Service and its director, Ms. Gloria Flora. She will also be in charge of the instruction and indoctrination of all present and future employees of the forest service. She is also authorized to utilize the services of the Bureau of Land Management.

It will be her duty that these employees learn to crush any opposition to bureaucratic regulations. They must be taught that the people are not sufficiently educated to know what is good for their welfare. It will also be explained to them that anyone belittling them is guilty of fed-bashing.

Those harassing or intimidating the officials will be guilty of racism. All employees will patrol the National Monument area armed with side arms and assault rifles. All idividuals in the area who are allowed to bear arms after background checks by the FBI, CIA, District of Columbia, Elko County and the National Rifle Association must have non-removable trigger locks installed.

All living creatures in the river flowing through the Monument area are declared endangered and must not be disturbed. These include all fish, snails, clams, crabs, worms etc. Since there are no cockroaches or termites in Elko County, the people of Elko County realize that they are an endangered species. They will be so listed. It will be a prison offense and fine for anyone killing them or interfering with their habitat.

All finished products which have raw materials obtained from the ground by mining or drilling is prohibited. Therefore, no building materials or heating materials are permitted.

Likewise, any article of clothing, or any food which is prepared by a genetic or chemically engineered technique is also prohibited. The piles of granite and marble which have been quarried from open pit mines to build monuments and buildings since the city was founded and which have degraded the once beautiful hills of the District must be removed and replaced in the pits from which they were quarried.

In the future, no quarried material will be permitted for building purposes.

All parks with their grasses and trees will no longer be tended, mowed, fertilized or treated with insecticides or pesticides. Irrigation is banned and only rainwater is permitted in order that they may maintain their natural state.

Any trees not native to the region will be removed, such as the Japanese cherry trees. It is expected and desired that this advanced management of the grasses and trees will result in overgrowth of dead material which will be good fuel for future fires. Fires are very beneficial to the land as has been demonstrated by the burning of 1 million acres of rangeland in northeastern Nevada in 1999. This is the result of excellent management by the forest service and Bureau of Land Management.

The large marsh area which was present before the establishment of the District of Columbia must be restored. There will be complete protection for all birds and other species using this marsh. All insect species, including the mosquito, aedes aegypti, which were formerly living in the swamp, will be reestablished to their former habitat. These mosquitos have been placed on the endangered species list and must be protected. Therefore, marshland must not be treated by any insecticides.

The yellow fever disease which is caused by a virus transmitted by this mosquito is an important historical illness. In 1793 and 1794 it killed one fourth of the population of Philadelphia. This illness must be allowed to naturally occur and must only be treated in the old historical ways. No chemically developed or genetically engineered drugs may be used in the treatment of yellow fever caused by this mosquito.

Mining is very harmful to the environment. In the future, no one in the Monument area is allowed to use tools, communication devices, transportation vehicles, power or illumination, which depend on materials from mines. This includes—but is not restricted to—copper, gold, silver, iron, coal and uranium. Drilling for oil and gas is also environmentally harmful and no product from this source is allowed. Any synthetic material, such as tires and plastic, which use oil or gas products in their production, is prohibited.

Genetically engineered materials for clothing or food consumption is prohibited. All such engineering is prohibited whether it is done by modern genetic methods or by old-fashioned natural selection. Hybrid corn is particularly prohibited.

Cattle and sheep are very damaging to the environment. It is important that they not be used for food and clothing in the Monument area.

There will be strict prohibition of supplying meat of these species or making clothing and other uses of their bodies: For example, leather and wool.

Only vegetables and fruit that contain worms and blemishes will be permitted for consumption. This is to ensure that no insecticides, pesticides or fertilizer have been involved in their production. Those without blemishes and worms were undoubtedly produced by using these prohibited substances and are not allowed in the Monument area.

No transportation on the river is allowed that can cause environmental damage. All boats using oil or gas for propulsion, or which create noise, are prohibited. Steel ships are also prohibited because they are a product of mining. Canoes are permitted as long as they are constructed of birch bark.

It has been demonstrated that federal ownership of 87 percent of Nevada has been very beneficial to the federal agencies, and to Politicians needing to establish their legacy.

Since we realize that this is a glorious and worthwhile purpose, it is therefore the intention of these intelligent people of Elko County to continue establishing National Monuments in the eastern states. We wish them to have the same advantages as Nevada and other western states.

Planned for this designation next year are 50 million acres in New England. Those regulations in force for Washington, D.C., will apply to all newly designated areas.

Each year a similar area will be so designated until all land east of the Mississippi River will have 87 percent under the beneficial and protective guidance of the U.S. Forest Service and the Bureau of Land Management.

Once this has been accomplished, similar designation of land west of the Mississippi will commence. Any objection to this improvement in the management of this land will be regarded as fed-bashing.

Those objecting will be designated by Ms. Gloria Flora as rebels and racists who do not appreciate the benefits that the benevolent government is providing for them. They must be forced to understand that this is progress and that they must obey and not object in any manner.

The use of shovels as a form of protest is especially prohibited.

For Elko County Citizens
    Signed this 31st day of January 2000

Document 2
Fact Finding Report

Work Environment and Community Relations
Humboldt-Toiyabe National Forest
February 4, 2000
1. *Work Environment*
The team determined that, except for one significant exception, most of the Humboldt-Toiyabe is similar to other national forests in the quality of community relationships and generally positive work environment. During our interviews with employees and members of the public we were told of posi-

tive working relationships and successful partnerships that exist with the Forest Service in many areas of Nevada.

The significant exception is in northeast Nevada where most employees view the work environment as unusual and antagonistic.

Employees there described numerous situations over the past three years where Forest Service employees and their families have been subject to various forms and degrees of intimidation, harassment, and verbal abuse.

Many current northeast Nevada employees and former employees reported being treated disrespectfully and being exposed to highly embarrassing situations by community members. Employees spoke of incidents where, while doing field work, they encountered people whose actions or language they considered threatening causing them to be afraid for their well-being.

In several instances, Forest Service employees either were refused service by employees of local businesses or were subjected to foul language by other business patrons. To their credit, business owners dealt with these situations when they were reported; however, these experiences were very troubling to employees. We heard from two Forest Service spouses who reported being ostracized from community groups and verbally abused and ridiculed in public. One spouse told us that her child's teacher made disparaging comments during class about Forest Service employees. The issue with the teacher was raised to school authorities and is being dealt with. In two instances, church members were said to have left congregations after Forest Service employees joined.

Antagonistic treatment appeared to be due to specific actions the Forest Service was taking or to being identified as a Forest Service employee or family member.

Of the approximately 35 employees we met with in Elko, the majority said that working and living in this setting affected their sense of well-being. Lack of community support in Elko, Nevada, has caused some employees in that area to minimize professional and social interactions. However, others reported that they considered dealing with this a normal and tolerable aspect of their jobs.

Very few employees wear their Forest Service uniforms. Many preferred to drive white and non-greenfleet vehicles while performing their duties. Employees stated that these actions made them less conspicuous, and therefore, less exposed to animosity.

We heard from both employees and community members that believe in the past the Elko Daily Free Press fueled anti-federal attitudes in Elko and around northeast Nevada, including articles directed at individual employees. The Elko Daily Free Press is the only daily newspaper published in northeast Nevada. A review of editorials on the Elko Daily Free Press web page indicates that the paper is strongly in favor of county, local and private rights and opposed to a federal presence in Nevada. The paper frequently featured headlines critical of the Forest Service.

Employees believed they had made good faith efforts to provide information of interest about the Forest Service to the community through the paper. They were frustrated that when articles on Forest Service activities did appear announcing Forest Service activities or programs they were frequently disputed in editorials and disparaged in opinion pieces by the publisher. Many employees expressed the opinion that the editorial content of the Elko Daily Free Press has devalued the role of the Forest Service in northeast Nevada and affects the working atmosphere.

During its visit to Nevada the team learned that the Elko Daily Free Press had been sold and a new editor appointed.

We heard of egregious incidents that occurred prior to 1996, including the bombing of the Carson City District Ranger's office and home. Some of these situations were resolved; others remain unresolved. Many employees have vivid memories of these events and continue to be troubled by them. Some incidents were never reported because the employee was not aware of the reporting process.

Many external contacts were troubled and angered by accusations raised by Flora in her letter and think the claims are unfounded or too all-inclusive.

The team found:

· Working relationships were generally good in much of Nevada. Where problems were found, Forest Service employees, elected officials and local publics expressed a strong desire to work together to improve relationships. An antagonistic work environment currently exists in northeast Nevada which has had an impact on Forest Service effectiveness. When considered cumulatively, the experiences employees described were beyond what is typical in work environments for Forest Service employees in other places. The work environment is difficult but is not considered dangerous.

· This finding of an antagonistic environment in northeast Nevada is consistent with the most recent Continuous Improvement Process (CIP) Survey. A

In a contest for control of Nevada's land, the shovel became a symbol of eastern Nevada's determination to remove any obstacle—even the federal government—from its exercise of freedom. Photo by Rachel Harvey

comparison between the 1997 and 1999 CIP survey indicates that while the results for the Humboldt-Toiyabe as a whole improved, results for the northeast Nevada Eco-unit declined. The CIP is designed to enable employees to provide input and give feedback about processes that affect employee performance, including work environment.

• No incidents of personal threats, violence, or abuse in the past several years that would cause the Forest Service to seek criminal prosecution through the Department of Justice.

• Concern still exists about the Carson City bombing to the extent that it affects some employees on a daily basis.

The Yucca Mountain Debate—*Spencer Abraham* v. *Kenny Guinn*

The Nuclear Waste Policy Act of 1982 directed the Department of Energy to find a site for a permanent repository for spent nuclear fuel. Within a year, the federal agency identified nine locations in six states as possible sites. Based on a preliminary report, President Ronald Reagan eliminated all but three of these: Hanford in Washington, Deaf Smith County in Texas, and Yucca Mountain in Nevada. Two years later, Reagan signed an amendment to the Nuclear Waste Policy Act directing the Department of Energy to stop consideration of all sites except Yucca Mountain, even though Nevada has no spent nuclear fuel and other locations were not fully examined to determine whether they would better serve the interests of the nation.

Presidential nominee George W. Bush campaigned in Nevada with the promise that he would not authorize a nuclear repository in Yucca Mountain without a sound scientific recommendation that the location would be safe for that purpose. Although many scientists regarded studies to be inadequate and inaccurate, President Bush authorized the building of the "Nuke Dump" at Yucca Mountain early in 2002. Governor Kenny Guinn subsequently vetoed the action of the president, returning it to Congress to override the veto. The two letters below were exchanged as part of this controversy.

Nevadans have frequently felt wrongfully used by the federal government. For example, an act of Congress known in Nevada as the "Crime of '73" resulted in a nineteenth-century devaluation of silver, hurting the state's mining industry. In the twentieth century, there have been numerous attempts to shift management of federal lands to state or local control. With nearly 87 percent of the state in federal ownership, Nevadans frequently feel surrounded and controlled in a way unmatched in the other continental states. The Yucca Mountain controversy serves in the minds of many Nevadans as yet another example of the federal government's ignoring the state's interests and rights, belligerently moving forward against the wishes of a clear majority.

—Ronald M. James

Thursday, January 10, 2002

Dear Governor Guinn:

This letter is to notify you, in accordance with section 114(a)(1) of the Nuclear Waste Policy Act, of my intention to recommend to the President approval of the Yucca Mountain site for the development of a nuclear waste repository. In accordance with the requirements of the Act, I will be submitting my recommendation to the President no sooner than 30 days from this date. At that time, as the Act also requires, I will be submitting to the President a comprehensive statement of the basis for that recommendation. First, and most important, that recommendation will include the basis for and documentation supporting my belief that the science behind this project is sound and that the site is technically suitable for this purpose. Second, there are compelling national interests that require us to complete the siting process and move forward with the development of a repository, as Congress mandated almost 20 years ago. In brief, the reasons are these:

• A repository is important to our national security. We must advance our non-proliferation goals by providing a secure place to dispose of any spent fuel and other waste products that result from decommissioning unneeded nuclear weapons, and ensure the effective operations of our nuclear Navy by providing a secure place to dispose of its spent nuclear fuel.

• A repository is important to the secure disposal of nuclear waste. Spent nuclear fuel, high level radioactive waste, and excess plutonium for which there is no complete disposal pathway without a repository are currently stored at over 131 sites in 39 States. We should consolidate the nuclear wastes to enhance protection against terrorists attacks by moving them to one underground location that is far from population centers.

• A repository is important to our energy security. We must ensure that nuclear power, which provides 20% of the nation's electric power, remains an important part of our domestic energy production.

• And a repository is important to our efforts to protect the environment. We must clean up our defense waste sites permanently and safely dispose of other high level nuclear waste.

As I indicated earlier, pursuant to section 114(a) of the NWPA, I will be submitting my recommendation to the President no earlier than 30 days from today, together with the other documentation the statute requires. I will provide you with a copy of those materials at that time.

Sincerely

signed

Spencer Abraham

Secretary of Energy

The Honorable Spencer Abraham
Secretary of Energy
Washington, D.C. 20585

January 24, 2002

Dear Secretary Abraham:

I was disappointed, to say the least, with your letter notifying me of your intent to recommend to President Bush approval of the Yucca Mountain site for the development of the nation's high level nuclear waste repository. Framing the decision in part as a "security" issue was somewhat surprising, since no analysis has ever been done to suggest that Yucca Mountain will contribute to national security.

It appears that the Department of Energy is the only entity familiar with the facts at Yucca Mountain that does not see your decision as premature. As you know, your own contractor Bechtel/SAIC, as well as the General Accounting Office, the Nuclear Regulatory Commission, the Advisory Committee on Nuclear Waste, the Yucca Mountain Technical Review Board, the National Academy of Sciences, and, recently, the International Atomic Energy Agency and the OECD's Nuclear Energy Agency, have each concluded that significant additional studies need to be performed before DOE can seriously consider whether to recommend the Yucca Mountain site for permanent nuclear waste disposal. For example, NRC has indicated that at least 292 major studies remain to be completed in 19 key areas, including corrosion of the waste packages, potential effects of volcanic activity, rapid groundwater flow rates through the mountain, large uncertainties in predicted repository performance, even the very design of the repository itself.

In particular, many of the organizations noted above have commented on DOE's newly improvised "total system" approach to nuclear waste storage at Yucca Mountain, an approach that appears designed to ignore the blatant unsuitability of the geology at Yucca Mountain for the isolation of radioactive waste. As you know, Nevada has taken legal action against DOE over this very issue on the grounds that DOE has abandoned the Nuclear Waste Policy Act's requirement that geologic isolation must be the primary form of containment. We know, as you do, that DOE retroactively changed its site suitability rules when it learned that the mountain's natural site features could not safely contain the waste. At the very least, the D.C. Court of Appeals should be allowed to rule on the merits of that action before any recommendation is made.

For the reasons set forth below, I respectfully disagree with each of your articulated reasons for rushing forward with Yucca Mountain.

Security Against Terrorism. This new rationale for rushing forward with Yucca Mountain was invented by DOE and the nuclear industry in the wake of the September 11 terrorist attacks. But what this rationale fails to acknowledge is that even if the Yucca Mountain project moves forward, spent fuel will continue to be stored at reactor sites across America for at least the next 50 years. Even on an optimistic schedule, Yucca Mountain will not be capable of receiving most of the waste for decades. Indeed, once at the site, much of the spent fuel will be stored *above ground* for the next 100 years. Instead of reducing any terrorist threat, rushing forward will actually significantly increase the potential threat by adding a massive new aboveground site in Nevada, in addition to the more than 100,000 shipments of spent fuel that will travel through the nation's cities. Upon examination of the facts, the terrorism argument does not ring true.

National Security. Yucca Mountain is not, and has never been, about national security and nuclear nonproliferation, as you suggest. Spent nuclear fuel and waste products do not pose a non-proliferation threat, since they do not contain separated fissile materials that can be utilized for nuclear weapons. If you mean to suggest that if Yucca Mountain does not open, the United States will be unable to dismantle its nuclear weapons or operate its nuclear submarines, I believe this is misleading. For example, I understand that DOE is currently building a brand new spent fuel storage facility in Idaho to house foreign research reactor spent fuel, and that this will be accomplished in a matter of only two years. If this can be done so readily to aid our foreign trading partners, I'm sure it can also be done to keep our nation secure should such a need arise.

Energy Security. During the next several decades, Yucca Mountain will contribute nothing to the nation's energy security. Nuclear plants across the nation are building inexpensive and safe dry storage facilities for their spent fuel, and successfully renewing their licenses as a result. They will continue to do this regardless of whether Yucca Mountain proceeds or not, since, even under the best of conditions, Yucca Mountain could not provide storage for several decades. DOE has even agreed with one utility, PECO Energy, to take title to its fuel on site, and to purchase and operate its storage facility.

Environmental Protection. It is simply untrue to suggest that Yucca Mountain is stalling cleanup of the nation's defense nuclear facilities. These sites are contaminated with massive quantities of low-level radioactive waste, which Yucca Mountain will not accept at any time. Higher-level transuranic wastes are already going into the successful repository at the Waste Isolation Pilot Project in New Mexico. DOE rejected efforts to develop additional low-level waste disposal sites in several states for defense cleanup activities. If environmental protection is DOE's main concern, perhaps the Department should explain to Nevadans why we should tolerate an uncertainty factor of 10,000 in the radiation dose projections for the Yucca Mountain repository system. Our slot machines have better odds than that.

Though you've clearly made up your mind, I remain hopeful that President Bush, when he receives your recommendation, will keep his promise to me and Nevada not to push the Yucca Mountain project forward against the imperatives of sound science. If that is not the case, however, please rest assured that Nevada will continue to pursue every means available to ensure that science and the law will ultimately prevail.

Sincerely,
Kenneth C. Guinn
Governor

SOURCES

Chapter 1 | Excerpt from Mark Twain (Samuel Clemens), *Roughing It* (New York: Harper and Brothers, 1871).

Chapter 2 | Excerpt from John C. Ewers, ed., *Adventures of Zenas Leonard, Fur Trader* (Norman: University of Oklahoma Press, 1959), 67–72, 130–31. Numaga's speech from Myron Angel, ed., *History of Nevada* (1881; reprint, with an introduction by David F. Myrick, Berkeley, Calif.: Howell-North, 1958), 151. Letter from Edmund Bryant to his father, dated May 31, 1860, on file at the Nevada State Historic Preservation Office, Carson City, Nevada, and in the Storey County Recorder's Office, Virginia City, Nevada. Excerpts from Sarah Winnemucca Hopkins, *Life Among the Paiutes* (Reno: University of Nevada Press, 1994), 11–12; *Gold Hill Daily News*, April 28, 1870; and *Alta California*, December 4, 1879. Parts of this introduction and excerpted documents were compiled from Sally Zanjani, *Sarah Winnemucca* (Lincoln: University of Nebraska Press, 2001).

Chapter 3 | Report of Captain Nathaniel V. Jones, April 16, 1857, from Andrew Jensen, "History of the Las Vegas Mission," in *Nevada State Historical Society Papers: 1925–26*, ed. Jeanne Elizabeth Weir (Reno: Nevada State Historical Society, 1926), 270–76. Original *Gold Hill Record Book* on file at the Storey County Recorder's Office, Virginia City, Nevada. Congressman James W. Ashley's (R-Ohio) reasons for Nevada statehood, 1865—from U.S. Congress, *Congressional Globe*, 39th Cong., 1st sess., 1865–1866, pt. 3: 2372–73. Ormsby letter from the Stephen A. Douglas Papers in the Manuscript Collections at the University of Chicago Special Collections. Copy of Lincoln's proclamation in the Nevada State Archives, Carson City, Nevada. Excerpt from the Nevada Constitution, Article 1, Section 2.

Chapter 4 | Excerpt from Mark Twain (Samuel Clemens), *Roughing It* (New York: Harper and Brothers, 1871), 210–14, 221–24. Excerpt from J. Ross Browne, *A Peep at Washoe and Washoe Revisited* (reprint, Balboa Island, Calif.: Palsano Press, 1959), 77–79. "In the Cradle of Hell," *Virginia Evening Chronicle*, July 9, 1877. Excerpt from

Dan De Quille, *History of the Big Bonanza: An Authentic Account of the Discovery, History, and Working of the World Renowned Comstock Silver Lode of Nevada, Including the Present Condition of the Various Mines Situated Thereon* (Hartford, Conn.: American Publishing Company; San Francisco: A. L. Bancroft & Co., 1877). Excerpts from the *Virginia Evening Chronicle,* April 15, 1867; *Gold Hill Evening News,* November 18, 1867, and July 6, 1870; *Territorial Enterprise,* December 10, 1878, and September 25, 1874; and *The Journals of Alfred Dolen* (Reno: University of Nevada Press, 1973), book 25, October 25, 1867. Julia Bulette's probate records are on file in the Clerk's Office at the Storey County Courthouse, Virginia City, Nevada. Extract from Mark Twain letter, the *Chicago Republican,* May 31, 1868. Extract from the *Journal of the Council of the First Legislative Assembly of the Territory of Nevada* (San Francisco: Commercial Steam Printing, 1862), 14–25. Frances Fuller Victor, "Nevada," *Overland Monthly* 3 (December 1869): 423–24.

Chapter 5 | Wovoka's letters are housed at the Nevada Historical Society, Reno, Nevada. Reports on Coxey's Army from the *Reno Evening Gazette,* April 4–7, 9, 1894. Address by W. H. Hall, published in the *Virginia City Territorial Enterprise,* April 9, 1870. Address by Alexander W. Baldwin, published in the *Virginia City Territorial Enterprise,* July 8, 1868.

Chapter 6 | Excerpt from Mrs. Hugh Brown, *Lady in Boomtown: Miners and Manners on the Nevada Frontier* (Reno: University of Nevada Press, 1991). Reprinted by permission. Theodore Roosevelt's admonition from the Governor Sparks Collection at the Nevada State Library and Archives, Carson City, Nevada. George Wingfield section from the *Sacramento Bee,* October 19, 1928.

Chapter 7 | James's letters from *Special Delivery: Letters from C. L. R. James* (London: Blackwell, 1998). Reprinted by permission. Excerpt from D. S. Dickerson, *Biennial Report of the Warden of the State Prison, 1923–24* (Carson City, Nev.: State Printing Office, 1925), 3–4. Billy Murray's "I'm on My Way to Reno" from Victor Record, #16475-B. Courtesy of the private collection of Anita Ernst Watson. Prohibition legislation from *Laws of the State of Nevada Passed at the Twenty-ninth Session of the Legislature, 1919* (Carson City, Nev.: State Printing Office, 1919).

Chapter 8 | Excerpts, Paul Hutchinson on Nevada gambling, from *The Christian Century,* 1931, copyright 1931. *The Christian Century,* reprinted by permission from the November 25, 1931, and December 9, 1931, issues. Erma O. Godbey, *Pioneering in Boulder City, Nevada.* An oral history conducted by Mary Ellen Glass, Oral History Program, University of Nevada, Reno, 1967. Reprinted courtesy of the University of Nevada Oral History Program.

Chapter 9 | H. M. Peterson's letter courtesy of the East Ely Depot Museum. Hank Greenspun on Senator Joe McCarthy from the Las Vegas *Sun*, January 8, 1954. Testimony from the Kefauver hearings from U.S. Senate, Special Committee on Organized Crime in Interstate Commerce, *Hearings, Part 10, Nevada-California*, 81st Cong., 2nd sess., 1950. Explanation of atomic testing from United States Atomic Energy Commission, *Atomic Tests in Nevada* (Washington, D.C.: Government Printing Office, March 1957), 1–3, 6–13, 35–36, 39–42. Thomas H. Saffer's witnessing of an atomic test from Thomas H. Saffer and Orville E. Kelly, *Countdown Zero* (New York: G. P. Putnam's Sons, 1982), 42–45. Arthur Miller on Nevada and *The Misfits* from Arthur Miller, *Timebends: A Life* (New York: Grove Press, 1987). Reprinted by permission. Grant Sawyer on gaming control from Grant Sawyer, Gary E. Elliott, and R. T. King, *Hang Tough! Grant Sawyer: An Activist in the Governor's Mansion* (Reno: University of Nevada Oral History Program, 1993), 81–94. Reprinted by permission. James B. McMillan on civil rights in Las Vegas from James B. McMillan, *Fighting Back: A Life in the Struggle for Civil Rights* (Reno: University of Nevada Oral History Program, 1997), 91–98, 137–39. Reprinted by permission. Sammy Davis Jr. on segregation in Las Vegas from Sammy Davis Jr., Jane Boyer, and Burt Boyer, *Yes I Can: The Story of Sammy Davis, Jr.* (New York: Farrar, Straus & Giroux, 1965). Reprinted by permission. Lena Horne on entertaining in Las Vegas from Lena Horne and Richard Schickel, *Lena* (Garden City, N.Y.: Doubleday & Co., 1965). Reprinted by permission. Paul Laxalt on Ronald Reagan from Paul Laxalt, *Nevada's Paul Laxalt: A Memoir* (Reno, Nev.: Jack Bacon & Company, 2000). Reprinted by permission. Jarbidge debate materials, *Elko Free Press*, February 11, 2000. Letters, Kenny Guinn and Spencer Abraham, from Governor Guinn's Web site (http://gov.state.nv.us/pr/2002/1-24yu8c.htm) and the Department of Energy Web site (http://www.energy.gov/HQPress/releases02/janpr/abraham_letter.pelt).

Alice M. Baldrica, author of the definitive treatment of Frederick West Lander and the Pyramid Lake War, graduated from the University of Nevada, Reno, with a B.A. and M.A. in anthropology. She has worked at the Nevada State Historic Preservation Office since 1981 and has served as deputy administrator since 1989.

Michael J. Brodhead is a professor emeritus, history, University of Nevada, Reno. He has also worked for the National Archives and Records Administration and the Nevada State Archives and is now a historian at the Office of History, U.S. Army Corps of Engineers, Alexandria, Virginia. His research interests include western American travel and exploration, military history, judicial biography, and American naturalists.

Dennis Dworkin is an associate professor of history at the University of Nevada, Reno. He teaches British and Irish history and cultural theory.

Bernadette C. Francke received her M.A. in American studies from Antioch College and is the author of several articles on Nevada history. She continues to research nineteenth-century Nevada photographers.

Cheryll Glotfelty is an associate professor of English at the University of Nevada, Reno, where she cofounded the Literature and Environment graduate program and teaches courses in American literature and Nevada literature. She coedited *The Ecocriticism Reader: Landmarks in Literary Ecology* with Harold Fromm and has published many essays on western American literature. She is currently editing an anthology of the literature of Nevada.

Michael Green is a professor of history at the Community College of Southern Nevada. He is coeditor of *Nevada: Readings and Perspectives;* editor and interviewer for *A Liberal Conscience: Ralph Denton, Nevadan;* book-review editor of the *Ne-*

vada Historical Society Quarterly; and a history series editor for the University of Nevada Press. He is the author of *Freedom, Union, and Power: Lincoln and His Party in the Civil War.*

Mella Rothwell Harmon is a historic preservation specialist with the Nevada State Historic Preservation Office, where she serves as coordinator for the National Register of Historic Places program. Ms. Harmon holds a B.A. in anthropology from the University of California, Berkeley, and an M.S. in land-use planning, with an emphasis on historic preservation, from the University of Nevada, Reno.

Rachel Harvey is pursuing her Ph.D. in sociology at the University of Chicago. Her M.S. thesis focused on the media coverage of the Jarbidge Shovel Brigade, and her doctoral research expands on her interest in Nevada by examining the state's gold-mining industry in relation to globalization.

Ronald M. James, historian and folklorist, is the Nevada State Historic Preservation Officer, having administered the agency since 1983. He is the author of four books, including *The Roar and the Silence: A History of Virginia City and the Comstock Lode.* He serves as adjunct faculty at the University of Nevada, Reno.

Susan James has an M.A. in history from the University of Nevada, Reno, where she taught for fifteen years. Her definitive article on Bulette appeared in *Nevada Magazine* in 1984 and is one of her many publications, including *Castle in the Sky: George Whittell Jr. and His Thunderbird Lodge,* a book recently coauthored with her husband, Ronald James.

Jeffrey M. Kintop has been a Nevada historian for twenty-four years and a state archivist for twenty years. His areas of interest include Nevada's territorial history and the political history of the state. He has contributed to numerous publications and projects concerning Nevada history.

Sharon Lowe is a full-time faculty member in the Liberal Arts Division at Truckee Meadows Community College, where she teaches American history and women's studies. She is currently completing her Ph.D. dissertation on a global study of women and drug use.

Michon Mackedon is an English professor and chair of the Communications and Fine Arts Division at Western Nevada Community College. A native of Nevada, she is working on a book that explores ways in which language has been deployed to "spin" nuclear events in the state, including the siting of Yucca Mountain.

Joxe Mallea-Olaetxe was born in the Basque Country and came to the United States in 1964. He received his M.A. at the University of Nebraska, Lincoln, in Latin American colonial studies in 1985 and his Ph.D. at the University of Nevada, Reno (UNR), in Basque studies/history in 1988. He has taught at UNR and Truckee Meadows Community College and has published three books. He currently does research at UNR's Center for Basque Studies.

Terri McBride, who has an M.A. in anthropology from the University of Denver, is an archaeologist at the State Historic Preservation Office. Her main areas of research include Native Americans in Nevada and New World archaeology.

C. Elizabeth Raymond is a professor of history at the University of Nevada, Reno. She is the author of *George Wingfield: Owner and Operator of Nevada* and coeditor with Ronald James of *Comstock Women.*

John B. Reid is a community college professor and chair of the Social Sciences Department at Truckee Meadows Community College. He holds an M.A. from the University of Nevada, Reno, and received his Ph.D. from Michigan State University with a specialty in African American history.

Tanya Reid, a native Nevadan, teaches English and humanities in the community college system.

Guy Louis Rocha has served as the Nevada state archivist since 1981 and prior to that worked for the Nevada Historical Society. He holds a B.S. in social studies/education from Syracuse University and an M.A. in American studies from San Diego State University and pursued postgraduate studies in history at the University of Nevada, Reno.

Elmer R. Rusco is emeritus professor of political science at the University of Nevada, Reno. He researches and writes on law and policy with a focus on Nevada.

Anita Ernst Watson earned a Ph.D. in history from the University of Nevada, Reno. She has published works focusing on women in Nevada and medical history in Nevada and the West; further research interests include American family life and stigmatized behavior. She is currently curator of education at the Stearns History Museum in St. Cloud, Minnesota.

Sally Zanjani is a Nevada historian and the author of eight books and many articles. One of her recent books, *Sarah Winnemucca* (2001), received the Evans Biography Award and the Westerners International Award. Dr. Zanjani is associated with the Political Science Department at the University of Nevada, Reno.